CW01240191

BREAKING AWAKE

BREAKING AWAKE

My Search For a New Life Through Drugs

P. E. MOSKOWITZ

BLOOMSBURY PUBLISHING
LONDON · OXFORD · NEW YORK · NEW DELHI · SYDNEY

BLOOMSBURY PUBLISHING
Bloomsbury Publishing Plc
50 Bedford Square, London, WC1B 3DP, UK
Bloomsbury Publishing Ireland Limited,
29 Earlsfort Terrace, Dublin 2, D02 AY28, Ireland

BLOOMSBURY, BLOOMSBURY PUBLISHING and the Diana
logo are trademarks of Bloomsbury Publishing Plc

First published in 2025 in the United States by Atria Books,
an imprint of Simon & Schuster, LLC
First published in Great Britain in 2025

Copyright © P. E. Moskowitz, 2025

P. E. Moskowitz is identified as the author of this work in accordance
with the Copyright, Designs and Patents Act 1988

All rights reserved. No part of this publication may be: i) reproduced or transmitted in any form, electronic or mechanical, including photocopying, recording or by means of any information storage or retrieval system without prior permission in writing from the publishers; or ii) used or reproduced in any way for the training, development or operation of artificial intelligence (AI) technologies, including generative AI technologies. The rights holders expressly reserve this publication from the text and data mining exception as per Article 4(3) of the Digital Single Market Directive (EU) 2019/790

Bloomsbury Publishing Plc does not have any control over, or responsibility for, any third-party websites referred to in this book. All internet addresses given in this book were correct at the time of going to press. The author and publisher regret any inconvenience caused if addresses have changed or sites have ceased to exist, but can accept no responsibility for any such changes

A catalogue record for this book is available from the British Library

ISBN: HB: 978-1-5266-5806-7; TPB: 978-1-5266-5808-1;
eBook: 978-1-5266-5810-4; ePDF: 978-1-5266-5807-4

2 4 6 8 10 9 7 5 3 1

Interior design by Erika R. Genova
Printed and bound in Great Britain by by Clays Ltd, Elcograf S.p.A

MIX
Paper | Supporting responsible forestry
FSC
www.fsc.org
FSC® C018072

To find out more about our authors and books visit www.bloomsbury.com
and sign up for our newsletters
For product safety related questions contact productsafety@bloomsbury.com

All around me are the shadows of the still living, and those who died heroes as if by choice.

**Eulogy for Gloria Moskowitz (my grandma),
given by Michael Moskowitz (my dad),
June 6, 2013, Port Jervis, New York**

CONTENTS

Introduction: The Narrative of One's Life	*1*
Interlude One: Accept Your Own Erasure	17
Part One: Breakdown	**19**
Chapter One: My Breakdown	21
Chapter Two: A Personal Breakdown	45
Chapter Three: The Unequal Distribution of Breakdown	77
Interlude Two: How to Externalize the Breakdown	105
Part Two: Stability	**115**
Chapter Four: Putting Myself Back Together	117
Chapter Five: A Tenuous Stability	155
Chapter Six: The Stability Trap	195
Interlude Three: Fear of Freedom / Freedom from Fear	227
Part Three: Rebirth	**235**
Chapter Seven: Becoming Alive	237
Chapter Eight: Searching for Collective Breakthrough	265
Afterword: Toward a New, Collective Narrative	*303*
Acknowledgments	*313*
Notes	*315*
Index	*343*

Monk: What is Buddha?
Priest: Three pounds of flax.

—Mid-thirteenth-century Zen koan

Monk: What is Buddha?
Priest: A Big Mac with cheese.

**—Updated interpretation,
posted on *NewBuddhist* Internet forum, 2014**

INTRODUCTION: THE NARRATIVE OF ONE'S LIFE

There are many bad things about nearly dying. Perhaps the only good one is that in leaving your life in ruins, it allows you to reconfigure it into something new.

On August 11, 2017, I drove from my home in Philadelphia down to Charlottesville, Virginia, with two friends, Erin and Xavi. This was the year Donald Trump became president the first time, and thus a year of massive resistance. We three were reporters and activists, and it felt important for us to be there to witness and fight back against "Unite the Right," a rally of hundreds of neo-Nazis and other varieties of white supremacists who were protesting the removal of the Confederate general Robert E. Lee from a small park named after him. I wanted to be a part of something bigger than myself. I wanted to be on the right side of history.

On the evening of the eleventh, Erin, Xavi, and I drank shitty wine in a room in a corporate hotel in a strip mall on the outskirts of the city. In the hallways, we saw dozens of police officers from other states, there to assist in the management of the next day's rally. We also saw people who were on the pro–Confederate statue side—big, bearded men with camo pants and shirts and MAGA hats. I thought it was funny that we were all there relaxing, knowing that tomorrow we'd all be fighting one another; troops getting lined up for battle. There's a picture on my phone from that night—us three friends clinking plastic glasses on the edge of the hotel bed, smiling.

I slept well.

On the morning of the twelfth, Erin, Xavi, and I entered the small college town of Charlottesville and wandered down its genial streets. Many of the homes there were built in the 1700s and 1800s, often by slaves; a reminder that day of what we were actually protesting against— not just the neo-Nazis, but an entire history of American oppression.

And then we came across the park at the center of the protest, where hundreds of protesters had gathered. I gawked at their semiauto rifles, their signs scrawled with words of hatred against immigrants and people of color and Jews. It terrified me that people like this existed. That there were so many of them.

Yet, for most of the day, I felt buoyant. Because outnumbering all these hateful idiots was our side—the counterprotesters. We chanted back at the Nazis. We surrounded them. We yelled at the police for being complicit, for not arresting anyone threatening to shoot us. We got tear gas in our eyes and witnessed fights break out and sent texts on encrypting messaging apps to track the white supremacists' movements. It was, strangely, fun. Yes, scary too. But mostly it felt exhilarating because, for most of the day, it seemed like we were winning. We were kicking the

Nazis out of town. We'd done our small part to make sure the arc of the moral universe continued to bend toward justice.

By the early afternoon, the police locked down the park at the center of the protest, so people began to march. Erin, Xavi, and I followed a group of thousands, chanting various slogans. Some people sang protest songs. Some banged drums. At an intersection a few blocks away from the park, another stream of leftists and progressives coming from the other direction merged into our group. We all cheered. It was loud. We'd banded together. And we'd won.

And then, as we turned a corner, marching up a little hilly street, there was an unplaceable sound, like nothing I'd ever heard before. A sound that should not exist, of screeching tires against concrete and metal against human flesh. Waves of bodies pushed into me; some flew a few feet into the air.

James Alex Fields Jr., a twenty-year-old neo-Nazi, had plowed his Dodge Challenger into the crowd. I was feet away. He then backed up and did it again.

All hell broke loose. The counterprotesters ran in every direction. In the chaos, I dropped my phone and lost track of Erin and Xavi. I pushed through the crowd trying to find them, passing a child, perhaps ten years old, lying on the ground with blood covering her torso and bone shooting through her kneecap. My vision was blurry. I felt as if I was watching myself from above. This, I'd later come to understand, was a sign of being in fight-or-flight. My mind had to dissociate from my body, direct it as if it was playing a video game, in order to ensure its survival. And entering this state, it turns out, can wreak havoc on you for months or years or a lifetime.

It was probably a minute, but it felt like an hour before I found my friends and my phone. We ran to the next block. Sat on a curb on the street. When I lit a cigarette, I noticed two things: One, that my hand was violently shaking. And two, that it still felt as if my brain was floating above my body.

The cops finally arrived. Then the EMTs. Dozens had been injured. And someone had apparently died—we saw the body of Heather Heyer, a thirty-two-year-old antifascist activist from a nearby town, being loaded into the back of an ambulance. I felt a deep well of anger in my stomach. But I was there as a journalist, and I had a story to file.

So I stopped thinking about it. I replaced my emotions with tasks—find my car, find some food, drive myself and my friends home, call my parents. I did call them. They asked if I was okay. I downplayed the situation; I told them I was farther away from the car than I was. I kept the details light. It was less about protecting them. I think, looking back, I knew that if I'd told them the full truth, the danger I was in, and how I actually felt, the anger and the rage and the fear, that their reaction would have forced me to accept what had really happened. It was about protecting me. So I just said I was fine.

And then, over the next few weeks, I internalized that emotional lie.

On the drive back to Philadelphia, and in the days afterward, as I went about my work and my life, I practiced that lie like I was memorizing for a test. I was fine. I was fine. I was fine. And it worked. I did not think about Charlottesville. And when I did, I'd force my brain on to something else. I wrote articles about politics and I got drunk with friends and I walked around Philadelphia aimlessly with my headphones on nearly every day. I had sex and I watched a million episodes of *30 Rock* and I cooked spatchcocked chicken with a side of broccoli rabe. I lived life. I did everything except stop and think.

And then I had a mental breakdown.

A month and two days after Charlottesville, September 14, 2017, I awoke alone in a hotel room in Oakland, California, where I'd traveled to give a talk about my work as a journalist. As soon as my eyes opened, I knew something was terribly wrong. I was in a completely different reality than the one I'd lived in for the first twenty-nine years of my life. My hands wouldn't stop shaking. I again felt as if I was floating above my own body. Except this time I couldn't make it stop. My nervous system was shot. If I stopped moving—pacing, tapping my legs, shaking my hands—whatever horrible energy coursing through me would rise through my hands and up my arms and through my throat and into my brain and cause me to start breathing irregularly to the point of hyperventilating; would cause my thoughts to race faster than I could understand them. I was going insane. Within five minutes of waking up that day, I thought for sure that I was headed for death—either directly from whatever was happening to me, or by my own hand, because another few minutes of that state felt deeply unsustainable.

Well. That state of life-ruining craziness, of PTSD, of nervous system deregulation, of dissociation, of breakdown—whatever you want to call it—lasted for years. It wasn't always as acute as it was in the hotel room that day. But it was always there. It still, on my bad days, is.

Yet I did not die.

I do not feel back to normal. I do not feel like I will ever achieve the same state of okayness that I had before my mental breakdown. And I am okay with this. More than okay. I am happy. I did not get better. I got different. I changed. My brain changed. My life changed. Even my gender changed. And all of it was necessary to move on, to make sense of what had happened to me, to continue to live, and to live better than

I had been—now more emotionally vulnerable, a little less stable, a little more raw, but in so many ways also more alive.

I do not feel grateful to my trauma for any of that. Because I would not wish that breakdown upon anyone. But I thank the tools I learned to use in recovery from that breakdown for saving my life, and for providing me with a new one.

Many of those tools were drugs. I'd used drugs for much of my life, both ones prescribed to me by psychiatrists and ones I'd found on my own at parties as a teen. And I knew that, whether illicit or prescription, they were often effective modulators of pain. And more than that, I knew they could help me understand my pain differently by helping me shift my perspective. To me, it didn't matter if the drugs were prescribed or illegal—they were all just different tools with different benefits and drawbacks. There were the downers to get me through the worst days, the mood stabilizers and antidepressants and ADHD meds to get me back to stability, the dissociatives like ketamine and the hallucinogens like LSD and psilocybin and 2C-B to help me envision life anew. I needed to throw them all at the wall and see what stuck.

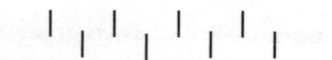

Until that day in Oakland, it had never occurred to me that my life had a narrative arc, that somewhere within me existed a story I'd told myself about my past, my present, and my future. I took for granted that I knew what I wanted in life, that I could envision myself one or five or ten years down the line, that my existence, in short, had an internal logic.

But then, very abruptly, I lost the narrative. I did not slowly veer off track. I did not look back and think, *Wow, my life is different than I expected*. Upon awaking that morning in Oakland, my life and everything leading up to it had simply stopped making sense. And my future, the story I thought I was living, was seemingly gone.

It's not that I hadn't struggled before then, but I always, until that point, had known, or at least thought I knew, what my life was like and would be like. There were ups and downs, but, until that point, my life felt readable. Like a story. There was the childhood, a good one—two stable and caring parents, a good home, good or good-enough schooling—that had led me here, the opportunities my upbringing had provided me and the problems it had rendered too, problems I could confront and conquer and grow from and move on from. And there was a destination, a future, or several possible ones: further my career as a writer, meet someone and fall in love and get married, try to help others along the way. A typical narrative arc, a "hero's journey," like the one I was taught in middle school English class, popular because it's effective and easy: something leads you to a challenge, you fight the challenge, you win, you learn and move on. The end.

But then all narrative logic was gone. I could no longer see the next paragraph on the page, nor interpret how the preceding ones had landed me here. I could barely understand the language I was supposed to be writing in. So I no longer knew what I was or who I was. It was terrifying.

For years after that sudden erasure, I attempted to will my previous narrative back into existence. Make myself fit the old plot. I'd cry in therapy about feeling like I was no longer a real person; I'd romanticize the before times, even the mundane things like being able to take a walk without feeling like my brain was spinning out of control, because, at least then, I felt on track. I attempted to become what I once was again, because that felt safe and knowable.

But willing myself back to the old story did not work. And it was painful to try. As I attempted to heal from my mental breakdown and the traumas that had triggered it, there was constant grief, because once I accepted there was no going back, I realized I was mourning a kind of death. Both a death of how my life had once been, and a future death, of all the things I had assumed would happen in my story.

There are many definitions of trauma, but the one that works best for me is about this narrative. Trauma is something that whacks you so hard that you completely lose the narrative arc of your life. It erases the book. And writing anew, finding a new narrative, is what's so hard about overcoming it.

But it's in there that there is hope. In the new draft.

I think many of us are struggling with something similar these days—a loss of narrative cohesion. Sure, some of us have it easier than others, but I think whether rich or poor or stable or not, unraveling is becoming a more and more common experience. The rate of depression worldwide increased by nearly 50 percent between 1990 and 2017.[1] In 2023, nearly 30 percent of adults in the US reported experiencing depression at some point in their lives, an all-time high.[2] Suicides and other "deaths from despair" (drug overdoses, alcoholism) are at highs too.

And so more than ever people are searching for tools to reconstruct their life narratives—to make sense of why they feel so hopeless.

Therapy is a kind of narrative process as much as anything else, a process by which people craft a story and draw a lesson from where there maybe is not one inherent. You take something horrible and senseless (or at least confusing) and give it meaning and flow. You impose a hero's journey. The innocent before times. Then the challenge, the trauma, the death, the depression, the whatever brought you to therapy. Then the triumph, the learning, the growth. That's what getting better means. Point A to B to C.

In that way, every diagnosis is a narrative too—to take a cluster of disparate and confusing symptoms and call them, say, depression, or bipolar, or PTSD, and then to get better from those symptoms via therapy or a pill or yoga. To take agency over your own brain is to make yourself the hero of the hero's journey, bravely slaying the demons of mental illness in your path until you reach your destiny of betterness, or at least stability. She was ill, then she worked hard to become un-ill, and now she is better. The end.

But, it turned out, therapy was not enough for me to regain a sense of story in my own life. Neither was diagnosis—no box could neatly contain what I was feeling. The severity of the narrative scrambling was too great. And this seems true for so many others too: despite record-high rates of prescription drug usage, despite record-high diagnoses of various mental health maladies, we are not getting better.

In crisis there is opportunity. When the narrative seems gone, we can invent a new one, construct a new self, and perhaps even construct a new world.

This, I believe, is the main problem with the way we talk about mental illness and trauma these days. We see these things as something to get better from, something to force one kind of simplistic storyline on. There's immense appeal in this—if we can place ourselves within a readily readable narrative, it's tempting to think that our journeys will be easier. But this limits us. It limits our ability to really change, to become weirder and wilder and more fully ourselves. We spend years or lifetimes attempting to "heal" back into a defined story, and in doing so, we disallow ourselves the liberation that can come from resisting false binaries of sick or well.

If we want greater freedom in our identities and lives and futures, we must work, as the psychoanalyst Avgi Saketopoulou writes, "to resist the narrative of restoration or repair, to refuse the idea that anyone ever returns to some prelapsarian moment, to the restoration of innocence before trauma..."[3]

Trauma is not good, of course, but it provides us with an opportunity to not only rewrite our lives, but to rewrite what a life is supposed to look like. And we can only do that if we stop attempting to get back to our pretraumatized states.

The person I am today would be unrecognizable to my prebreakdown self. This fact used to terrify me. Now I am glad. I am stronger, I am weirder, I am more conflicted, I am less readable, I am different, and that is good. The trauma itself has changed me, but so has the healing process—the drugs I used to find solace, the acid trips and nights out during which I completely re-understood the purpose of my life—reshaped me into a new person.

I am not necessarily happier or more confident than I once was, but I am more confident in my lack of confidence, and more content with life's always-too-short moments of joy. I accept uncertainty more. I accept that life is messy, that it is often filled with grief and rage, but that those things must be experienced to experience the outer limits of ecstasy. And most important, I now accept that life cannot be controlled.

In reading other accounts of trauma and transformation, I found that this was a common thread—that losing the plot, eventually, becomes opportunity. In Marianne Williamson's *A Return to Love*, for example, she writes of a period of years in which she felt "as though my skull had exploded. It seemed as though thousands of little pieces of it had shot into outer space."

But in here, she found a capacity to grow: "While my emotional brain was so exposed, it seemed to be rewired, like I'd had some kind of psychic surgery," she writes. "I felt like I became a different person."[4]

She credits these years with putting her on a new path, one in which she could help others and spread the gospel of what she believed in.

I began to see this psychic rewiring everywhere. When I heard things like this, not from psychologists or mental health experts, but from normal people who had found life after experiencing horrible things, it made me think that we all are, in some ways, repressing what we all inherently know: We have an incredible individual and collective power to change, if we're allowed to get a little weird with it. If we can resist rebecoming the people we were told—and told ourselves—we were supposed to be, and instead give ourselves the freedom to rewrite our lives exactly as we please.

How sad, then, that we've reduced these narrative-shaking experiences to a very narrow framework of healing. We spend incredible effort and a lot of money attempting to box up what can be transformative—into labels like PTSD or CPTSD or depression, into simple stories about becoming better and overcoming our trauma.

It's what the critic Parul Sehgal calls "the trauma plot"—our ever-increasing tendency to frame all human experience into a one-size-fits-all narrative of linear trauma-to-healing, backed by an ever-growing literature of "trauma studies."[5]

To Sehgal, the imposition of simplistic narrative structure on life's inherent complexity flattens human experience and disables us from finding new forms of being and expression. We are trapped by the insistence that our lives be turned into a readable story. What if, she argues, we began to see our lives less like a hero's journey, less like a story with a beginning and end, and more like a Picasso painting—perhaps unknowable in words but nonetheless affecting and effective at getting to personal and collective truths.

"The narrating self, very often the adult self—who shapes story out of raw hunks of observation and partial understanding—is typically privileged, congratulated for its discernment and given all the good lines," Sehgal writes. "But that unstoried self understands a great deal in its commotion, in its inability to keep anything compartmentalized, and it loses something when experience is squeezed to release trickles of insight."[6]

What if we accepted that much of life, as Sehgal writes, is the "narrative equivalent of dark matter"? What more could we learn by embracing the dark? What more could we glean from ourselves, our psyches, our collective lives, if we did not insist that they follow a familiar and tried-and-true story format?

To accept the messiness, the dark matter, the unnarrativizable, then, is to embrace that no one story will ever contain all the possibilities of life.

There are many ways to come to this acceptance, to come to a state in which we embrace change rather than attempt to box it up or apply an overly simplistic plot to it. Good therapy can do this. Bodywork of various sorts can help do this. But, I've found, some of the most effective tools are psychoactive substances.

If trauma erased the book of my life, and therapy attempted to give me a new story, what drugs ultimately did was allow me to dispense with my need for readability and find comfort in a messy narrative. That, at the end of the day, is what has kept me fascinated by drugs—not their ability to heal wounds, but their ability to *transform* them into places of meaning and beauty.

This book is a collection of stories, mine included, that push back on the current, mainstream conceptualization of drugs. We've been told by politicians and the media for so long that drugs are always detrimental, always dangerous, and never worth it. But in my own life, and in my reporting on dozens of other drug users, I've found a different perspective on these substances—one in which they are sometimes good and sometimes bad, but most often neither. Instead, they are tools that, like almost any tool, can be used in productive or damaging ways. At their best, they can be used to help us survive lives of depression and despair, and even help us envision new lives on a personal and societal level.

This is not a self-help book, at least in the traditional sense. But I hope it can encourage people to find the story that works best for them. As scary as losing the plot can be, as scary as it can be for one's life to not make sense, I think there is immense freedom in that; in realizing we can write our lives anew, individually and collectively.

So, then, what follows are stories about losing the plot, finding the plot again, realizing the limitations of the tried-and-true plot, and then dispensing with the plot completely in search of something greater or more meaningful or more beautiful. In each of these stories, drugs are a tool of narrative construction and destruction—they help people find solace when their books of life are erased, they help people find stability and begin redrafting their books, and they help people see beyond stability and into something messier and, often, through this messiness, more hopeful and radical and important.

The first section of this book is about losing the plot, what I call "breakdown." I tell the story of how two events in my life, September 11 and Charlottesville, caused me to feel like I had to begin anew, and how drugs helped me not die as I stared at my life's blank page. And I tell the stories of a society that has seemingly lost the plot—in which many feel totally alone, without purpose, ground down by capitalism and its demands, and unable to find narrative stability—and discuss how drugs have been used by these people to survive these terrifying circumstances.

The second section is about finding a tenuous stability—rewriting the narrative and making sense of one's life again, and about the drugs people use to do this, specifically prescription drugs that have been sold to us with the promise of allowing people to live well-adjusted lives. Here, I explore the allure of stability, as well as its limits—how attempting to adjust oneself to a normative narrative of life can hinder our healing on both an individual and societal level.

And the third section is about narrative breakthrough, about pushing beyond this stability—attempting to dispense with the safety of predetermined storylines and find our own, outside of what society considers normal. And about the drugs people, including me, have used to do this. I explore whether drugs can help us, on either an individual or collective level, envision a present or future radically different from the ones we've been taught are possible.

I resist easy conclusions in all of these stories, but I do hope that through them I find some truths—about what it means to live in what can feel like a particularly depressing era of human history, and about what it can feel like to transcend beyond that history in search of something better.

In this moment I hear many questioning the point of work, the point of our political systems, the point of grinding on for what feels like diminishing returns, the point of living life with global warming and fascism on the horizon. We're questioning whether the narratives we've been given about our past and present are even true. And, because of all that, we're questioning our place in things, our own identities, our own senses of self.

There can be sheer terror in that. And, as I've found, immense possibility.

The page is blank. Where do you want to start?

INTERLUDE ONE
Accept Your Own Erasure

The first time my brain left my body, the first time I became acquainted with total dissociation, I was thirteen years old, in eighth grade, and running from the first collapsing Twin Tower in downtown Manhattan, 100 percent convinced that all my friends and I were about to die. The second, third, fourth, fifth, and sixth times were less dramatic—a moment in tenth-grade science class when a tinge of panic began crawling through my stomach and up through my esophagus as I realized I was attracted to the boy sitting next to me; a moment in college in rural Massachusetts, seeing a flyer in a gender-neutral bathroom, put up by some university anarchists, that declared you could be any gender you wanted to be. The thousandth time was again dramatic—running from the neo-Nazi plowing his car into us in Charlottesville.

It turns out you can grow accustomed to feeling inhuman, feeling like a ghost floating through a material world. Until, apparently, it all becomes too much or, really, all becomes too little—until life no longer matters because you are in no meaningful way alive.

There's a Looney Tunes cartoon starring Daffy Duck I saw when I was maybe seven, sitting alone on a dog-fur-covered couch before my parents woke up. In the cartoon, an unseen cartoonist is being rude to the duck, and keeps changing Daffy's body and background, erasing and redrawing, until Daffy is no longer a duck, but a catlike creature with a flag for a tail, or until Daffy is no longer on land, but suddenly sinking into the sea. In one scene, as the world around Daffy is erased completely, Daffy yells at the unseen cartoonist, until the artist's pencil comes down over the frame and begins to erase Daffy himself until he is nothing but a head floating on a white background. "Well," Daffy says, at this point more perplexed than angry. "Where's the rest of me?"

PART 1

BREAKDOWN

1

MY BREAKDOWN

THE DAY I LOST THE PLOT;
HOW KLONOPIN KEPT ME ALIVE;
AMERICA'S LONG SEARCH FOR SOMETHING
TO SOOTHE THE BREAKDOWN

Straight to hell. Everything around me death sculptures—the beige walls, the overly large flat-screen television, the plasticky pillows. Their auras threatened me, a cumulative Satan with an invisible pitchfork chasing me around a tiny room at the Courtyard by Marriott. There was no God. There was no salvation. There was only me, on 130 square feet of itchy carpeting, in Oakland, California, at 9:20-ish a.m., Pacific time, on September 14 of 2017, having what I would later refer to as "what happened," or "it," or "that time," or "my mental breakdown."

I could not comprehend how six days ago I had been at a club with a dear friend in New York, dancing to unidentifiable techno and doing pea-size bumps of cocaine every half hour; how five days ago I had had a normal dinner with my parents, chicken; how sixteen hours ago I had excitedly boarded a flight to California, convinced that this was the ultimate sign that my life was headed in the right direction—I was being paid to travel and give a talk about my writing. Wow.

But, I guess, the rumbles were there. The disquieting feeling on the plane, despite its smooth sailing, very brief but scary, in my stomach, like I'd just dropped down the first hill of a roller-coaster. I'd ignored it because I could not comprehend what it was, and because it was gone before I had reason to investigate. The strange twilight sleep I'd had that night. No thoughts infiltrating my mind, but something keeping me from full unconsciousness, something in me that knew what was about to happen, or was trying to prevent it from happening, maybe.

But then it happened.

I awoke with my hands violently shaking. I tried to make them stop. I couldn't, this in itself terrifying—that I was no longer in control of my own body. My eyes darted around the room, like they were looking for a hidden predator.

You are not in danger, I told myself over and over again. I attempted to sit down on the edge of the hotel bed and take a few breaths, but every time I stopped moving it felt as if I would combust from the excess energy coursing through me, a harsh, electric sensation shooting up my spine and into my brain, telling me to *run, run, run*. So I did. I darted out of the hotel room and down to the lobby and out to the sidewalk. Maybe fresh air would help. It did not. My breaths were shallow. My chest tight. I had experienced many panic attacks in my life—moments of overwhelm during breakups, or big moves, or big work deadlines; this was not one of them. Yes, there was panic, but it was more a sense that I was about to die, that my brain was in the process of some sort of explosion.

I had no clue what was happening to me, but even in those first few minutes of my breakdown, I knew that this wasn't going to be over soon. I knew that my life had irrevocably been changed in an instant.

As I paced back and forth on the street outside my hotel, I called my therapist in Philadelphia to tell him I was going insane. Dennis, a forty-something jovial gay man whom I'd started seeing a few months prior, picked up and asked me what was going on. I told him I did not know. All I knew is that I felt like I'd lost my mind. He told me, in his high and comforting voice, that I would be okay.

I imagined him sitting in his beige office chair, wrinkly polo and slacks on, gentle and understanding, a slight smile on his face. This thought brought me a small amount of solace. As I sobbed into the phone, he repeated the words: You'll be okay. You'll be okay. I highly doubted that, and yet him saying it calmed me down, just by a percentage or two, just enough to be able to concentrate on what he was asking me—if something had happened recently that might've triggered this state. I couldn't think of anything. It did not occur to me that this state made perfect sense for what I'd been through. But, I guess, that's the extent of denial I had been in—I'd pushed down so much for so long, cramming more and more into the limited space in my brain until the pressure built up, until the walls I'd erected to prevent psychic pain and discomfort could no longer hold . . . and then *boom*.

Dennis talked me through the next steps: As soon as I got back to the East Coast, I'd come see him to talk through what was happening.

I'd also maybe go to a psychiatrist as well to see if any new medication would help. But for now, I needed to figure out how to get through the next twenty-four hours in California, until my flight the next morning. The bigger problems: We could deal with all those later, Dennis said. We would figure out exactly what the hell was happening, he assured me. My mission now was just to stay alive and well enough to get home.

My panic rose as I thought about how I'd do this. My nervous system was so shattered that I could barely steady my hand enough to type out a text, much less think about the logistics of cross-continent air travel. But then Dennis said the magic words: take a Klonopin.

Ever since I'd had my first panic attack, about five years before that day in Oakland, I traveled with a few of the little blue pills. Just in case.

I rushed back to my hotel room to see if I had them on me. I thanked God like he'd rained down manna from heaven as I pulled out my pill case from my travel bag. I swallowed it with a swig of water from one of those little plastic hotel cups. God bless Klonopin. It saved me that day. It did its job, the same job it's been doing for millions of people for seven decades—quelling the feeling of breakdown.

Klonopin, aka clonazepam. A benzodiazepine, a lifesaver, a highly addictive substance. A little pill that within an hour eases all of life's problems. Back then I did not know how Klonopin worked, but I knew it could temporarily lessen the pain; not get rid of it, but turn the volume down at least, from eardrum-splitting screech to a low hum. Always miraculous to me that something so small could tame feelings so large.

After I swallowed the pill, I paced, and breathed jaggedly, waiting for it to kick in. Ten minutes. Twenty minutes. Pace. Pace. Pace. And then I could feel my breathing begin to smooth. A clarity in my mind returned. I still felt crazy, but at least I did not feel as if I was being chased through a Marriott by a pack of wolves.

The talk I was supposed to give—on gentrification and urban development, the topic of my first book—was in thirty minutes. It was a miracle I was able to make it—or, really, Klonopin was the miracle that enabled me to make it. Years later I searched the Internet for photos from that talk. Sure enough, there's me, eyes glassy and wide, in shock, but medicated into something resembling normalcy.

A local friend who'd come to the talk spotted me after I walked off the stage. I grabbed his shoulder and whispered to him that I was having a mental breakdown, that I needed to get out of there, that I could not stop shaking. So he took me where he was going: to a protest against his Bay Area university for hosting a talk by a far-right provocateur. Strangely, being around so many people, around the anger, the frustration, felt calming. It was like my mind had been externalized.

After the protest, back to my hotel room, half a Klonopin more, a shot of whiskey from a bottle purchased at the grocery store across the street, television set to some mindless something or other, itchy sheets, curtains closed, more Klonopin, another shot, more Klonopin, until I pass out, wake up, am somehow on a train, then a plane, more Klonopin, landing, relief, but only a little, lotion on a third-degree burn, still feeling like I do not belong in my skin; but at least back on the East Coast, in New York City, where I was born, in a car, to my parents' apartment; get there, I sob. More Klonopin.

I sat across from them in the living room of their apartment. The same apartment I grew up in. The chair I sat on had been there for most of my twenty-nine years. But now it felt different; foreign. Everything did. Like I was playing a video game of my own life. Later, I will learn to call this "dissociation," or "depersonalization." Back then, it all just felt like various parts of the same big thing: going insane.

I hoped the fact that my parents are psychologists would help me as I sat across from them; that they'd have some magic words to say that would make this all go away, or at least make it make sense. I asked them what was happening to me. They looked back at me with a mixture of empathy and concern, which made me panic more. Of course they didn't know what was happening to me. No one did. I cried harder. I am dying, I told them. That is the only explanation. No, you're not, they said. Yes, I am. No. I wanted their reassurance, yet when they gave it, it made little difference. I was too far gone. The only comfort they could give me was to tell me that stuff like this happens. That sometimes people go through periods of high stress and turmoil. Okay, I said. This did not provide much solace either—like telling someone in the midst of being squeezed to death by the world's largest vise that sometimes people feel pressure. I needed immediate relief. And words could not provide that. The only thing that could was Klonopin.

After an hour or so of crying, I retreated to bed in their small guest room, my older brother's former bedroom. A room I've stayed in a million times. But now it felt like a prison. Like the walls were closing in on me.

I somehow fell asleep. Dream: I am in a pastoral setting, a cabin my family spent a lot of time at when I was a kid. It's nice. And then the tornadoes and fires and mudslides show up.

At 4:30 a.m., I awoke in a panic, like I was being chased through the woods by some army, like I was about to be killed and could not stop running, like there were bullets whizzing by my head. Breath more jagged than ever. Alone in that small room not much bigger than the size of the full-size bed I rocked back and forth on as I told myself this was all temporary.

Somewhere in the back of my mind I knew it was not, or that temporary is relative; temporary can mean a long time. Mountains are temporary.

I racked my brain for answers—perhaps it was a delayed reaction to using cocaine a few days earlier. Perhaps my mind's chemicals were knocked off-kilter by that. Perhaps this is like what happened to me in college when I got off my ADHD medication Adderall the first time, a kind of withdrawal? Perhaps it's because I was planning to move back to New York from Philadelphia, had just broken up with my boyfriend, had just ended another relationship with a shitty friend whom I felt controlled by; perhaps it was because I had begun realizing I was trans, had begun realizing I was not happy, that there was an ennui within me that I hadn't addressed. A few days before the breakdown, in my diary I had written that I *was* happy. Yet I'd also written, "It's this feeling of death basically like walking around and not being in the real world at all. Totally removed." Perhaps the dissonance was too great; that I had become so dissociated, as if on top of a balloon, floating up and up, so many feet in the air, and somehow, I had just realized I had no way back down. Or maybe it was because of my short stint on antidepressants a few months earlier; maybe they'd permanently fucked up my brain and I was only just realizing it. Or maybe I was punishing myself for being happy, free, independent of the controlling friend, on my own and out of New York for the first time in my life, ready to be me for the first time. All explanations seemed plausible; none fully accounted for my state of near psychosis. As if explanations even mattered. Explanations are not cures, and they're certainly not fast ones.

All I could think, over and over and over again, was, *What the fuck is happening to me* and *When will this go away?*

The next few days inched by in a blur—slow and confusing and literally blurry because my brain was in such overdrive that my eyes could not properly focus. I tried to reassure myself. I kept trying.

Better today than yesterday.

Better yesterday than the day before.

Better tomorrow than today.

That became a new mantra, though it wasn't true. Each day felt equally bad, often worse than the day before. So I found a new mantra, one I'd heard repeated on the Internet and by therapy-minded friends over the years: "Progress isn't linear." Things don't have to be going well for them to be getting better; you could feel bad and still be healing.

This was not much comfort either.

My head was filling up with mantras, which in itself felt like a sign of a severe brain disorder—I was, all of a sudden, a person who needed platitudes to get through the day. I felt silly. Like, where's the switch to turn this whole cuckoo thing off? Stop shaking. Stop, just stop. Eventually, maybe five days in, sitting on that hard mattress in my brother's room, browsing deep into the Web forums, like page 45, of people struggling to maintain their sanity, I found a mantra that actually made sense to me: "Life is," a woman wrote. From what I could gather she was some kind of nurse. I made up more details about her to make her more real: her name was Jane and she had a scraggly-haired small dog and two kids and got too drunk at Thanksgiving dinners. "Life is. Life isn't good or bad, it just is. There are good parts, and bad parts. The sooner you stop expecting life to be good, and accept that it just *is*, the less you will battle against yourself, the more you will calm down." Something like that.

It was something I could chew on. Something I could work on accepting. A mantra good enough. I would repeat it to myself endlessly in the next months; I even got it tattooed below the crease of my right elbow. A constant reminder when I looked down: LIFE IS. Life is. Stop fighting. Life is. That's what the next days and months and years would be. Learning to accept. Learning to accept there was no going back. That I could not rebuild my brain in the same, pre-Oakland configuration. Learning to accept that it would take years, and in some ways a lifetime, to understand what had happened to me. Life is. Life is. Life is.

When the mantra didn't work, at least the Klonopin would.

I spent the next week in my parents' apartment, as I found being in familiar surroundings weakly comforting. The smells—their dog-fur-laden couch; the shampoo my mom used, the same one she'd always used, wafting out of the bathroom in a cloud of steam at six thirty in the morning as she got ready for work; even my dad's coffee breath—all little reminders that I was still in the same world I'd always been in, even if my mind had entered a new and terrifying one.

My dad, Michael, a full head of brown, wavy hair down to his neck, a big nose—in his seventies, but still looking like the Jewish hippie rebel he'd always been. And my mom, Sally, her gray and bouncing curls she refused to dye, her nearly all-black wardrobe, both signs of her unwillingness to bend to what the world thought women should be. I loved them both. I respected them both. Yet I also found myself angry at my parents for not being able to tell me what was happening to me.

Both Jews from Holocaust-surviving families. Which inspired both to study Sigmund Freud and his contemporaries and become psychoanalysts. They wanted to understand their own traumas and their families' traumas and how those two things intersected. And through that, they wanted to understand the world and its horrors—how people could carry on cycle after cycle of violence against one another; mother or father against child, government against populace. Psychoanalysis was how my parents made sense of everything. To them, the world was awash in violence and despair because the world was awash in repression and unaddressed trauma.

Yet they couldn't make sense of what I was going through in that moment. I do not blame them now; now it is obvious that *no one* could really understand what I was going through. But in the early days of my breakdown, I resented them for not being able to fix me. I resented that the most they could do was give me a hug, or tell me that it would be okay, or share a bit of my angst about my recent ex-boyfriend and our breakup, or encourage me to call my therapist during the worst of my panics.

Five or six days after Oakland, I sat in their living room and told them as much, my voice quivering, asking, pleading for them to help me figure out why I had woken up one day in a completely altered reality. And they couldn't. All they could say was that they were so sorry. I saw tears form in my mom's eyes. I started crying too. She could see how bad it all was, but she must've felt helpless. And her helplessness sent yet another jolt of panic down my spine—if she and my father, two people with decades of experience helping the mentally ill, could not fix me, then I truly was fucked.

After a week, I decided to leave their apartment and go back to Philadelphia and my own life. I was curious if getting back to a routine would bring me further solace. I wanted to get back to walking my dog, Remi—a big and goofy pit bull I rescued when I was twenty-two—each morning and afternoon and night; I wanted to get back to my own desk to write, or at least attempt to write—to see if I could still perform my job as a journalist; I wanted to get back to my own bed. But mostly I wanted to get back to my therapist. If anyone could tell me what was going on, it was him.

Except, I discovered, he couldn't. Not really. Or not in the way I want—not in the here's-how-we'll-fix-you-immediately way.

I sat across from him in his office in Center City, Philadelphia, and I asked him the same question I kept asking everyone: What the fuck is happening to me?

We went over the possible suspects: the current tumult in my personal life—friend drama, wanting to move back to New York, my breakup, all of that; general life stress and malaise—feeling directionless and unsure of what I wanted my future to look like; and then, oh yeah, Charlottesville. Dennis told me it made sense that a few weeks after this traumatic event I would have feelings about it.

I agreed, but I still couldn't really comprehend how the event, no matter how scary, could displace my entire being, making me feel like I existed in some parallel and terrible universe. Well, Dennis said, isn't this the *second* time you've almost died?

That was true. The first was when I was thirteen, on September 11, 2001. The day I saw people covered in dust and blood. The day I saw bodies falling from the sky. The day I thought for an hour that the rest of my school was dead. The day my parents couldn't find me for several hours.

Well, Dennis asked me, couldn't that be contributing to this? Charlottesville triggering the panic from back then—my body already prone from an early experience with fight-or-flight being easily kicked back into it?

And, Dennis asked, what about the whole familial aspect—the Holocaust-surviving grandparents and the trauma they passed down to my parents and then perhaps to me. Dennis told me surely all this was enough to make anyone feel troubled. A "perfect storm," he called it.

Yes, on paper, this all made sense. Trauma plus trauma plus trauma. But making logical sense of things did not help me with what I needed right then and there, which was relief.

I woke up each morning still feeling like I was being chased. It was not clear to me how discussing a trauma from sixteen years earlier, or even one from a month earlier, was supposed to change that feeling.

So, at a certain point, Dennis's calm demeanor and gentle insistence that we would figure this all out, however long it might take, began to anger me too. He, like my parents, was supposed to understand me. I thought he, like my parents, would have the best shot at fixing me. And it seemed he couldn't.

Two weeks into my breakdown, I broke down to Dennis. I sobbed and began yelling in desperation: Who the hell cares about my childhood and my traumas and how they might interact in my psyche? Can't you see I am on fire? Can't you see that all I need is someone to put it out?

Please, I begged him. He tried so hard to help. But he couldn't help with that. He couldn't put out the fire. At least not immediately.

After that session, I called my parents and asked them to send me the number of a psychiatrist—someone who could prescribe me drugs. I was in desperate need of a quicker fix.

I traveled back to New York the next day to see her. I sat in her cushy office on the Upper West Side of Manhattan and did the only thing I seemed capable of those days: I sobbed and told her I felt I had gone insane. She looked over her glasses at me, calmly. I don't remember exactly what she said, but it was essentially the same thing everyone seemed to be saying: these things happen, you'll eventually get better. She also told me it seemed like I had a lot of anger. No shit. After fifteen minutes she prescribed me Lexapro, a selective serotonin reuptake inhibitor, an SSRI, an antidepressant. I swallowed the first pill with an immense amount of hope that this would be the thing that finally made me feel like I wasn't on fire.

It wasn't.

Two days after starting, I was worse than ever. I spent the day back in Philadelphia writhing in bed, calling friends and crying. That night, I went on a bike ride to clear my head. As I gained speed down a hill into the charming and rich and quiet Old City neighborhood, as the fall breeze rushed past me—I felt, for a split second, something like an emotion other than pure dread and panic. The speed and the air against my face, forcing me to focus on just biking, momentarily took my mind off everything else. And then that feeling vanished. The recoil shocked me, like I'd been holding on to a life raft in the middle of a vast ocean and thought I might be saved . . . and then some cruel God just yanked it away.

I passed under the Benjamin Franklin Bridge. I thought about jumping off it. I'd entertained the idea of suicide as a kind of what-if in past bouts of depressions, but kind of like it was a fun little thought experiment like *wouldn't that be nice*. It gave me as much concern as whether to order Chinese food or pizza. But this time was different. This time it was as if there was another me within me, telling me to do it; as if it wasn't really my decision to make, but a directive from some terrible gremlin pulling the wires around in my brain.

I took a Klonopin to get to sleep.

The next morning, I decided not to take the Lexapro.

The days passed slowly and painfully. I could not write, because writing required thinking, and I could barely do that. Even looking at social media felt like too much for my brain. I'd lie in bed watching sitcoms; I'd call friends and they'd come over and sit with me for a bit, watch TV with me for a bit, try to make jokes. I felt grateful, but also pitied by them and jealous of them. I imagined that after they left me they'd talk to one another, like, "What happened? Their life seemed to be going so well!" In my head, I was now one of *those* people—the people who are talked about through small frowns and concerned whispers among friends, the people worthy of a moment of conversation among normal people before the normal people get to move on to more fun topics, before they then go grab a beer or see a movie or fuck one another or the myriad other beautiful things people can do when they're not mentally incapacitated.

Another day. Another therapy session with Dennis. We began by talking about the same things—Charlottesville, running from the Twin Towers when I was thirteen, my family's traumas. Something still wasn't making sense. "Is there anything else you feel like might be happening?" he asked. I hesitated to bring it up. It felt so . . . minuscule compared to almost dying, twice. But for whatever reason it bubbled up through my throat and then I felt it leave my lips: I had been wondering about my gender. I remembered going into my gender-bendy roommate/friend/sometimes-fuck-buddy's room when he was away a few months prior and putting on one of his skirts. I looked in the mirror. I felt . . . *something*. I waited for Dennis to look surprised, or to judge me, or to say, "Oh, wow!" But he just asked if there was anything else I wanted to say about it. I couldn't. Not then. Not because I didn't want to, or because I felt ashamed (though that too) but because that's all I knew right then—which was basically nothing. It all felt so random. Just another little thing to add into the mix of all the possible reasons I could have been feeling insane. The cherry on top.

The next day. The next session. We talked about the same things. Now with gender thrown into the mix. I told Dennis I was frustrated again. Like, how many times could we talk about trauma before it all clicked? But that's the process, Dennis said as calm as he always was—you keep addressing the same topics over and over again, but eventually, they begin to hit differently; you get deeper into them, you make connections where you saw none before, you find perspective where there once wasn't any. Perhaps that's why suddenly gender had come into the mix amid the endless trauma talk. Because we'd found a new angle; because the process, as frustrating and slow as it was, was working.

And perhaps that's why I cried harder than I ever had that session—tears and snot running down my face for thirty minutes. I was beginning to understand: This was not a matter of getting back to normal; this was going to be a matter of months, and years, of finding all the doors to get us beyond the walls I'd built up to protect my brain from all the things I was scared of—trauma, gender, everything. And not only finding those doors, but finding out which keys—which combinations of words and analyses of dreams and embodiments of emotional states—would finally unlock those doors. Endless possibilities. Dizzying. Painstaking.

After our session, I wandered the streets of Center City with no destination in mind, trying to internalize what Dennis had told me; trying to practice acceptance of my temporary-but-probably-long-lasting insanity; trying to see this crisis as something I could not quickly escape from, but as something to work through slowly. Very slowly.

That night, as I sat in a shitty Mexican chain restaurant and attempted to eat a burrito, I tried to think back to before Oakland—to remember what my brain felt like before then—and somehow will myself back into that state. This, of course, did not work. I almost threw up my burrito as I realized just how far I was from that pre-breakdown self. So I cried more in a drizzling rain as I walked through the city. I biked around again in the dark for a few hours, trying to get the stress out of my nervous system. I called my ex-boyfriend and asked him why I felt this way, as if he would know. He was nice, if unhelpful, but not notably so. No one could really help. What friend would be able to tell me: Well, it's obvious that you are processing several traumas, a recent one which triggered one from long ago, plus a family history of trauma that predisposes you to being triggered, oh, and plus you're probably trans?

So on top of feeling in deep pain, on top of feeling in crisis, I also just felt . . . alone.

That, I guess, is one of the dilemmas inherent in being human—that we're all different. No two histories or traumas or brains are the same, and those things can combine and manifest in your psyche in a trillion different ways. We can relate to one another over the broad feelings of stress or misery or despair, we can deem their overlaps a disorder or a syndrome or a diagnosis. But at end of the day, even if friends and professionals and communities are necessary to the healing of one's problems, your problems are yours and yours alone. And that is deeply isolating.

I got back to my small and dusty Philly apartment that night and lay in bed and tried to let it all wash over me. *No rush*, I told myself. *This will take a while.* Maybe what my parents and the psychiatrist and Dennis kept telling me wasn't some empty platitude they'd all conspiratorially settled on; maybe it was what they actually all knew from experience— that regardless of their inability to truly understand my specific circumstances, they could tell me with confidence that it would get better.

But it was all too much. I pulled my covers over my head and cried again. And then the panic started all over—knowing I would be crazy for the foreseeable future, and knowing that my journey would be a lonely one.

So I popped a Klonopin. And waited. And thirty minutes or so later, it all got better. Somewhere deep down, beyond the drug's effects, I knew that it was not actually better—that I would awake the next morning in the same place, with the same brain, with the same feeling of being chased by animals as soon as I opened my eyes. But Klonopin at least allowed me to live in a temporary fantasy of calmness; and, more important, it allowed me to see a world in which I could actually feel better. Like the split second of okayness on the bike a few nights before, Klonopin was not just a respite, but proof, however brief, that there was another side.

THE CONSTANT SEARCH FOR CALM

As long as humans have experienced emotional crisis (which is to say: for all of human history), they've attempted to ease their pain with drugs—plant-based psychoactives like marijuana in preindustrial societies, alcohol during the Industrial Revolution (quickly industrializing late nineteenth-century London, population 1 million, consumed an estimated 200 million quarts of beer, 50 million quarts of wine, and 10 million quarts of rum each year, for example).[1] What's new about our modern era isn't drug consumption, it's that drugs have become much more specifically formulated to ease each form of pain we experience in modern life. As capitalism has invented ever more ways to be miserable, so too has it invented ever more specific ways to ease that misery.

In an essay examining the origins of trauma and PTSD, the writer Will Self argues that mental trauma and the anxiety and despair it causes are inherent to the invention of modern, industrialized society. Self writes that technologies like the railway and the factory, and the very organization of life by a clock, were so destabilizing to our preindustrial rhythms that they caused a body- and mind-altering anxiety.[2] In this understanding of modern capitalism, the PTSD caused by war, or, say, a neo-Nazi plowing an American muscle car into a crowd of protesters, is not unique; it is just the furthest node on a spectrum of the trauma that essentially *everyone* experiences under modern capitalism.

Which perhaps explains why it was at the height of industrial America that an industry dedicated to calming people down blossomed.

The 1950s saw the introduction of the first popular, industrially made anti-anxiety drugs. First with an antipsychotic called Thorazine, and then, most popularly at the time, with meprobamate, aka Miltown, a sedative with mysterious chemical properties (to this day no one really understands how it works)[3] that immediately flooded American culture and bloodstreams. Newspapers called it a "wonder pill" and "emotional aspirin." Pharmacies made signs that said "Miltown Available

Tomorrow" to temporarily ward off the growing hordes of people coming in to get it.[4]

"Fashionable ladies and hard-driving male executives alike kept their supplies close at hand," historian of science Anne Harrington wrote in her book *Mind Fixers*. "Greeting card companies created cute Valentine's Day designs that incorporated the drug, and bars introduced the Miltini—a martini with a Miltown tablet in place of the traditional olive."

By the late fifties, one in three prescriptions in America was for meprobamate. Fifty tons were being produced a month, and a billion tablets had been sold within a few years.[5]

And then, as fast as they took over America, the pills disappeared, not because people realized that consuming vast quantities of drugs was bad, or because the government regulated their use, but because a new class of drugs, promising even fewer side effects and less potential for addiction, took over. And those pills, developed fifty years ago as a replacement for Miltown, are what sit in my bathroom cabinet, and in a small pill case in my bag wherever I go in case I have a panic attack.

Klonopin is a benzodiazepine—a class of central nervous system depressants first synthesized by a man named Leo Sternbach at the drug company F. Hoffmann–La Roche in 1955. Sternbach was notoriously messy; his bosses did not like him. He was hardheaded, convinced he could find a new tranquilizer despite the company's insistence he move on.

His research wasn't going anywhere. Eventually, his bosses ordered him to clean up his disorganized lab, start from scratch, get it together. As he decluttered, his colleague Earl Reeder noticed a "nicely crystalline" compound, labeled RO-5-0690, sitting around that had gone untested for twenty years, so, on a lark, they decided to give it to some lab mice, just to see what it would do. Immediately they noticed that it relaxed the little animals; their muscles loosened, their movements slowed. By 1960, RO-5-0690 was on the market, branded as Librium.[6] And three years later, the company released diazepam, branded as Valium, named after the Latin word "*valere*," which means "be strong." The drug became so popular in such a short time that a few years later the Rolling Stones released a song about it called "Mother's Little Helper."[7] By the late 1970s, Americans were consuming 2.3 billion Valium tablets a year. Billion. With a *B*. Somewhere between 10 and 15 percent of all Americans were on the drugs, as were somewhere between 4 and 8 percent of Europeans. By 1984, an estimated 500 million people worldwide had taken a benzo.[8]

After Roche released its little miracle pill, drug companies, searching for their own patentable versions, began pushing out as many benzos as they could. In 1975, clonazepam, aka Klonopin, came to market.

As is more common than you'd probably like to think with psychoactive medication, no one, including the scientists who made them, really understood how benzos worked, even as doctors prescribed millions upon millions of the pills to patients.[9] But in the late 1970s, researchers began to learn that the drugs helped flood the brain with gamma-aminobutyric acid, or GABA, which in essence blocks your nervous system from receiving too many activation signals.

There are dozens of different benzos, but they all work in basically the same way—forcing your nervous system into a kind of low-power mode. The main way they differ is in how long they last. One of the most popular, and notorious, alprazolam—more commonly known as Xanax—has a half-life of only twelve hours. You get high fast, you withdraw fast. That leads to more addiction. Klonopin, on the other hand, has a half-life of between twenty and eighty hours. The withdrawal is much slower. You're not zapped back into your normal brain so quickly.[10] And that's why doctors prescribed it to me. The disadvantage is that it takes longer to work.

Which is why I would pace back and forth in my Philadelphia apartment, heart beating a thousand beats per minute, for ten, twenty, thirty, forty minutes, until I felt a heaviness overtake me. My eyelids would droop. My thoughts, instead of feeling like they were being released via machine gun, felt like they were launched from an old-timey pistol shot underwater, the propulsion forcibly slowed. I would drift off to sleep, wishing I could build a world out of Klonopin, like a gingerbread house—the walls and floors and tables and chairs a dusty blue; a Klonopin lamp, a Klonopin rug, a Klonopin dog. Peace on earth.

And then I'd wake up the next morning and, of course, the terror would be back.

Seeing my trauma and my drug use in this historical context—Charlottesville not as a one-off event but just a particularly nasty instance of an entire system set up to traumatize, and thus a system that encourages people to find relief in chemical cures—made me feel less alone.

In their 2014 manifesto, the European leftist collective Plan C wrote that each age of capitalism comes with an attendant affect.[11] The Industrial Revolution brought widespread misery in the form of brutal factory working conditions. The early and mid-1900s brought crushing boredom, as lives became increasingly suburbanized, individualized, standardized—think of the prototypical depressed and stressed housewife and the businessman husband who cheated on her to add excitement to his life; stamp-size, pesticided grass yards, all cut to the same length, on which children would attempt to add any kind of spontaneity to their lives. The children of this era would go on to lead the next affective era in the form of the 1960s—which in many ways were a fight against this boredom, a call to reclaim the excitement of communalism, of revolution, of queerness and chaos. But as repression killed these movements, and capitalism moved on, a new era emerged: the age of anxiety, which we've been stuck in since the 1970s. An age where as a society we have enough, even too much—food, housing, work, entertainment—but these things are precarious, always at risk of being stripped away. Homes sit empty as the homeless population grows. Wages flatline as productivity skyrockets. We never know what the next year will bring, when our rent will go up, when the next war will start, when inflation will take food off our tables.

After my mental breakdown, I began to see this internalized precarity everywhere I looked. I saw it in friends who lost jobs and then turned to drugs to ease the anxiety of their financial uncertainty; I saw it in the news, in statistics about suicide and addiction, and I saw it in myself—this feeling that the world and its violences had been placed into me, into my nervous system and psyche, an unwanted osmosis of energy.

For me, that osmosis was direct and obvious—the violence of fascism all represented by one man, James Alex Fields Jr., driving his car into a crowd and infecting me and so many others with his energetic sickness. For so many others the osmosis is slower and less conspicuous—the constant stress on one's nerves from underpay and overwork and the rent being too high and our world, generally, being wholly unfair. But it is nonetheless damaging. We carry that stress in our nerve endings. We become bodies with constant excitation without release.

Klonopin does not permanently extinguish this excitation, but it tames it enough so that you can temporarily ignore it.

It's not an exaggeration to say that drugs, both illicit and prescription, saved my life. They helped me when nothing else would. It's hard to see through the haze of propaganda, the false divide that's been placed between medications and illegal substances. But, to me, that divide is much less clear. People use illicit drugs for the same reason they use prescription ones—to quell pain, to help them focus or get through the day, to ease their depression and anxiety. What differentiates these drugs is less a matter of their purpose, and more a matter of how our laws and media treat these drugs. They've associated them with the ravages of poverty, they've criminalized them so that users of these drugs end up in a constant cycle of violence. We've been led to believe that drugs cause the breakdown, when in truth they are part and parcel of it. If our minds are constantly burdened, constantly being reshaped by the trauma of capitalism, of course we're going to need ameliorants. Of course we're going to need a break.

Drugs can be used in ways that end up breaking us, that end up keeping us closer to the trauma than we should be. The systems we have set up in this world often do not allow people to use drugs in healthy ways, and to stop using them when they want to. But the reason people use drugs is simple: it's because they help. And the world, it's bad. So we need help.

When I was at my worst, when drugs were the only thing that would help, I took a kind of sick solace in that: that so many others were in the same place.

There was one good night in my life that first year of breakdown. Like, one memory I actually look back on fondly.

It was perhaps a month in. And my friend Bobbi came over to my apartment. We watched a movie, but I do not remember which one. We ate dinner, but I do not remember what we ate. I just remember her, this butch lesbian with short hair and an aura of calm about her, sitting next to me, holding my hand as I stared at the TV in a daze, under the influence of a broken nervous system and 1 milligram of Klonopin. At some point I got sleepy from the downer in my bloodstream. I asked to go to bed.

Bobbi came with me. I lay on my side, curled up like a baby on top of the covers, and Bobbi pushed up behind me, her strong arms holding me tight to her stomach and big breasts. She smelled like lavender and sweat.

My eyes closed and then opened and then closed and then, when they opened again, it was two hours later and she was still there holding me.

That was the only moment of true comfort in my life for a year, maybe more; the only moment where my brain truly felt like it could turn off.

I would chase that feeling. Of ensconcement from everything evil in this world. And chasing it is what would keep me alive during my darkest moments. In some ways, it's still what's keeping me alive—the knowledge that with people to hold you close (and perhaps a chemical flowing through you that allows your brain to feel the comfort of that), the other side is visible, reachable, already here.

2

A PERSONAL BREAKDOWN

THE INS AND OUTS OF A PERSONAL BREAKDOWN;
OPIOIDS AS BREAKDOWN-SOOTHERS;
WHY PEOPLE NEED DRUGS

For weeks and months and years after my breakdown, I felt alone in my pain, like I was the only one who had ever experienced such depths of sorrow. Yet I also knew that statistically, I was far from being the only one struggling—suicides have become the twelfth-leading cause of death in the US, and the second-leading cause of death of people between 25 and 34, and ages 10 to 14[1] (the only thing more deadly for kids is homicide[2]). The suicide rate increased 35 percent between 2000 and 2018. In 2021, 32.8 percent of Americans were depressed.[3] That's a third of the country. And doesn't include anxiety disorders and all the rest. Nearly a quarter of Americans are on psychoactive meds for depression, anxiety, ADHD, or another mental health condition.[4] A 10 percent increase in just a few years.

Things aren't much better elsewhere: In the UK, for example, one in four people experiences a mental health issue like depression or anxiety each year.[5] According to a survey of 150,000 people worldwide, researchers estimate that one of every two people across the globe will experience a significant mental health issue in their life.[6] Something is very wrong.

So many people in various states of pain, many of whom seek ameliorants in the form of substances. So why did I feel so alone during my breakdown? Why, as I paced back and forth in my apartment in a panic, waiting for my preferred downer—Klonopin—to hit so that I could feel the pain a little less acutely, so that I could get a little break, did I feel like I was the only one, when there were undoubtedly others like me down the block, on the street, in the apartments on either side of me?

Even as I recovered from the worst years of my life, I was stuck with a kind of anger at that. That I had been made to feel so isolated. I wanted to know how that happens—how someone, even someone with support and friends and money and a job, can be left to ameliorate their pain in complete isolation, left, essentially, to die.

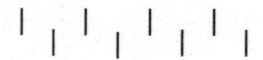

※ ※ ※ ※ ※

I'd known about Lucas for a few years; he ran in the same circle of New York queers as me. We'd never really talked, but as I recovered from my own breakdown and began my search for others whom I could relate to, people kept telling me to talk to him—that he had a lot to say about using drugs to cope with pain.

So, on a gray, spring day in 2022, I went to his apartment in north Brooklyn. It's in one of those gentrification buildings—small, boxy apartments with new but cheap appliances, a big window looking out onto nothing. Lucas's place is untidy but not terribly so. The dining room table is scuffed. The small bedroom, where he and his longtime boyfriend sleep, has clothes all over the floor. The boyfriend is at work. Lucas, in his late twenties, wears a baseball cap that says WINE DIVA on it, and a T-shirt with the logo of the band Nirvana, but the shirt is designer, Marc Jacobs. Lucas was employed by a tech company until he was laid off recently. So he passes his time watching daytime TV. *The View* is blasting through his very large television with a sound bar underneath it when I walk in. He loves *The View*. He watches it while he takes his pills.

Lucas buys what are marketed by his drug dealer as Percocets, a pain medication that's a combination of oxycodone (an opioid) and acetaminophen (Tylenol), usually prescribed to people in a lot of physical pain. But Lucas knows that they're not Percocet, or not primarily Percocet, but fentanyl—his friend who uses the same dealer tested them with a little fentanyl test strip a few weeks ago and got a positive result. It's not surprising; basically everything is fentanyl these days.

The problem for Lucas, one of many, is that fentanyl is 50 to 100 times more powerful than morphine,[7] which makes it much more cost-effective for producers and dealers—no need to smuggle huge bricks of field-grown poppy-turned-heroin through borders when you can produce batches dozens of times smaller in a lab. There were nearly 70,000 opioid-related overdose deaths in 2020, and fentanyl was responsible for 46,802 of them.[8] That's partly because it's so strong, but also because it really has taken over everything. It's nearly impossible to buy real heroin anymore, or pressed pills that claim to be things like Percocet, without getting some fentanyl.

Which pisses Lucas off because he knows the danger of fent; he'd rather have the percs, but they're just not available.

The percs he takes today are 15 milligrams each. Each pill costs $20. When I arrive, he quickly pops four into his mouth, chews them up (they hit faster and harder that way), swigs from a tall glass of water, and swallows. He lies back on his gray IKEA couch, his foot tapping. I vape my little nicotine pen and take notes as we chat.

Lucas feels in a pretty good place with his drug use that day, he tells me. A year ago, when the pandemic hit, he spiraled and went on a monthslong bender, from June to Halloween.

"The first few months were fun," he told me. "But then it became a problem financially, and physically—you always have to take more and more to feel the same thing. And once I was taking a lot, then it puts me in a kind of psycho state. Usually when I use I'm, like, happy and fun and bubbly, but I would just be aggro and mean."

When he'd get really high during that time, he'd break things, throw glasses, drum on the wall, talk almost like, as he described it, he had Tourette's.

"When you do it too much, it just becomes not fun anymore," he said. "That's when I try to regulate it."

His boyfriend has been very understanding, though Lucas knows some would call it enabling. But to Lucas, it's more that the boyfriend doesn't judge him for his use. He'll get mad at him about finances (at their worst, they were behind on a few months of rent), he'll get mad when he gets a mess, but he never makes Lucas feel bad for being a drug user. They've used a few times together, but the boyfriend's not really into opiates, so, usually, Lucas uses alone.

"He said its difficult to connect with me when I'm feeling the best I've ever felt in my life and he's just had a normal day," Lucas said.

Those were a hard few months. The messy months. Lucas started kind of blacking out from his drug use. Before then, as long as he had used, he'd never felt like he had reached a place where the drugs were a threat to his life. But those months were different. He was buying up to thirty percs a day. He was spending $10,000 a month on drugs. He was going through horrible withdrawals. "You're hot and you're cold. You're feverish. You have tremors. Your nose runs. And you have this depression and insomnia. It's not like normal depression. It's like I literally have no ability to connect with or care about anything on earth. It's fucking horrible, it sucks."

Lucas clawed his way back from that dark period. He didn't go to rehab. He didn't quit. Instead he used a combination of self-control and Suboxone—a drug prescribed to opioid users that contains buprenorphine and naloxone. Buprenorphine is a partial opioid agonist—basically it gets you a little high, and thus prevents you from going into deep withdrawal, and also, theoretically, works to lessen your cravings for opioids. Naloxone, aka Narcan, is an opioid antagonist. Used alone in a higher dose, it can quickly reverse an opioid overdose. It works 100 percent of the time if used soon enough and at the correct dosage, blocking your brain's opioid receptors so that the opioids cannot latch on. It's a miracle drug. It's saved countless lives. And when a low dose of it is combined with buprenorphine, it, in theory, prevents people from getting too high. It works, though many people hate it because of the naloxone part—your brain constantly trapped in a battle between feeling better and being blocked from feeling better.

But the Suboxone was effective for Lucas, he said. He didn't stop using opioids. But he'd use Suboxone for a week or two, then use percs for a few days, then Suboxone again, until he got to a place where his use felt sustainable, where it felt like a positive part of his life again. Now he uses a few times a week.

As Lucas tells me all this, he comes up—starts getting high. His eyelids droop a little bit, but he's animated, even excited. A common misconception about opioids is that they make everyone into a kind of zombie—in my experience with opioid users that's simply not true; most people relax but also feel up and loose.

"I'm at the beginnings of the high," Lucas says, smile on his face. "I'm tingly in my chest. When you shut your eyes you can kind of hear the flutter—or the shutter of your eyes, or blood vessels or something. Its like this *swoosh* and that's when you know you're getting high."

It's been about forty minutes since he first popped the pills, and he says he's about as high as he'll get. He craves another one or two pills, but not in a fiendish way, he says, just in a kind of wishes-he-had-the-money-for-them-but-is-okay-with-not way. He thinks this feeling will last about two hours, and then there'll be an afterglow all day.

Lucas is committed to not going too far, because he wants to be able to keep using—he wishes he could get on a maintenance program where they give you regulated, tested, clean heroin, so he could just be high in a safe way. They do that in some other countries. But not here. So Lucas, like basically every opioid user, is stuck regulating his intake himself, trying to ensure he can keep using something that brings him some semblance of satisfaction without going too far.

The opioid overdose statistics are horrifying, but they also belie the fact that many, many more people don't die from their use than do. Most people are like Lucas. They're not on front pages. They're not splayed out in the street. They're managing. Just trying to give themselves a break from life via chemical alteration. And keep themselves alive and well, or well enough, with very little help from anyone else.

"It's hard for me to structure my day without it," Lucas tells me. "So many days I just feel like I'm bored. And with the shit, psycho landscape we're living in right now, I don't want to deny myself joy. I know I'm using chaotically or problematically or whatever right now, but it's a source of joy in my life. I have something that makes me happy. You can say it's fake happiness or chemical happiness, but so is fucking everything."

Sure, there have been dark periods, but mostly he's been okay, he tells me. Employed. Stable enough, all things considered. (I mean, who is really stable these days?) He's been fine enough on opioids for a long time. He's been using since he was thirteen.

DRUG USE IS NATURAL, DRUG CRISIS IS NOT

It'd be easy to see Lucas's story as solely a story about opioids. But to me, Lucas's story is more complicated than that. Opioids may be the tool Lucas uses to quell his pain, but Lucas, like other opioid users, would likely not have become addicted to opioids if he wasn't in pain, and if there were other tools more readily available to help ease that pain. While my breakdown was different from Lucas's, and Lucas's different from that of any other drug user, what unites us all is that pain, and a search for an ameliorant.

What has changed in the past few decades is not only the availability of opioids—humans have used opioids for thousands of years—but the safety net available to people who are struggling.

The familiar story we've been told about the opioid crisis ("opioid," by the way, refers to all chemicals that affect people's opioid receptors; "opiate" refers to only natural ones like heroin and morphine)[9] is that it is a relatively recent phenomenon, largely caused by one corporation, Purdue Pharma, which helped flood the streets of our cities and towns with unneeded prescriptions for OxyContin, hooking people on the drug. When the prescriptions dried up, people turned to cheaper and more readily available opioids—heroin, fentanyl, and the like. This story is partially true, but incomplete. The crisis is not one perpetrated by one class of chemicals, but one perpetrated by humans—the policies they create, their indifference to death, their fealty to economic gain over human life.

When you swallow a Percocet, or inject fentanyl, or perform whatever your preferred method of opioid administration may be, the opioid flows through your bloodstream and into your brain, where it attaches itself to your nervous system's opioid receptors. And those little receptors are some of the most fundamental components of the human brain and body—their activation protects us from excessive stress and prevents us from feeling too much pain when we're physically injured. They're integral to our bodies' internal reward systems, to basically every base-level function we carry out.[10] Somewhere along the path of human history, we discovered that you can activate these receptors chemically. That through ingesting a substance, we could find the pleasure associated with sex or food much more easily, and much more intensely. Opioids trigger our most basic pleasure centers. That's why opioid use has existed for as long as human history has. They're that integral to our development.

It's why the Sumerians, back in 3400 BC, called the opium-producing poppies they grew "joy plants."[11] It's why one specific poppy plant, *P. somniferum*, is the one that made it to dozens of countries stretching from the Middle East to Europe to East Asia, hundreds of years before the world would declare itself to be in an "opioid epidemic."

The prevalence of this particular poppy plant the world over, one of only two poppy species that produce sizable amounts of opium, out of the 250 species of the plant, has led some historians and scientists to argue that *P. somniferum* was purposefully engineered, cross-bred generation after generation to become more and more narcotic, and then traded around the world thousands of years ago.

But we have coexisted in relative peace with opioids (and many other drugs) for much of human history. Radiocarbon dating has found opium existed between 5900 and 3500 BC in the Mediterranean. Evidence suggests its usage quickly spread across Europe and much of the world from then.[12] Greek, Egyptian, and Roman art and writing is rife with references to opium: a statue of a goddess from 1500 BC depicted with poppy capsules in her hair, her eyes sedate[13]; medical texts from 1000 BC that suggest the use of opium as an analgesic and pain reliever; it's referenced even in perhaps the most famous book of all time (besides the Bible), Homer's *Odyssey*.[14]

The historian D. C. A. Hillman, in his exhaustive account of drug use and representation in Greek and Roman societies, writes that much of the literature from the time references opium poppies, along with many other drugs. Pliny the Elder, the Roman author (and also naval and army commander general; everyone seems to have been both a writer and a warrior back then), born twenty-three-ish years before the switch from BC to AD, counted opium poppy as a "garden variety" plant grown in Roman families' backyards. People were getting high while Jesus was being born.

Aristotle references opium, along with several other drugs, in a short work titled "On Sleep" ("they all [mind-altering substances], whether potable or edible, for instance poppy, mandragora, wine, darnel, produce a heaviness in the head; and persons borne down [by sleepiness] and nodding [drowsily] all seem affected in this way, i.e., they are unable to lift up the head or the eye-lids."[15]) Aristotle was describing nodding off in 350 BC.

Hillman argues that part of the reason we've forgotten or ignored that drug use has been a constant for much of human civilization is that we've applied a modern, prohibitionary lens to the past. Scholars leave much of ancient drug use unmentioned in their histories, as if, Hillman says, they are ashamed of it. Which is strange, because within the texts themselves, there appears to be no shame, no stigma attached to these mind-altering substances. They are simply a fact of life, like food.

Ancient texts also make it obvious that people knew the dark sides of these drugs, knew that people could go too far, become dependent, withdrawn, despondent because of them. But while addiction has followed drugs wherever they are from the beginning of time, the idea of an addiction crisis seems much more recent, a result of both the modern prohibitionary mindset which shames drug users into isolation and desperation, and the exponential power of the newer drugs modernity has given us.

The number of people who use drugs like opioids fluctuates, the response to that use fluctuates, but it seems as long as the drugs are available, there will be some people who use them, and some percentage of those people who need help when that use goes too far. Yet despite this constant use it wasn't until 1821 that we got our first truly popular account of drug use, when the English essayist Thomas De Quincey published what we'd now call an addiction memoir, *Confessions of an English Opium-Eater*.

The book, the first of its kind, paved the way for a new understanding of drugs in the English-speaking world. That world was already awash in drugs, especially opium, but few talked about it, and when they did, they did so with a heavy dose of racism, envisioning drugs as a foreign threat, something that only concerned the lower classes and immigrants. Respectable English people were fond of saying that all Turkish people were opium users, even as the Brits ingested loads of the stuff—Robert Morrison writes in the 2013 introduction to *Confessions* that opium was cheaper than alcohol, legal, and sold as a cure to basically any ailment one could think of—from cholera and cancer to diabetes and depression.[16]

De Quincey had his own racism too, casting his drug use as somehow different, or more intellectual, than that of people from other ethnic backgrounds. He posited that a Turk could not experience the same pleasure that he did from opium. In this way, De Quincey's book was successful partly because it allowed Europeans to admit they sought forbidden pleasures too, while also allowing them to see themselves as erudite for doing so. It created a binary that exists today: the good drug user who uses for intellectual pursuits, and the bad one who must be punished. That binary is still present in nearly every media story about the opioid epidemic; it's why we seemed to only recently realize, after the past opioid surge that came via the overprescription of OxyContin, that people were being killed by the drugs, because, all of a sudden, the public face of use and abuse was white.

Of course, the book was more than racism. *Confessions*, which was first published as a series of essays in a London magazine, was an overnight sensation for the same reason so many addiction memoirs today still are: he allowed a fundamentally prudish society to admit that drugs had an allure, that even with all their potential downsides, their life-ruining potential, there was a reason behind their use—namely that they provided pleasure, and that for those in great pain, they provided something more important than pleasure: solace.

De Quincey was aware that he would scandalize a nation with his work. But that's what he wanted. "Nothing, indeed, is more revolting to English feelings, than the spectacle of a human being obtruding on our notice his moral ulcers or scars, and tearing away that 'decent drapery,' which time, or indulgence to human frailty, may have drawn over them," he wrote.[17]

And that's what he did: tear away that decent drapery, in painstaking detail telling readers that many more people than polite society wanted to admit were druggies.

"Here was a panacea—a 'drug to quiet all pain and strife'[18]—for all human woes," De Quincey wrote. "Here was the secret of happiness, about which philosophers had disputed for so many ages, at once discovered: happiness might now be bought for a penny, and carried in the waistcoat pocket: portable ecstasies might be had corked up in a pint bottle: and peace of mind could be sent down in gallons by the mail coach."

What a scary thought for a society so focused on the nobility of hard labor and silent suffering, that one could simply make their own happiness. De Quincey told the world it was not only possible, but that a large fraction of society was already doing it—going to the pharmacy and buying laudanum (opium dissolved in water), and getting high.

De Quincey felt opium connected him to his life, to God, to his own mind. He did not retreat from society, but enjoyed it more—he wanted to hear music, see performances, celebrate the best that his culture had to offer. And his book is much like an opera, with a crescendo detailing the heights of his pleasure: "Thou only givest these gifts to man; and thou hast the keys of Paradise, oh, just, subtle, and mighty opium!"

And then, of course, came the crash.

And it's in De Quincey's downfall that we see the dangers of opioids, and really all drugs: they can help us ameliorate our states of breakdown, but in societies not built to help drug users out of their states of distress, in which drug users are isolated and shamed, drugs can compound that isolation and shame. Addiction becomes a feedback loop and keeps people in their breakdown states for longer than they should be. In De Quincey's downfall, I see Lucas's story. I see the story of millions who understandably turn to drugs to ease their pains, and then who are left to suffer with little to no outside help.

For De Quincey, the addiction felt inevitable. There was no other option: "I could not have done otherwise," he wrote. Facing a series of personal crises and a seemingly undiagnosable physical torment, he began using opium constantly. He would successfully taper down from 320 grains of opium a day to one-eighth that amount, but every time he did he would experience "the cloud of the profoundest melancholy." He began to feel trapped: "I seemed every night to descend, not metaphorically, but literally to descend, into chasms and sunless abysses, depths below depths, from which it seemed hopeless that I could ever re-ascend."

He felt his traumas were carved deep into his brain; sometimes separated by a veil, or many veils, but always there. He would walk on a sunny summer's day, and only feel death.

"It was not for the purpose of creating pleasure, but of mitigating pain in the severest degree, that I first began to use opium as an article of daily diet," De Quincey wrote.

For De Quincey, opium was an effective solution to this. It allowed him to experience happiness. It allowed him to walk in the sun and feel something other than death. It allowed him not only to numb pain, but to lift the veil of that pain so that he could experience joy.

Enough people could relate to that to make De Quincey's book a global sensation. People began blaming the popularity of *Confessions* for an increase in opium use, and for opium deaths for years after its publication.[19] Other writers said they were influenced by the book—influenced in their writing style, or influenced to try opium, or both.

None of this benefited De Quincey himself. He for years struggled to make money, and was sued over debts several times. His physical health continued to deteriorate, and so did his mental health.

Joel Faflak, literary historian and biographer of De Quincey, argues that the book and the reactions to it would foretell much of the industrialized world's subsequent attitude toward drugs and mental health. People were fascinated by a substance's ability to alter our interior states, and simultaneously terrified of the implications that could have on a society scared of the very idea of sharing our pains with one another. It was easier for people, even as they gobbled up De Quincey's writings, to dismiss him as a dangerous madman.

His book showcased the "habit of diseased introspection ... so tolerant of its own deformities as to lose all sensitiveness about them," read one obituary shortly after his death, calling him the "most unhealthy and abnormal mind to be found amongst modern writers."[20]

De Quincey died at seventy-four, in 1859, screaming for his sister, who had died during his childhood. He was penniless and alone.[21]

He had provided the world a truth about drugs, and thus a truth about ourselves, about our psyches and pains and how we seek to ameliorate them, and received little in return.

But in that way he told us one more important story, one about the future beyond his life: that drug users are able to shine a light on the parts of our societies and our selves that we most want to keep hidden, and that in return for that, we often relegate them to loneliness and death.

It became clear to Lucas only in retrospect why he started using opioids so young—that he was trying not only to numb himself from pain, but to create a happiness that wasn't available to him.

Lucas grew up in a relatively conservative town in Virginia. By middle school, Lucas was already experiencing a lot of anxiety. It was less one big, dramatic event that caused his unease, and more just an ennui, an apathy to his life and his surroundings that seemed constant. He felt outcast and isolated by his queerness.

"I was bullied for being gay before I even knew I was gay," he told me.

But he also just felt like something was missing in his life, like he wanted something more.

The summer before eighth grade, his grandfather, who was dying of cancer, moved in with Lucas's family so that Lucas's parents could take care of him. Lucas's grandpa was supposed to be there for a summer, but he passed away within a month.

He left behind six bottles of painkillers, Vicodins.

"Witnessing someone die really quickly in front of me probably tipped the scale," Lucas said. Lucas began taking the pills without telling anyone.

"I literally didn't even know what they were, I just wondered if they could get you high," Lucas said. "I didn't know they were, like, the most powerful drug in the world. I was thirteen. And after taking one I was obsessed. I was like, OMG this is the best thing I've ever done."

Lucas weighed less than a hundred pounds at the time, so the supply was enough to last him a year or two; he needed just one pill to get "high as hell."

"I was still reckoning with my sexuality; I was bullied. The Vicodin just evened me out and made me happy . . . it took away the negative," he said. "Some people describe it as like a warm hug, or like a heavenly experience, and that's certainly been my experience—a stress-free, all-around happy experience, no matter what's going on, just unequivocal happiness. Which, at thirteen, is very dangerous. Because after a couple of years, I knew there was never going to be anything better for me."

As Lucas's grandpa's stash was running low, when Lucas was in high school, one of Lucas's best friends, a football player, injured his shoulder while on the field. The friend was prescribed something like 150 Vicodin by a doctor, which the friend readily shared with Lucas. Sometimes they'd take them together, and sometimes the friend would sell Lucas a few for a few dollars. So through pure luck, or really through the US's insanely lax drug prescribing practices at the time, Lucas ended up with an uninterrupted ten-year supply of Vicodin, from the age of thirteen through college.

Still, Lucas didn't use every day. He'd use for a while. Then stop. Then start. Then stop again. But when he'd stop using for a week or two he wouldn't go through withdrawals. Not yet. So he didn't consider himself an addict.

But then, junior year of college, Lucas was introduced to Xanax, and things started taking a turn. He'd mix the benzos with the opiates and then he'd black out, steal shit, fight people. He went on a two-week binge that ended with an intervention from his family. He got into a Suboxone program. He stayed on Suboxone for six months and then started using again.

Lucas has repeated this cycle from senior year of college in 2018 until now—Suboxone to hydrocodone or oxycodone and back again. At periods of peak use, the withdrawals have been horrible, so he tries not to take the pills too many days in a row. But he is, mostly, comfortable with his use, he says. Even with the withdrawals, even with the money problems. He's been using for so long that he doesn't really know what else to do, except use as safely as he can.

"I have a kind of harm reduction model for myself—if I'm not really blowing my money or really endangering my health and I'm not using daily, I'm holding myself to a standard that a little bit of use can be enjoyable," he told me. "Because it's been in my life so long, in so many incarnations, it's kind of second nature to me at this point. I don't think my goal will ever be pure abstinence, unless the consequences are so intense that that really has to happen."

Two weeks after our first meeting, the consequences start to pile up. When I come to meet Lucas, dried blood leads me from the lobby door of his apartment building to Lucas's apartment. There's more blood inside, on the floors, and other stains across the wall and ceiling. Lucas, already pretty high, is pacing back and forth on a half-mopped floor that he's attempting, only slightly successfully, to continue mopping. He stops every few seconds to talk, and then mops over the same spot again. There has been, he tells me, an incident.

A few days ago, Lucas was home alone. He only had enough money for three of his regular pills. So, after buying them, he decided to snort them, to get a more intense high; more bang for his buck. The high was too intense. He went into a kind of fugue state. He broke glasses, he took a shower while singing and screaming. And somewhere in that time he cut his foot. When he got out of the shower, there were cops in his apartment. Apparently, to his neighbors, the glass crashing and the screaming sounded like domestic violence. The cops saw the blood. They began searching for someone whom Lucas had hurt, rifling through his closets. But it was just Lucas, doing the damage all on his own. And once the police realized this, they told Lucas he needed to go to the local hospital for a psychiatric evaluation.

Lucas did not want to, but was put in handcuffs, put in the back of an ambulance, and taken to a local ER, and guarded by cops anyway. There, he waited eight hours to see a doctor, who took a brief look at Lucas and said he could go back home.

"Every time something like this happens, it's because I couldn't figure out the strength of the pills," Lucas told me. If he had a regular supply, a regulated supply, he said, this would not have happened.

But Lucas also knows it's not only the reliability of the pills that's changed. His use has too—partly because the pills are stronger, so he's become more accustomed to higher doses, and partly because that's how addiction works. What was once a helpful ameliorant can spiral into something dangerous very quickly. I see this happen in real time. In the few weeks since first starting my interviews with Lucas, he's gone from a relatively stable, though still dangerous, pattern of use, to using almost every day.

It's gotten to the point that when Lucas goes for thirty-six hours without using, he becomes so sick, the withdrawals so intense, that for the first time in a long time his boyfriend starts giving him a little bit of money to get just a little bit high, to stop the pain. It's made the relationship tense.

The next time I interview Lucas, about two weeks after the hospitalization, he tells me there's been yet another incident. The night before, at three a.m., he and his boyfriend got into a fight—there was more screaming. Lucas walked outside to cool off. But he was too high again. He wasn't in control of his own body and mind—he began screaming again, babbling to himself on the street. He sat on a mailbox outside his neighbor's house. Apparently, the neighbors saw him and were concerned. Within a few minutes, several squad cars pulled up and told Lucas he needed to go to the hospital again. The cops asked to search Lucas's phone, but he'd left it in the apartment. The hospital was less bad this time around, Lucas tells me—less waiting around.

But the incident is enough to shake him, and me. When I see Lucas that following morning I am worried. He hasn't slept in a day, only a few hours removed from the psych eval, and he's nodding off from the drugs—every few sentences punctuated by his eyes closing and his head drooping and his mouth going a little slack for a few seconds, before he suddenly perks back up. He hiccups and burps, and he's worried he's gonna throw up—maybe something weird is in this batch, he tells me.

I want to leave, but I stay there for a while to make sure he doesn't overdose, checking to make sure I have Narcan in my backpack.

As Lucas comes in and out of full lucidity, local news plays loudly on the TV in front of him. *The View* ended twenty minutes ago and he hasn't bothered changing the channel. The news, as always, is bleak. Shootings, missing people, hit-and-runs—two of them within ten minutes of each other on Long Island. A segment on the anniversary of the police murdering George Floyd. Then, a segment about how there will be more hurricanes this season because of higher water temperatures. It is, apparently, the seventh above-average hurricane season in a row. Then, a commercial for some nonprofit that wants to end drug addiction. Then, a commercial for New York City's overdose prevention services—they want to encourage people to carry blue nylon bags containing Narcan, the same blue bags that sit in Lucas's cupboard, and in my backpack, and in the bags of dozens of friends I've told to always keep on them, and in hundreds of restaurants and bars and crisis centers and hospitals and basically everywhere (though still not in enough places), because that's how pervasive this epidemic is.

The local news depresses Lucas. He knows this shit happens but he doesn't want to hear about it all the time. Life is hard enough. Later he tells me that this is the kind of ennui-inducing stuff that keeps him using—less one traumatic event and more the fact that life is constantly stressful, especially during Covid, when he felt particularly isolated and unable to live a fulfilling life. Lucas would watch his friends accomplish things—have successful relationships and careers.

"I felt very stuck," he told me.

But when I was interviewing Lucas, the stasis of his life and use of opiates had become a self-perpetuating cycle. The more he took painkillers, the more chaotic that use became, the more he was unable to do all the things he felt he was missing out on in life—and that became all the more reason to find fulfillment chemically.

That day, the one after his second hospital visit, as Lucas comes into a brief moment of coherence before nodding off again, he tells me he too has become concerned about his use. He wants to ramp down. He can't go off completely without intense withdrawals, but he thinks he can stop using so much. Yet as he says this, he decides to chew another blue pill; it tastes "cardboardy," which to Lucas means it's not as professionally made as the previous batch.

"I feel like the last time I saw you I was in a good place," he says. "Now I'm like, I definitely want to slow down and get this shit under control. It needs to stop—the screaming, that's not even fun. I never want to get to that point."

An hour later, when I'm confident, or semiconfident, that Lucas will not die, I leave. I hope his boyfriend will get back soon. I check in on him via text throughout the day.

I get back to my apartment and pop my ADHD medication, Adderall. Also blue. What is it with pill manufacturers and blue? I wonder. I try to put the depressing situation out of my mind. I don't like seeing people like that. Yet I feel I cannot judge him, as I am drug-dependent too. We both take little blue pills nearly every day. My pills are just more regulated and thus safer, less likely to kill me.

As I interviewed Lucas, and as I reported in this book, that central unfairness stuck with me. Everyone I talked to had turned to substances for similar reasons: to quell the pain inherent in our existence, whether that pain was sudden and acute, as was my case with Charlottesville; or more diffuse and dull, as it was for Lucas and many others I'd interviewed. The differentiating factor in our outcomes—whether we were able to live lives of relative safety; whether we could keep our careers and relationships and friendships going and not spiral out of control—seemed less about our specific psychologies and more about our specific circumstances: which of us had access to tools like therapy and supportive families and money, all of which can help keep drug use in check, and which of us didn't. Which of us gravitated toward drugs that were deemed by the government to be ameliorants worthy of legal protection and regulation, and which of us didn't.

Lucas and I both used drugs on a near-daily basis for the majority of our lives. But my use, especially of the more potentially addictive drugs like Klonopin, was, generally, overseen by a team of professionals. And those drugs were professionally manufactured and consistent in strength. Lucas, on the other hand, was pushed into an isolating spiral of use without any oversight or support. And his preferred substances were, largely because of decades of negligent and punitive government policy, made as strong and as inconsistent and as dangerous as possible.

So it was no surprise to me a few weeks later when I got a text: Lucas had overdosed. It was through a combination of luck, and the one policy the government *has* gotten right (at least in New York State) in relation to opiates—the proliferation of free Narcan—that he survived.

A WORLD ATTEMPTING TO MANAGE PAIN

The majority of people who use opioids, even today, when they are more potent than ever, do not become addicted to the drugs—estimates vary, but somewhere between 3 and 19 percent of those who take prescription painkillers develop a dependency on them.[22] Yet more people are dying from opioids than at any point in human history.[23] If opioids are a constant in humans' search for ameliorants to their pain, then perhaps what has changed in the past few decades is not just the availability or potency of the drugs, but the amount of pain that people are attempting to ameliorate.

Though of course no two struggles are the same, a society with a fraying social safety net accentuates the desperation of nearly everyone. In many Western countries, pay has stagnated, worker protections have been systemically weakened, and housing prices have skyrocketed. In the US, housing prices ballooned by nearly 120 percent between 1965 and 2020, while incomes rose by only 15 percent.[24] In the UK, the same economic factors have translated to nearly 50 percent of people turning off or rationing heat in the winter.[25]

Homelessness and poverty are perhaps the most obvious signs of social decay, but I see it everywhere. Statistically, we are becoming more isolated, lonely, depressed, and anxious as each year passes. I see that decay in the faces of friends who can't find steady work, who spend their days alone numbing themselves with opiates and other drugs. I see it when I get a text at nine a.m. on a Sunday telling me that a friend has overdosed on a club drug the previous night—the second weekend in a row; an occurrence among my queer community that seems more and more common these days. I see it in Lucas's story—how, despite a boyfriend and access to work and an apartment, he was left with so few places to turn as his addiction spiraled. And I see it in my story—the deep loneliness I felt as I struggled to rebuild my life from a breakdown. Loss—grief, heartbreak—is inherent to life. But the amount of loss we all face—an amount that can become untenable to the point that people develop severe addictions to cope, untenable to the point that people die young from overdoses and suicide more each year—is not inevitable.

We are social creatures, and this feeling of social loss thus hurts us at our deepest levels. In 1920, Freud wrote that a child feeling detached from their mother will result in a pain that is emotionally identical to a physical injury.[26] Since Freud's writing, scientists have been able to prove the veracity of his claims: that emotional pain is, to our brains, very similar to physical pain. Psychologists have found that grief produces physical symptoms: fatigue, shortness of breath, abdominal pain.[27] A 2021 study found that a common physical pain suppressant, acetaminophen (aka Tylenol), lessened not only physical pain but emotional pain too, suggesting that the same chemical processes govern both.[28] One researcher found that widows were more likely to die within six months of the loss of a loved one—the ultimate physical price for an emotional problem.[29] Another researcher found that parents grieving the deaths of their children experienced frightening physical symptoms—one parent described an excruciating pain, as if her limbs were being chopped off; others had headaches and stomachaches so debilitating they could not move.

I've experienced this connection between physical and emotional pain as well. On the bad days, even years after my mental breakdown, I would get body aches that made me feel as if I'd just run a marathon. I would feel like I had the flu. I'd need to lie down for an entire day. I'm sure a doctor could have diagnosed me with chronic fatigue syndrome or fibromyalgia. At certain points the physical pain was so intense, and so consistent, that I was convinced I had a rare disease, maybe a brain tumor, or Lyme disease. I would walk for a few blocks and then need to rest for hours. The stereotypical image of a depressed person that you see in movies and in antidepressant commercials—lying on the couch, immobile—has some truth to it, but perhaps the reason they cannot move is not because they are simply sad, but because it is physically painful to do so, because their psychic pain is physical.

So it makes sense that opioids are so popular these days. That we are in an opioid crisis, because we are in a crisis of pain both physical and mental.

I tried many things to quell my physical pain—exercise, yoga, acupuncture, breathing exercises. All worked a little, though none that well. What I ultimately settled on to help me was a drug: kratom, the leaves of the *Mitragyna speciosa*, a tree indigenous to Southeast Asia, ground down into a fine powder. Laborers in Malaysia, Indonesia, and elsewhere have for hundreds of years used kratom to help them get through their physically demanding days. The tree is closely related to the trees that produce coffee beans. Some varieties of it stimulate you, others sedate. It's legal in some states in the US, illegal in others. Internet forums are filled with thousands of testimonials from pain patients, chronically ill elderly people, people with injuries, the depressed, those going through opioid withdrawal, all thanking the drug for helping them. That's how I found the drug. On an Internet forum. And, while not classified as an opioid, its chemical compounds act in a similar way to opioids, stimulating the body's and brain's opioid receptors. Kratom is more mild than most opioids, but it can still cause dependency[30] for the same reason opioids do—your body acclimates to the chemical attachment, and you withdraw when the chemicals are no longer there.

And I am dependent on it. Every day I pour a scoop of the green powder into a cup, mix it with hot water and oat milk, and drink it while working, or reading, or watching TV. I feel a slight sense of calm wash over me. It is a mild high, but it is still a high.

I choose to view my dependency as no different from those who are dependent on an antidepressant, and no different from those who are dependent on illegal drugs like heroin or fentanyl. I, fortunately, have found a drug dependency that feels less catastrophically life-changing than other dependencies might—I won't rob a bank to get more of kratom, I won't cut off my family because of it. But whichever drug someone is on, I believe we're all playing the same game of whack-a-mole—attempting to manage lives of varying degrees of pain, attempting to mitigate the societal breakdown all around us.

If it were not for my relative privilege, the fact that I could afford therapy and a gym membership and yoga and acupuncture and time off from work, time to collapse in bed and allow my body to rest from the pain, it's likely I would need a stronger opioid agonist, like so many do. What has saved me from the worst parts of addiction is access to nonnarcotic solutions to my pain, solutions many people do not have the time or money for. Yet still I must use those nonnarcotic solutions in combination with narcotics to feel okay enough to make it through the day. Given that, it feels impossible to judge anyone who uses drugs stronger than kratom. And it feels inevitable that for some, no matter how many ameliorants they may have access to, the pain will be too great to manage.

Beginning in 2015, Princeton economists Anne Case and Angus Deaton began investigating a curious trend: After decades of steady increases, the life expectancy for some Americans was declining. For white Americans, particularly those without college degrees, deaths were skyrocketing. As of 1999, the mortality rate for white people with less than a college education was 30 percent lower than for Black Americans, which is what you'd expect in a country with a racist medical system and economic policies that have historically privileged white people. But by 2015, the numbers had flipped. The mortality of white people without a college education was 30 percent higher than Black people of the same educational demographic.[31] The numbers were puzzling to researchers—how could a traditionally privileged group (at least comparatively privileged to people of other races in the US) be dying en masse, and in such a short period of time? What they found was that for middle-age white Americans, the vast economic shifts in the country over the past few decades came as a kind of shock to the system. After decades of relatively steady employment and wages, a combination of outsourcing jobs to other countries, depressed wages, and the subsequent breakdown of communities and families that relied on those jobs had pushed people into a collective hopelessness. Suicides, drug overdoses, alcohol-related deaths all skyrocketed. Case and Deaton called them "deaths of despair."

A nagging question for researchers looking into these deaths was how white people could be dying at higher rates than people of color from these self-inflicted deaths. Black mortality and Hispanic mortality are still significantly higher than white mortality in the US.[32] People of color have less access to medical care, and less access to sufficient and nutritious food. But, as of 2015, it seemed that nonwhite communities had better insulated themselves specifically from these deaths of despair. In the face of the inherent and constant racism of the United States, communities of color had found coping strategies that enabled them to weather oppression. That, to one researcher, explained why poor Black Americans were significantly more optimistic than poor white

Americans[33]—white people were simply not used to being on the losing side of this country's economic equation.[34] So, to numb the loss of their status and stability, many turned to alcohol, to drugs, to suicide. This might also partly explain why men commit suicide at a rate 3.88 times higher than women—women, oppressed for eons, have developed effective coping strategies for the stress of their lives.[35]

It is perhaps a hard pill to swallow, that it is not only the amount of pain, but not being accustomed to that pain, not knowing how to effectively mitigate it, not knowing where to turn, that causes addiction and death.

In the past several years, politicians and the media have finally decided to address the opioid crisis. To do so, they've largely singled out the corporations that made billions selling opioids like OxyContin and made billions more by ensuring nothing—doctors, the government, insurers—got in the way of their distribution. And to be sure, without those corporations, we'd be facing a much different crisis. Without them, there's no way the number of opioids dispensed in the US could quintuple from the early 1990s to 2012.[36]

But in directing the public's attention only to the supply side of the crisis, we've continued to ignore the demand side—the fact that people are seeking out these drugs because more and more people are in deep emotional pain, and do not have the skills, community, time, or money necessary to address that pain.

Opioid prescriptions have been declining dramatically—down 44.4 percent from 2011 to 2020.[37] It's now relatively difficult to get an opioid prescription—pain patients complain that the pendulum has swung so far in the other direction that doctors are reticent to prescribe opioids even for extreme physical pain. But deaths from opioids continue largely unabated. Stopping the flow of one source of opioids won't stop the crisis, because the crisis isn't the drugs, the crisis is the despair.

│ │ │ │ │
 │ │ │ │

About six weeks after we'd last met, Lucas was doing okay, he said. He was using slightly more than he wanted to, but still felt in control.

But then, one hot summer day, Lucas and his boyfriend got into another fight about his use. Afterward, Lucas was feeling angry and ordered some pills, the usual—fentanyl-disguised-as-Percocets. He got high. Then he ordered some more. At some point he lost track of how many he had taken.

"I always thought if I was ODing, I'd be able to identify it and stop it, which was kind of stupid because I don't think anyone can really do that," Lucas later told me. "But I'd been using for so long without a problem that I always had this idea that I could pull back."

By ten or eleven that night, Lucas was in that place that he never likes to be—he was being loud and rowdy, stomping around the living room again. The noise woke up his boyfriend, who was asleep a few feet away in the bedroom. From bed, the boyfriend heard clangs and shouts and bangs and then, all of a sudden, silence. Lucas had no clue he was ODing, had no chance to stop it. It happened in a split second. If the noise hadn't woken his boyfriend up, the subsequent silence may have gone unnoticed. Lucas would have likely died.

Minutes later Lucas awoke with his boyfriend above him. It was only then that he realized he had overdosed. The boyfriend had used naloxone, aka Narcan, in the form of two nasal plungers you insert into a nostril and push down on. They were the only two doses in the house. For many people who overdose on fentanyl, three or four or more doses are needed. With heroin, it used to be you only needed one. Thankfully, in this case, two was enough.

Waking up from a Narcan overdose reversal is not a pleasant experience—all your opioid receptors are suddenly blocked by the drug, and thus you go from being really, really high to completely sober, like going through a week's worth of withdrawal in a few seconds. So, like many others who are Narcan'd back to life, Lucas woke up feeling insane—he was dizzy and disoriented; he could barely move. He lay down in his bed, and then a few minutes later the cops showed up, and then, a few minutes after that, the paramedics. It's always a good idea to go to the ER after a Narcan reversal, because it can theoretically wear off and the overdose can once again take hold, something Lucas knew. But the presence of all the responders was nonetheless disorienting.

"I went from being so high to such an immediate withdrawal that I was acting crazy," Lucas told me. "I was yelling at the EMTs. I was going off on them, cursing at them, and then being like, 'OMG I'm so sorry I don't know why I said that,' but I couldn't stop."

Lucas felt very ill for an hour or so. He arrived at the ER and threw up. He was hooked up to various machines to make sure his vitals were stable. And then, about two hours after it started, it was over—Lucas was fine again. He felt okay, but shaken.

But in a strange way, Lucas told me the OD and Narcan reversal made the subsequent weeks easier—Lucas didn't have to go through the long process of physical withdrawal because he went through it all in a couple of hours. He also didn't have to wait to start Suboxone—usually you have to wait a few days, until the opioids are out of your system, to get on the drug, but because of the Narcan, Lucas could start right away.

So, a few months later, when I talk to Lucas, he says he's in a good place. The Suboxone is doing what it's supposed to do—giving his brain enough opioids to keep it satiated, but blocking enough receptors to prevent a high. He's having very few cravings. He's starting to focus on the bigger stuff—seeing a therapist, finding other coping mechanisms for life. He has a new job at a media company helping make advertisements. He loves it. He was only a week into the job when he OD'd, but he got right back to it, and feels like he's doing well.

But then, a few months after that, I talk to Lucas again. He's still doing okay, he tells me. He's about to head to Berlin with his boyfriend for a joint birthday trip. His financial situation has stabilized. The job is still going well. But he's started using again.

Just a little bit, he says—once every two weeks or so. He'll stop the Suboxone for a few days, wait for it to be out of his system. Then pop the pills. Then, a few days later, get back on the Suboxone. He knows his triggers—financial insecurity seems to make him want to use more. So does taking Adderall, because the opioids help with the comedown.

"I wouldn't call it a relapse," he tells me. "It was more like I wanted to do it one day, so I did, and then it kind of just seeped back into my routine."

He hadn't planned on the pills seeping back into his routine so quickly after the overdose. But they did. And, he tells me, he accepts that. In an ideal world, he'd be in some kind of maintenance program, getting pure and tested drugs that are much safer, directly from the government, he says. Like they do in Vancouver and a few other places. But Lucas doesn't live in that world.

Still, he doesn't think that he'll get back to that dark place he was in a few months ago. But he knows the chances of that aren't nil. The line is always there, waiting to be crossed.

He likes where he's at now. He likes being able to use. He feels stable. He feels in control. He has years of using, without much problem, under his belt; he's confident he can have years more.

"I've always leaned on them for help," he says. "I think it's less about pain and more about boredom. Like existential boredom," he tells me. "The world is boring. It's nice to have this."

But the next time I hear from Lucas, he tells me he's overdosed and nearly died again. Every time I hear from him since, I am glad he's still alive. The fact that he is makes him one of the lucky ones.

3

THE UNEQUAL DISTRIBUTION
OF BREAKDOWN

THE CENTER OF A BREAKDOWN CRISIS;
ARE WE IN ADDICTION OR JUST IN PAIN;
ATTEMPTING TO PULL PEOPLE OUT OF
BREAKDOWN

After Charlottesville, after my breakdown, my privilege became incredibly obvious to me. Each therapy session with Dennis cost $175. My medication was covered by insurance, but my visits to various psychiatrists were usually not—those ranged between $100 and $400 a session. Years after my breakdown, when I began seeing a somatic therapist, each session cost $300. Yoga. Acupuncture. It all cost money. Then there were the less obvious costs: the work I couldn't do because I was busy writhing in bed in mental anguish, or taking long walks through Philadelphia to calm my nerves, or scheduling my days around those various mental health practitioners.

I was able to use drugs like Klonopin and kratom and Adderall without developing a life-ruining addiction, and thus able to work on my recovery, because my life had guardrails.

Societal breakdown affects us all, but it doesn't affect equally. The conditions that created the Nazi who drove his car into a crowd and completely deregulated my brain and nervous system were the same conditions that were making others face increased housing precarity, longer working hours, homelessness—all part and parcel of a violent and decaying capitalist society. But I had the tools and the money to attempt a recovery; I had the space to rebuild a life.

Between one in four and one in five Americans was on some kind of medication for their mental health in 2020, though that number likely rose through the Covid pandemic.[1] And more than one in five American adults and teens used illicit drugs in 2021.[2] Drug use transcends race, class, and gender. Yet only those of us with sufficient resources can prevent ourselves from dangers of drugs use, and thus can use drugs in ways that can help maintain our lives, and even rebuild them.

We are a society wholly dependent on drugs to quell the misery that capitalism inflicts on people. Whether those drugs help one's life or end it depends less on the drug than it does on things fully out of our control—our race, our class, where we were born. We are united by breakdown, united in pain, and united in using drugs to ameliorate that pain, but divided by everything else.

That's why I wanted to travel to a neighborhood of Philadelphia called Kensington.

Five miles from where I lived in Philadelphia during the worst years of my life—the years in which I used a plethora of drugs to help subdue my pain—was a neighborhood that seemingly every politician had framed as the center of America's social rot, where Senate candidates go to for photo ops with used needles.[3] More than one in every hundred people who die from an overdose death in the United States die in Philly. Kensington is the fentanyl capital of America.

In this mess of abandonment and neglect are people—not very many, a few dozen perhaps—who have made it their mission to attempt to stem the tide of America's drug crisis, to lessen the impact on those who face the brunt of it. But in order to do that, they have to convince everyone else that this is our crisis too—that Kensington and every other neighborhood like it are not something that can be looked away from or dismissed as un-human.

"Everything feels like it's just getting worse and worse, and we've all just accepted that," Shoshana Aronowitz, an organizer with SOL Collective, a volunteer group that hands out clean needles and other supplies in Kensington, told me. "Every aspect of our lives, everything that's offered to us, just feels like crap. People are seeing that and feeling that, but they're fed this story that it's *these* people who are the problem."

The day I visit Kensington, it's spring and it's hot and overhead an elevated subway is screeching down the main avenue. The neighborhood looks like a lot of Philly, and like a lot of the urban United States—blocks of small, brick row houses snaking out from a few main avenues where restaurants and shops are, or used to be, before they started closing. I pass dozens upon dozens of people sitting on the street, or in tents, several of whom are buying drugs or shooting up in public. I see a boy, likely no older than sixteen, nodding off in the middle of the sidewalk, his head bobbing down to his waist and then back up again. There are cop cars everywhere but the cops do not seem to be interested in much except sitting there. Of course, arrests are often made, though these have done little to address the crisis. In 2017 politicians and the police made a big deal of closing down "El Campamento," an encampment near the freight rail tracks in Kensington. Multiple national media outlets came to cover the removal of dozens of tents and the cleanup of thousands of needles. The only effect this had, Aronowitz told me, was to force drug users onto the residential streets of the neighborhood.

My first destination for the day is at the center of all this. A large former church, stained glass and all, is now the home to Prevention Point, the city's largest nonprofit that practices what's called "harm reduction"—a philosophy that dictates that instead of punishing people for using drugs, people should be given tools like clean syringes and medical supplies and access to medical care to help ensure that drugs don't cause them undue harm or death. Outside, around a hundred people wait in a line at the church's door. Each of them is instructed to walk down to the church basement, where about ten employees and volunteers of the organization sit at plastic folding tables. Other workers filter down the stairs and then back up, directing their clientele, rushing to get the medics when there's an emergency, cleaning the stray needles and empty bags of chips off the floor. This is a harm reduction assembly line; they've gotten it down to a science—how to serve, with such limited resources, the most people. They have a few million dollars in grants a year, and with that manage to give out 6 to 7 million syringes a year, and usher around 250 people through a medication-assisted therapy program.

Today is a needle exchange day. One at a time, people take a ticket, like at a deli counter, then walk down the stairs to the basement and stop at the first plastic folding table. There they answer a few anonymized questions about their drug use and how many needles they've used in the past week. At the next table, they drop off any used needles they have. And then at the next they pick up packs of new ones—ten or a hundred needles at a time. Some people use them all in a week. Some give some to their friends. The clients can get Narcan here too. And fentanyl test strips, not that they're of much use—Hilary Disch, the head of communications at Prevention Point, told me that basically all the "heroin" on the street is fentanyl these days. And nearly all of that fentanyl is accompanied by "tranq"—the street term for the animal sedative xylazine, which is used by dealers to potentiate their supply on the cheap. Tranq is horrible—drug users don't even like the high, Narcan doesn't work to reverse its effects since it's not an opioid, and injecting it is known to cause skin ulcers.[4] Now a large part of Prevention Point's work is helping drug users with open wounds, often the size of baseballs or even larger, on their legs and arms.

Within an hour of opening, there's a line out the door. Shawn, a bearded guy who looks like he could be in a nü metal band, takes down people's basic demographic info. They'll probably serve 600 or 650 people today, he tells me. That's about average.

One guy, white, middle-age, in a baseball cap, waiting in line for needles, strikes up a conversation with a woman next to him—he wants to get off dope again, he says, but methadone barely does anything anymore. Maybe you'd need 30 milligrams a day back in the nineties for it to prevent withdrawal. "Now you need four hundred, and you still get sick."

Another guy, forty-three years old, says you need at least three doses of Narcan to revive someone these days. He's had to reverse two overdoses in the past month, and he's here to stock back up. A younger woman sings a song, something about "hold on, hold on to each other," as she waits in the needle line. A kid, can't be older than fifteen, waits behind her. He's nodding off in line, his head drooping down past his abdomen, and then back up again.

Many residents of Kensington, the homeowners of this once-more-put-together neighborhood, are not fans of Prevention Point, or of the concept of harm reduction writ large—they see distributing needles and Narcan and other supplies to drug users as enabling the crisis on their doorsteps. But to the people working with drug users every day, there's not much radical about what they're doing; they are, as the term applied to their work suggests, simply attempting to reduce the harm caused by an unsafe drug supply and an ever-growing overdose crisis. And they're doing all this while knowing that it's not nearly enough.

"We need schools and food and health care and housing and public parks," Aronowitz said. "All of these things—they're not completely incompatible with capitalism but they're clearly incompatible under the capitalism we currently have going."

My second stop of the day is a few blocks away from Prevention Point. Down a more residential and quiet street. Few are given the exact address of this two-story brick house, which looks identical to the ones surrounding it, by design. The people who run it are trying to keep potential trouble—the cops, anti-harm-reduction residents of the neighborhood, the media—away.

This is Serenity House, a service center on the opposite end of the harm reduction spectrum—no big nonprofit, no board, just one woman who is paid, and not enough at all, to run it, and a few volunteers who help her out. The woman is LaDonna Smith; the people she serves are all sex workers like her. Nearly all are homeless; all use drugs, mostly fentanyl. They come by for food and clothes and support from one another. In one of Serenity House's rooms are makeup and beauty supplies for the taking. In another, medical supplies like bandages and condoms and rubbing alcohol. In another, clothes from various thrift stores that people who come here can take. In another, two pine bunk beds with thin mattresses. No one is allowed to live here, but the girls who come can take a nap for a few hours, or, on rare emergency occasions, stay overnight. Downstairs the walls are decorated with butterfly stickers and inspirational posters—live your dream, follow your heart, laugh out loud, fall in love, today is the day, stuff like that. A small black-and-white cat runs around. The kitchen is stocked; LaDonna cooks food—fried chicken, veggies, spaghetti—for the visitors.

They're only open two days a week officially, but if one of the girls calls on an off day—maybe they really need to take a shower—LaDonna will go open up the house.

LaDonna, small and skinny with a big presence, dressed in a minidress and proud of her femininity (she wears a shirt that says FEMME DADDY in big letters across the chest), grew up in Philly. Her dad wasn't around a lot, LaDonna tells me, so LaDonna was raised mostly by her mother and grandmother. She preferred hanging out with guys over girls, and when she started dating, it was mainly drug dealers. By sixteen, she had a daughter. By seventeen, she was smoking weed and occasionally crack, and then crack became a bigger and bigger part of her life. She'd have sex with various clients to make ends meet. And she still does—that's how LaDonna has enough time and money to work at Serenity House.

"Even though my name means 'the lady' in Italian, I've always been a whore," she tells me with a smile.

And that's what lets the girls she helps trust her. LaDonna had spent years working with the larger nonprofits in the city that were helping drug users. But she said so many of them had white savior complexes; and their end goal was often to get their clients to stop using drugs, or doing sex work.

"People say to meet people where they're at, but no one really does that—you have to go to where people are using, where the girls are tricking," she says. "This is my definition of meeting them where they're at."

On days when the house is open to the public, anywhere between five and thirty women stop by. They get their medical supplies. They clean their wounds. They get Narcan. They take showers. Mostly they decompress. LaDonna says the women know that she knows how much better it feels once you've showered, once you can get the smell of the last trick off you. And that's the main point of this place—not to try to lecture or get people off drugs or off the streets, but just to provide people with a little bit of time, a little solace from the shit outside.

"I provide a space that allows a level of consciousness that allows them to make sound decisions," LaDonna says. "There's no expectations, no rules for what you must be or can't be."

If you're hiding from the police, she doesn't care. If you take the free clothes and then sell them to get drugs, she doesn't care (though she'd prefer that you didn't). The philosophy is: the girls know how best to survive, Serenity is just there to help them.

But fentanyl and tranq have made that calculus harder—girls come in with wounds from their knees to their ankles, like "something from a horror movie," LaDonna tells me. People OD a lot more these days and need more Narcan to be revived. No one, LaDonna says, even likes fentanyl. It's fucked up, she says, that everyone who was using heroin was basically forced to switch over to it—a worse high, a shorter high, and more danger and death.

LaDonna tells me she knows she can't change the world, but she can make some people's lives a little bit better when the entire system has abandoned them. Sitting in a plush, comfy, slightly ratty armchair on Serenity House's first floor, LaDonna told me that's all she can do—no one gives a fuck about these people, she said. At least a few people can show they care.

"I like this secret society," she said. "You go down this path, and it's so deserted. And then boom, it's like the Batcave. . . . I want these women to receive the same respect as Michelle Obama. I want them to see themselves that way."

Prevention Point and Serenity House are two of a dozen or more harm reduction centers in Philly. They're little rays of hope in a world where escaping this constant breakdown feels impossible. But they're not enough, not by a long shot.

After I returned from Philadelphia, back to New York, I felt a bit shocked by the level of desperation I'd seen in the city.

I went to a friend's birthday party at a nice bar. People were happy, a lot of which was chemically induced. I couldn't stop thinking about how different the two worlds were. There, in Philly, everyone using drugs and left for dead. And here, in New York, at that party, everyone using drugs too—cocaine and 2C-B and ketamine and GHB passed between friends, joyously, with no stigma, no death; even glamorized, written up as "party reporting" in the same newspapers running story after story about how no one can figure out what to do about the opioid epidemic, the same newspapers that dryly report on the millions dead as if there is no cause, a mysterious disease that has taken over our society. For some it's a party, for others an epidemic.

I came to see all those stories—the glamorous ones in the Styles section and the distant and emotionless ones on the front pages—as lies, or half truths. Because they're the same story, separated by race and class. We're all desperate for a fix, to take our minds off reality, to remove our brains from this hellish world we're forced to exist in. But some of us get the support to do that—the money and the care and the therapy and the yoga and the acupuncture and the psychiatry, and, crucially, a less deadly and adulterated class of drugs, and also crucially, the narrative that we are good people. And that allows us to prosper even as we use. And others, by chance of where they are born, by the chance of their race, by the chance of being poor, get none of that. They get cops and death, and maybe a little, temporary hope from people like LaDonna.

A few months after Philadelphia, I got news from a Serenity House volunteer. LaDonna Smith had unexpectedly passed away. The cause, people think, was heart failure, though no one seems sure. She left behind three children and a deeply heartbroken community. She was forty-seven.

Those close to Serenity House and LaDonna raised over $10,000 in just a few days in her honor, to help her youngest child, her seventeen-year-old son, and to help with her funeral costs. People commented on her donation page about how much she'd meant to them, how much she'd helped those around her. But there were no obituaries in the national papers, nor in the local ones. No big memorial. No commendations from politicians. No public acknowledgment at all of her work. A hero to many, lost in the ever-deepening breakdown of the world that surrounded her.

HOW WE JUSTIFY SOCIETAL BREAKDOWN

Opioids may be everywhere, drugs may be everywhere, but who ends up with a life ruled by their relationship to them, and who ends up dead because of them, is not random.

Curious, then, that in recent years, we've come to view addiction as a disease. A disease that's an inherent part of one's brain, that leads one to become dependent on substances—something you either have, or don't. In 2014, the United States government officialized this framing, promoting the idea of addiction as a disease in several policy papers. The US Office of National Drug Control Policy even went so far as to say that viewing drug use as a personal moral failing instead of a disorder was a large impediment to addressing drug use in the US, and suggesting that words like "addict" and "addiction" should be dropped in favor of terms like "substance use disorder."[5]

There is, to be sure, some scientific rationale behind this framing: brain imaging has shown that addiction can change the way the brain functions, rewiring reward pathways, decreasing levels of neurotransmitters like dopamine.[6] In that way, the National Institutes of Health argues, addiction is much like any other serious medical condition such as heart disease: "Both disrupt the normal, healthy functioning of an organ in the body, both have serious harmful effects, and both are, in many cases, preventable and treatable."[7]

But if addiction is a disease, then it's a strange one, one in which there is no clear line between having it and not. Is it the lack of dopamine or serotonin in your brain that is the disease? If this is the case, then anyone with lower-than-average levels of dopamine or serotonin could be said to have a disease too, whether they are addicted to something or not. Or is it the compulsive behavior—the repeated drug use itself—that's the disease? This also doesn't make sense; we know that smoking cigarettes can cause cancer, but the act of smoking cigarettes is not itself cancer. Is it the reliance on a substance for functioning that is the disease? If that was true, anyone on an antidepressant could be said to have a disease. Sure, you can say depression is a disease too, but no one would argue there is a disease called antidepressant-use disorder. There's no disputing that repeated drug use changes the brain. This is scientific fact. But so does repeated exercise, and repeated reading and writing. To paraphrase neuroscientist Marc Lewis, if addiction is a disease, then so is love and religion.[8]

If addiction is a disease, it's also a very fluid one—one that plagues men more than women, one that plagued white people more than Black people until recently. It's a disease that has vastly expanded and infected more people over the past few decades, and one that seems to spread as poverty and misery spreads. And it's a disease that, unlike most others, can often be cured, or at least managed, by getting nonmedical support—going to meetings or seeing a therapist or improving one's material circumstances. Heart disease and addiction may share some attributes, but you cannot talk out heart disease with a therapist.

The disease framing is attractive because it removes the blame from those who struggle with drug use—it's no longer their fault, but a problem with their brains, their wiring. Lessening the stigma of addiction is an explicit reason the National Institutes of Health prefers the disease model.[9] The framework was developed by medical experts, along with antidrug groups like Alcoholics Anonymous, as a direct response to previous popular understandings of addiction as a moral failing.[10]

Addiction-as-disease is an improvement from past decades' targets of blame: poor people and immigrants. King James I blamed the introduction of tobacco in feudal England on the "wilde, godlesse, and slavish Indians."[11] In both England and the US, the press, politicians, and polite society writ large blamed opium addiction on the lower classes, especially Chinese people. In the 1800s, the *New York Times* would regularly run sensationalistic stories about opium den raids that uncovered "pretty" and "fashionable" women controlled by menacing Chinese lovers. The first antidrug laws in the United States were passed at the same time that lawmakers passed laws limiting Chinese immigration. The first national opium law was passed as part of an 1881 treaty that prevented Chinese immigration to the United States. It made opium smoking illegal for Chinese nationals, but not US citizens.[12]

Race and class infected every iota of Western civilization's understanding of drugs, leading some substances to be deemed "drugs" and others "medications." Opium was for the poor and immigrants, while morphine (which has essentially the same effects as opium) was considered a modern medical marvel. As drug historian David Herzberg points out in his book *White Market Drugs*, the entire pharmaceutical industry was born out of this false divide between drug and medicine, with the government sanctioning and promoting the use of the latter (usually for richer, white people) and severely punishing the use of the former. When it turned out that many people prescribed morphine actually *did* become addicted to it, then it and its chemical cousin heroin were relegated to "drug" status, and prescription drug companies came up with new drugs like Demerol and Dilaudid that they promised were not as addictive,[13] in order to maintain this false divide between bad and good substance. "No longer any excuse for becoming a dope slave," one newspaper ad for Demerol stated in bold lettering, with an attached advertorial that cautioned against the evils of morphine.[14] (Turns out, Dilaudid and Demerol both have similar potential for addiction as any other opioid, whoops.)

This never-ending cycle—bad people use drugs, good people are prescribed medications—meant that every decade or so, a new blockbuster drug that promised to, somehow, be different from all the opioids before it, came to market. In the mid-1900s it was Percodan— oxycodone and aspirin in one pill. Sales increased 500 percent between 1955 and 1960. "People are eating Percodan as though it were popcorn," one medical journal warned. And, the journal said, they were people "normally not associated with the illicit drug traffic."[15] Those unable to get Percodan or other white-market drugs were relegated to the illegal markets, where heroin use was skyrocketing (perhaps not a surprise after several decades of millions of Americans getting a taste for opioids through their doctors).

And that's how something like OxyContin was allowed to flourish for years essentially unchecked—because, until the number of deaths became impossible to ignore, it wasn't really considered a drug, but a medication.

"American drug control was too weak to restrain Purdue Pharma, but so strong that it sent countless people to prison," Herzberg writes. "How was it possible for drug laws to have both problems at the same time?"

This false divide also allowed the media and politicians to frame the Oxy crisis as something new, as if addiction had suddenly left its containment zone of the urban poor and jumped into an undeserving host community of white people who live in the suburbs and rural areas. The reality is that many white Americans have been dependent on drugs (or "medications") for centuries, and, according to Herzberg, probably *more* dependent on drugs than people of color and the poor for much of that time: 65 million barbiturate prescriptions were written in 1965 alone, along with 85 million for tranquilizers, and 26 million for amphetamines. By 1967, 31 percent of American women and 15 percent of men had used a stimulant or sedative within the past year. And, as Herzberg writes, use among whites was nearly two times more common than among Black Americans.

But the crucial difference is that white Americans were largely getting their drugs legally—produced by drug companies, dispensed by doctors, and underwritten by insurance companies. As drug historian David T. Courtwright argues, the majority of American drug addiction throughout all of US history has been facilitated not by street dealers, but by doctors doling out prescriptions for powerful opioids and other drugs.[16] In the 1960s and '70s, far more people were dying from prescription opioids than from illegal heroin, yet the majority of media and political attention was paid to heroin use.[17]

Those privileged enough to enjoy their highs from the white market were given special protections: their drugs would be professionally manufactured, free from impurities, dispensed at regular dosages from safe stores, come without the threat of jail time, and often be paid for by insurance companies. Which explains why, even during the peak of OxyContin, overdoses were much lower than they are today: when the United States and much of the world decided to crack down on opioid prescriptions, they did not stop people from using drugs, they simply pushed them from the white market to the illegal market, and thus revoked the plethora of privileges that came from having access to that market.

This divide still exists. The drug I am prescribed for attention deficit hyperactivity disorder, Adderall, a combination of amphetamine and dextroamphetamine, is chemically similar to crystal meth, but I am prescribed it in a low and measured dose. (I've heard anecdotally from meth users that if you take enough Adderall, it feels pretty much the same as taking meth—the difference between the drugs less a question of chemical makeup and more of concentration, like drinking a glass of wine versus downing a bottle of whiskey.) Opiates are still prescribed regularly, though with less frequency than they used to be, while tens of thousands are arrested for using drugs that are very nearly identical on the streets.

Now that addiction has been acknowledged to exist among the rich and the white, it makes sense that the disease model has come back in favor. Because while this country has had no problem attempting to imprison its way out of drug use when the drug use was thought to occur only among the poor and people of color, it's much more reticent to do so when the victims are white.

After opioid prescriptions skyrocketed in the 1800s (there was a tenfold increase in opium use from 1870 to the 1890s alone),[18] a similar turn toward disease explanations occurred: in 1877, for example, after years of blaming Asians for opium, the *New York Times* wrote that morphine addiction, unlike opium addiction, was "a disease produced not through the culpability of its victims but in consequence of their physical and mental ailments, and chiefly through the instrumentality of their physicians."

For literally hundreds of years, we have maintained the same attitude toward drugs—that drugs are bad, and can be policed out of existence (four hundred thousand Americans are currently locked up on drug charges,[19] and Black Americans are incarcerated at a rate of nearly five times that of white Americans.[20]) And that medications are good, and do not have the same potential downsides as drugs, but that, when they inevitably end up having those downsides, it is not anyone's fault, but the symptom of a disease that must be medically instead of carcerally managed.

Though addiction-as-disease allows for less-punitive approaches to drug use, it doesn't allow for an exploration of the societal factors that lead to use in the first place. It doesn't account for the under-regulation of the prescription drug industry, and the ever-increasing power of drugs manufactured by that industry—fentanyl, after all, was created not by drug dealers, but by Janssen Pharmaceuticals, later bought out by Johnson & Johnson[21]; heroin, morphine, and virtually every other opioid more powerful than opium were also created by the industry. And, most critically, the disease model does not account for the ever-widening breakdown of our society and its supports.

Canadian psychologist Bruce Alexander's "dislocation theory of addiction" posits that we are all, rich and poor, of all races and genders, increasingly alienated from community, from meaning-making and spirituality, so it makes sense that addiction and death have increased dramatically across races and classes in the past several decades. To Alexander, addiction is not an accident, but a rational search for an effective ameliorant to this dislocation.[22] So if addiction is a disease, then it is like a cancer that comes from living next to a power plant. It has a direct cause. And we've tried everything except shutting the plant down. We've abstracted cause and effect, the focus on our biology and chemistry acting as a smoke screen between the plant and our house.

This smoke screen is no accident. It allows the power plant to keep operating; it forces us to deal with the disease it causes at an individual level, instead of just shutting the damn thing down.

This is what, in 1845, Friedrich Engels called social murder—deaths that have an obvious cause but are obfuscated by our refusal to name that cause. "When [society] deprives thousands of the necessaries of life, places them under conditions in which they cannot live—forces them, through the strong arm of the law, to remain in such conditions until that death ensues which is the inevitable consequence—knows that these thousands of victims must perish, yet permits these conditions to remain, its deed is murder just as surely as the deed of the single individual," he wrote.[23]

Engels, focusing specifically on London nearly two hundred years ago, wrote of a society in which food did not nourish, living quarters produced stress, jobs provided neither meaning nor purpose, pollution created sickness, social ties were broken. "How is it possible, under such conditions, for the lower class to be healthy and long lived? What else can be expected than an excessive mortality, an unbroken series of epidemics," he wrote.

The same could be said of today's society, except now the drugs, the ameliorants to this vast pain, are far more powerful.

I have, at various points in my life, been dependent on drugs. Was my excessive use of cocaine when I was a teenager a disease, or a response to the conditions of my life—the traumas of growing up queer, of witnessing 9/11 at thirteen years old, the isolation from community I felt? Is my reliance on Adderall now a medication for a disorder, or is my ADHD and the speed I require to deal with it a response to the conditions of my life—the expectation that I be able to do what humans have never done until very recent history (sit still in a chair for six or eight or ten hours a day) to make a living? Is my dependence on kratom and Klonopin a disease, or a response to the conditions of my life—a nervous system deregulated by the violence of a white supremacist?

I have been able to use these drugs safely because of my various privileges. But the same conditions of violence that I faced have more devastating consequences for those born without the same guardrails my life has had.

Poverty, homelessness, inequality, despair—as these increase so too will deaths from people trying to ameliorate their pain. The least we can do is attempt to establish some guardrails for those who have none.

I'd been told by many activists and drug users that there was one place to go if I wanted to see those guardrails being established in real time. Which is how I found myself at the center of a neighborhood in which thousands of people use drugs openly on the street, on the Downtown Eastside of Vancouver, just blocks away from the gleaming business district and residential neighborhoods where houses sell for millions of dollars.

There, in a little office on the first floor of a decrepit building, I held $10,000 of meth in a Ziploc bag. The crystals looked almost like icicles, white and translucent, the bag heavy and crunchy. It felt like holding a very dangerous box of cereal in my hands.

As I marveled at what was in my hands, two workers at this harm reduction clinic sipped coffee and waited for me to refocus my attention. This was just another day for them, in an office that could have been the office of any nonprofit—a desktop computer, papers covering a desk, some ratty chairs. But there was also a steel gate across the front door to prevent people, especially cops, from getting inside, and a very, very heavy safe, and also $30,000 worth of heroin, cocaine, and meth in bags scattered around.

The Big Bag of Meth will get weighed out into individual doses and put into tiny cardboard boxes, labeled with its contents, purity, and the logo of DULF—the Drug User Liberation Front.

The office's location is not on any maps or findable by any search engines, but it's not exactly secret—Vancouver's government, the cops, drug users, and maybe even dealers all know where it is, and, it turns out, that's been pretty much fine, despite the fact that the people inside it are buying and selling felony-level quantities of drugs every week.

Such is life in Vancouver, where the drug problem has been so bad for so long that the authorities here have, reluctantly and with a lot of pressure, begun to allow for a kind of radical experimentation not really going on anywhere else.

The Downtown Eastside is like many downtrodden neighborhoods in other cities—homeless people set up tents on the sidewalks, people use drugs in the open, people deal drugs in the open, and a thousand nonprofits and churches have swooped in to attempt to help those who live or frequent here. It's like Kensington in Philadelphia, or Skid Row in Los Angeles, or the Tenderloin in San Francisco. Places of, to crib a term popularized by prison abolitionist and geographer Ruth Wilson Gilmore, "organized abandonment"[24]—places the state has essentially given up on, leaving people to fend for themselves.

But unlike in those other places, here, there has been, dare I say, hope.

Not hope because things are going well. They're not. There are hundreds of overdose deaths every month in British Columbia (the province that surrounds Vancouver), and that number keeps going up.[25] At the height of the Covid pandemic, more people were dying from overdoses than from Covid each month here.[26] But hope that things can change. That people can commit to battling the breakdown even when the rest of society has given up.

It's precisely because things are so bad here that people have decided to go against the grain, experiment with radical solutions to the drug overdose epidemic not seen anywhere else. And it doesn't get any more radical or experimental than DULF.

"This is our last-resort effort to stop the death of people in this community," Eris Nyx, one of DULF's founders, a thirtysomething tattooed woman in tattered shorts, tells me. "After years and years and years and years of trying everything else, we're just giving people drugs."

Eris worked in the shelter system for years, and in nonprofits that focused on overdose prevention, and then for the government itself. She handed out needles and got people signed up for services. But at a certain point she realized no one was addressing the base problem: the drugs were bad; inconsistent in their potency, sometimes heroin and sometimes fentanyl, sometimes other shit that's even worse like tranq, or other synthetic opioids that are even *more* powerful than fentanyl.

"The crux of this whole issue is the regime of drug prohibition, that's what's causing the spikes of death—it's the volatility of the drug supply," she said. "If you give people drugs with predictable contents, they stop dying. So I spent all my time in nonprofits and governments saying, 'Someone should be giving people drugs with predictable contents,' and then I thought, *Well, fuck it, I'll just do that.*"

Eris and her main DULF partner, Jeremy Kalicum, formed DULF in 2020 and since then have been running the entire operation essentially by themselves. They collect money, buy drugs on the dark web, send them to labs to be tested for purity using mass spectrometry and other technology, then box them up and distribute them. Sometimes they give out the drugs as part of media events, what they consider a kind of theater, to draw attention to the overdose crisis. But as of a few months ago, they've begun a more official program, enrolling forty people in a study to prove how much safer well-regulated drugs are than what you get on the street. The study is simple: twenty people who use heroin, cocaine, or meth are allowed to come to DULF and pick up their drugs for below-market rates, what they call the "compassion club." The other twenty, the control group, continue buying their drugs as they always have, on the street. They all fill out extensive questionnaires about their backgrounds, their lives, their use and overdoses. So far, DULF has found that no one in the compassion club arm of the study has overdosed, fatally or otherwise.

The compassion club serves two purposes: it keeps twenty people (and more in the future, they hope) safer from overdose than they would be buying their drugs on the street, and it also acts as a model—one they hope the government can't ignore: If DULF can keep its users alive better than any other harm reduction program, why wouldn't a government supposedly dedicated to the safety of its inhabitants follow the program's lead?

What is perhaps most remarkable about DULF is how much support they'd originally received from places usually actively hostile toward drug users—much of the public health apparatus in the city, from the medical officers of hospitals to heads of medical departments of large universities and even the mayor of Vancouver, has advocated for them to get an exemption from Canada's federal government that would allow them to deal the drugs legally.[27]

When I first go to DULF, on a Tuesday in August, Eris and Jeremy are busy planning a media campaign, march, and street concert to bring attention to the overdose crisis, and to commemorate International Overdose Awareness Day, which is the following day. Eris is also futzing with the computer, trying to get the illegal drug–selling website to load so that they can re-up their supplies. They buy in bulk, like hundreds of grams at a time, and break down each bulk order into hundreds of little boxes, which sit securely in the safe so that, according to Jeremy, "If someone tries to rob us, it'll take at least five minutes to get the safe open."

The heroin they sell goes for $128 (Canadian) a gram, the cocaine for $66, and the meth for $16.50. DULF prices their drugs to be at or below street prices, but they offer more than a good price: they're the only ones selling *actual* heroin, not the stuff called "down," which is usually fentanyl mixed with tranq and infinite possibilities of other chemicals, and which is basically the only heroin-esque substance available on Vancouver's streets these days.

On the days they're open, usually all twenty people in their compassion club come in to buy, sometimes more than once a day.

"Who wouldn't want hundred percent pure cocaine," Jeremy asks. "It's like getting a free taco. A free, delicious taco."

An email pops up on the computer from the lab—the test results of their most recent batch of heroin. It has some acetylmorphine in it, which isn't dangerous but a sign that the heroin was less professionally produced than some batches. It also means the heroin smells a little weird, like ammonia.

Shawn, a fifty-year-old compassion club member, stops in and buys a little cardboard box of heroin. He pays, exits the small office, and picks up some supplies sitting on a counter in the hallway—two needles and one syringe, some cotton, a little metal dish that you cook the heroin on. He mixes some of the tan powder with a bit of water, heats it up with a lighter, drops in the cotton, draws up the liquid with one syringe, then switches the needle on the base of the syringe (every time a needle is used, it gets duller, meaning it's more likely to tear your skin and cause infection, so harm reduction advocates often tell people to use one needle for drawing and one for shooting), and finds a vein on his left arm. He shoots up. It all takes less than a minute.

"DULF is awesome," he tells me as the liquid enters his arm. "I don't like fentanyl at all, I just like heroin, and it's impossible to get real heroin these days."

Shawn has been using since he was fifteen, on and off, never at a level to consider himself an addict, until about two years ago, when his use increased to every day. He'd try to find heroin and end up with fentanyl. He'd never know what he was really getting. One day, he OD'd. Someone had to Narcan him back to life.

"I had this vision of floating upward, but something was holding me back on earth preventing me from leaving completely," he told me.

But he's watched plenty of people OD and not make it. "Fentanyl is destroying things," he says.

That's one of the biggest limitations DULF faces right now—now that everyone has grown accustomed to a drug so much more powerful, it's hard to get people off fent and back onto good ol' heroin. So DULF wants to start selling fent too. Near DULF's office, a doctor named Christy Sutherland prescribes it free of charge, with the government's consent. Sutherland stops by to talk shop with the DULF people that day. Mostly she and Eris discuss how it's hard to source as much fentanyl as they need—for the hundred-plus people Sutherland sees, she needs kilos. There aren't enough legal, regulated manufacturers of the stuff.

The fact that small amounts of hard drugs are decriminalized here, that DULF is allowed (or not exactly allowed, but not not allowed) to sell them, that Sutherland can prescribe them, that there's a vending machine that dispenses Dilaudid (a prescription opioid) down the street from DULF, that people can shoot up in the open—has obviously drawn some criticism. Conservative city council members rail against the harm reduction practitioners. Right-wing websites write horror stories about the Downtown Eastside. But there's less pushback than you might think. To the people doing this work, it's all very rational. The government already regulates and allows the sale of one of the most deadly substances in the world—alcohol. Eris points out that during Prohibition in the United States, people didn't stop drinking, they simply started dying from alcohol contaminated with other chemicals. Heroin, fentanyl, meth; why is it any different?

"We're a drop in the bucket, piss in the ocean," Eris says. "You really need the government to be doing this. Like a liquor store. We're a pilot program, and we're a PR firm for this method of tackling the crisis. But we're two people. And this is a UN-level kind of problem."

She envisions a future in which heroin and every other drug are handled similarly to alcohol—regulated, free from impurities, legal, and available to the public. She does not see any other way out of the crisis. Everything else we've tried has simply not worked.

The next morning, about a hundred people gather on the Downtown Eastside for the march DULF helped plan. The marchers pass block after block of tents, they pass an under-construction development that'll house a bunch of wealthier people. An Indigenous activist asks the crowd how many more hair salons and coffee shops the neighborhood needs. They pass a police station and yell, "Fuck the police!" A lot of people who take the mic end up crying, relaying stories of loved ones lost to overdose.

Vince Tao, one of the organizers of the march, tells me how interconnected it all is—the gentrification (the median rent in Vancouver is nearly $2,500 a month),[28] the real estate development, the abandonment of people here, the policing, the drug war. Two sides of the same coin, or six sides of the same die.

"The people whose bodies are employed to do the work as part of our housing crisis, their bodies are destroyed through that work, squeezed in a thresher to build condos, so they end up turning to drugs, and then the people displaced by the housing crisis, who are evicted and homeless, end up on the Downtown Eastside too," he says. "The entire political economy of the city is connected to the drug crisis."

Which is why, for Tao, harm reduction is good, but not enough. He wants people to politicize their pain, to realize that their lot in life, their place in the center of this mass breakdown, is not only because they are drug users, but because they are considered disposable within a capitalist economy, and so must fight back against that.

"Capitalism has always been about the distribution of pain, and the uneven distribution of that pain," Tao tells me. "Pain has existed forever, and so have people's forms of managing that pain, but capitalism creates very unequal distribution of that pain."

With a crumbling welfare system, stagnant wages, bad health care, bad jobs, it's inevitable that people will turn to drugs. What's happening on the Downtown Eastside, Tao tells me, is not a drug crisis, but a crisis of insufficient, and unequal, pain management.

INTERLUDE TWO
How to Externalize the Breakdown

The last time it happened, I was hungover on a Sunday morning. There was no one trigger, more just a feeling that welled in my body slowly, quiet and slow enough for me not to notice until it was too late. The hangover was a contributing factor—the haze of the aftereffects of alcohol not dissimilar to the feeling of PTSD-induced dissociation. So I was already down maybe 20 points from 100 percent perfect mental health. It's easy to look back in hindsight and see other contributing factors—the weather was unnervingly warm that day, which perhaps caused me to feel overwhelmed by the state of the world and its seemingly negative trajectory. I had had a fight with a good friend, which perhaps made me feel shaky, like life wasn't on solid ground. Who knows. I've given up trying to determine the exact concoction necessary to set it off. Sometimes it just happens.

As I watched *30 Rock* and ate a breakfast burrito and drank coffee, I felt that familiar creeping sensation—literally creeping, like the energy was crawling through my skin, from my toes upward, to my arms and then my chest.

Time to initiate the protocol, I told myself.

Breathe in, breathe out. Four/seven/eight breath. This means four seconds inhale. Seven seconds holding. Eight seconds release. My mom taught it to me. A yogic trick for calm. It works sometimes. But in that moment, it did not. On to the next step of the protocol: I paced and shook my arms out. I did a few push-ups to try to get my energy levels up. The creeping sensation continued, though. I walked outside my apartment to get some fresh air. But my breaths felt jagged. The feedback loop had already started, and now I felt there was no way to break it: jagged breath—that means I cannot breathe—that means a heart attack. No matter how many times I told myself in that moment that I was fine, it was too late—my nervous system had already decided I was in a crisis. The peak of the crisis that day is the same peak every time I have an anxiety attack—I realize I feel just as crazy as I did that morning in Oakland, the day I went insane, and I convince myself that it's all happening again, that my life is over again. And then I hyperventilate. And then, blessedly, I remember I have Klonopin, and take one, and wait.

It kicks in, and I realize that I will be okay. That this day sucks, but I will not be crazy tomorrow. Just a temporary hiccup. "Recovery is not linear," as all those Instagram infographics keep telling me.

I used to hate these episodes, and still do, but now have come to see them as inevitable; as a release of pent-up energy—too many neurons firing in my body too quickly. They must discharge somehow. The shit I experienced—the societal breakdown that led a Nazi to try to murder me and my friends—it lives in me. It causes my nervous system to go haywire randomly. And it's now my responsibility to expel it, it's now my breakdown to deal with.

I have more support to do this, to attempt to externalize the breakdown within me, than most do. I have therapists and a supportive family and well-regulated medications and the kind of job that allows me to have panic attacks throughout the day without getting fired. Yet it's still hard. Because the breakdown is still all around me. It feels and, I think, *is* impossible to fully heal into a world that by design causes so much stress and desperation, and that leaves people on their own to deal with it.

So I've become a body without sufficient release; and we've become a populace without sufficient release. What Freud called cathexis, the buildup of energy in the body that must somehow be emancipated, the body looking to return to stasis.[1] If it cannot, the energy ricochets around its host, tearing holes; the host develops neuroses, depression, anxiety, psychosis—too much energy stored, nowhere for that energy to go. That, at a personal, and at a societal level. A worldwide crisis of cathexis. Masses and masses of energy stored in our bodies and minds with nowhere to go.

We already know that unemployment directly leads to a 20 to 30 percent increase in suicides.[2] We already know that the stress of work directly leads to more heart attacks, to premature deaths, to depression and anxiety disorders.[3] But we can't see the bigger picture—panic attacks, suicides, drug overdoses, depression are not isolated incidents; they are predictable outcomes of worsening living conditions. No wonder we turn to drugs, to try to regulate, to try to find a sustainable neutral in a world that makes that a near-impossible feat.

"The more a person curbs his aggression towards the external world, the more severe and hence more aggressive he becomes in his ego-ideal," Freud wrote.[4] In other words, the better we become at repression, the more we take the repression out on ourselves; it infects our minds, driving us crazy.

Building on Frantz Fanon's work, the philosopher Kelly Oliver writes that we can think of our psychic space as colonized in the same way that physical space is.

This is of course more true for some populations than others, but it affects nearly all of us, dehumanizing us, disabling us from finding an effective outlet for our anger at the world around us.

"Without the discharge of bodily drives into language and other signifying systems, we become cut off from the world of meaning on which we depend for meaningful lives," Oliver writes. "Diminished psychic space results in bodily drives and affects turned inward, which ultimately leads to depression and self-hatred unless these very affects can be turned or returned into resistance and fortifying strategies."[5]

This is already often obvious to us on an individual level—if you're in an abusive relationship, if you're at a bad job, if you've been traumatized in some way, much of the healing involves getting out the energies, the anger, the frustration, that have been placed in you. The somatic therapist Peter Levine writes that PTSD is essentially just that—what he calls "residue of energy" that's trapped within our nervous systems. That's why therapy helps—because you can talk it out. That's why mental health professionals recommend bodywork like yoga or running or boxing—to get the energy out.[6]

But it's much harder to do that on a societal level.

The Downtown Eastside of Vancouver, Kensington in Philadelphia—these are places where this internalization of the oppression we all face is incredibly obvious. Where the lack of an outlet to express the rage and despair makes itself known.

What Kelly Oliver is saying is not so different from what Vince Tao said in linking the gentrification of Vancouver to the drug crisis: displacement, financial precarity, disruption occur, and that produces intense pain, both physical and mental. But we have nowhere for that pain to go. It remains in us all, and in some more than others, unevenly distributed.

When a corporation builds something, say, steel beams, and that something pollutes, say, a river—in economics, this is called an externality.[7] We can see our brains and bodies in the same way. We hold the externalities of a violent society.

"Anyone who has a pistol can kill us or imprison us; anyone who controls the means of our livelihood can starve us or force us to do his bidding," the psychologist Erich Fromm wrote. "Inasmuch as we want to live, we must submit or fight—provided there is a chance—and there often is none. Precisely because power decides upon life and death, freedom and slavery, it impresses not only our bodies but our minds."

We hold the psychic damage of the rich and powerful, those who control the shape of not only our physical but mental spaces.

After Charlottesville, I was tasked with carrying the weight of a psychopath, and also the weight of the world that created that psychopath. I was tasked with slowly remediating those externalities that were placed within me. Klonopin and kratom and many other drugs helped with that. As did the therapy—to be able to feel and expel my pain through tears; to be able to think through my anger and despair and contextualize it. I was slowly able to externalize the externalities. But for others less fortunate than me, their task is much larger. How does one remediate an environment that is constantly being polluted? How does one reverse the flow of energies when there is no space to breathe?

The theorist Judith Butler noted that in those dealing with the loss of their friends from AIDS, there was no place for their grief to go. They were not only dealing with the mourning and anger and fear inherent in the AIDS crisis, they were dealing with a society that did not even want to acknowledge the crisis, much less the emotions it caused in those affected by it. So those emotions turned inward: "Insofar as the grief remains unspeakable," Butler wrote, "the rage over the loss can redouble by virtue of remaining unavowed."[8]

To Butler, the solution to internalized grief was the creation of collective institutions through which to process that grief. Political organizations like Queer Nation functioned not only as vehicles for political change, but as vehicles for the transformation of individualized, internal grief to externalized and collective grief.

Today, we have few institutions for collective grieving. We are increasingly isolated from one another, lonely, with no outlet for the anger at what the world has done to us. Even the inadequate institutions we once had for a collective sharing of grief and pain are disintegrating—the workplace and its unions replaced by the isolation-causing gig economy; the church (for all its faults, still a place of collective sharing of emotion) on its way out. Where do we turn, except inward?

In an oft quoted but oft misunderstood passage, Marx wrote of how religion acts as a valve for the oppression people face. "Religious distress is at the same time the expression of real distress and the protest against real distress. Religion is the sigh of the oppressed creature, the heart of a heartless world, just as it is the spirit of an unspiritual situation. It is the opium of the people," he wrote.[9]

The church, to Marx, served a function under capitalism as an outlet for people's distress. But this caused a problem: it allowed that psychic violence to continue. Workers would be overworked and abused and underpaid in factories, and then expel that energy through the church, giving them little reason to rebel against the conditions of their oppression. Marx said the church was like placing flowers around chains—it made the chains feel better, but it did not do anything to remove the shackles themselves.

Drugs today may function similarly to how organized religion functioned in Marx's time—a necessary set of flowers to make the fact of our chains bearable.

If we want to stop people from dying from overdoses, if we want to stop drugs from being used in ways that endanger people, we must create a world in which we are asked to carry less grief and pain and anger; and a world in which that grief and anger can be adequately expressed, a place where we can release our cathexis. Until we create that world, whatever it may ultimately look like, we will, to greater or lesser extents depending on our privilege, continue to internalize the horrors, and thus need ameliorants for our psychic pain.

To stop what we see in Kensington or the Downtown Eastside of Vancouver, we must create the chance to fight and express; a world in which people are able to live, to make known both their anger and their joy, to externalize the energies placed in all of us. To attempt to create this world, to attempt to create space for people, to give them a moment of relief from the constant internalizing of externalities, as DULF does, as Serenity House does, is a radical act. None of these small projects are enough on their own, but they are the start of something. By allowing people in egregious need reprieve from precarity and scarcity, they allow psychic space to grow, they lessen the burden just a little bit—a necessary precursor to larger-scale social change.

There's a reason this kind of reprieve is so hard to come by, though. There's a reason we have so few chances to let our psychic spaces grow: because to do so would be dangerous to the social order. Those in power have a vested interest in preventing us the time, the space, the energy to thrive—to make art or protest or fuck or simply chitchat.[10] To allow for those things would be to allow us the space to change the entire world.

"If desire is repressed, it is because every position of desire, no matter how small, is capable of calling into question the established order of a society," the philosophers Gilles Deleuze and Félix Guattari wrote in 1972.[11] Desire, they said, had the potential to be "explosive."

If we were to release our desire on a mass scale, if we were to say, "I no longer want to do this anymore—to work long hours for low pay and degrade my body and mind in the process," the world as we know it would be forced to change, to reorganize itself to our needs and wants. The more we start externalizing, the more dangerous we become.[12]

In the meantime, drugs can temporarily soothe us; their use is inevitable in a world in which there is often no space for emotional release, a world in which desire and hope for something better are so often not given the chance to flourish, a world in which we are all, to varying degrees, tasked with carrying the externalities of the breakdown. My Klonopin and kratom, Lucas's pills, the opioids people on the streets of Philly and Vancouver take, they lessen the burden of our collective cathexis. But they are not enough. Without a vision for a brighter future, without the creation of a world in which our desire is acknowledged and actualized, we will feel stuck, depressed, anxious, and unsatisfied, no matter how many flowers we place around our chains.

PART 2
STABILITY

4

PUTTING MYSELF BACK TOGETHER

FINDING STABILITY;
ANTIDEPRESSANTS-AS-STABILITY-ENFORCERS;
THE POLITICS OF BEING SAD

Two months after my mental breakdown, on a Tuesday, I entered the decaying gray office building in Center City, Philadelphia, and brushed past the doorman, who, because he saw me three to four times every week, knew who I was. This embarrassed me. I was one of *those* people now. A therapy person.

I patiently waited for the rickety elevator to deliver me to the sixteenth floor and then clomped down the dim hallway to the office and took a few deep breaths. Today, I'd decided, was the day to tell my therapist that this wasn't working—that I was still insane, and that it was taking too long to not be, and that it was his fault.

Dennis, as always, was waiting for me with a smile that instantly made me feel better. My plan wasn't off to a great start.

The session started as it always did: Dennis sat in front of me, maybe five feet away, in his rumpled polo and glasses, and asked me how I was. I wanted to tell him that I was beginning to hate him. That I was furious at him for not being able to cure me already.

Instead, I started sobbing.

I took a tissue from the box next to my chair and attempted to collect myself, but I heard what came out of my mouth and it was much louder than I'd intended: "Why can't I get better?" I was practically screaming. "Why can't I get better? Why can't you fix me?"

Dennis answered calmly: This process takes time. Eventually, you will get better. And, he said, you already *are* better than you were just a few weeks ago.

I took a moment to consider this. He was, despite my protestations, right. It might not have felt like it, but my state of craziness in that moment was significantly less crazy than the state of craziness from a few months prior. My hands were no longer constantly shaking. I could go to sleep most nights without Klonopin (though I still would wake up in the middle of the night in a full-on panic attack most nights). I still felt nothing like my old self, but I had settled into a new routine that was more compatible with my state: Lots of therapy, less work, daily calls with friends. A life dedicated to healing. Not a good life, but a life aiming at stability.

Yet Dennis's insistence that this was progress did not comfort me. I could not accept that this was how long progress takes. If it required two months to get from a level 10 on the Richter scale to, maybe, a level 8, then how long until we got to 0? Two years? Five? Ten? This thought terrified me.

As my sobs subsided, I managed to tell Dennis more calmly what, exactly, my concern was: I no longer spent every waking second thinking I was going to die, but I still did not wish to be alive, because I did not feel alive in any of the ways that matter—the ones that involve joy and contentment and fun and being cozy under a blanket as you watch a movie, instead of sensing a dread so deep and overpowering in the pit of your stomach every second of the day that every movie felt like the worst movie ever.

I felt like a car with a dead engine, I told him—there and hulking and existent but useless. I wanted the engine to restart already. And Dennis was, in so many words, telling me I'd have to completely take the engine apart, strip it to its individual components, find the broken pieces, and rebuild the whole thing by hand before that could happen.

Just get me back on the highway, I told him. I want to drive again. But that was the catch-22 of it all: Every time I tried to drive again—every time I attempted to live life as if nothing had happened, as if my nervous system wasn't in a severely damaged state—I could feel the engine breaking into pieces, metal against grinding metal. I was not well enough to live the life I once lived. I needed more time in the garage. Somewhere in me, I knew that.

So, by the end of the session, Dennis had convinced me that this process—slowly getting better, allowing myself the time I need in the garage—was, whether I like it or not, the only process.

I thanked him. I left. And I decided I would try to find something else to speed that process up.

In the next few weeks, participating in any mundane activity that I used to enjoy pre-being-crazy became further proof that I needed *more*, that psychoanalysis was not enough. One beautiful afternoon, I walked around the city aimlessly, perhaps once my favorite thing to do—and instead of filling me with calm or wonder at the humanity around me, it filled me with nothingness. The spark was gone. And that—the fact that walking no longer did anything for me—filled me with dread.

One night, I went to a party in North Philadelphia, a poetry reading with a bunch of queers, my head sunken in my oversize hoodie, unable to face the world head-on. Maybe, I thought, jump-starting my social life would reenergize me. But as soon as I entered the living room, I knew I was mistaken. The lights in the house felt too bright. My conversations felt like I was watching television, like I was on a couch watching my own life. This was a terrifying sensation, maybe one you've experienced while too high on weed. But for your brain to do this on its own, no drug needed, was much more jarring. The unreality made me panic. I walked outside without saying bye to anyone. The streets were dark and empty. I dry-heaved on the corner and felt thankful no one saw me. I ran to my car. I drove home, which did not feel like home, but someone else's home—nothing felt mine because nothing felt real. *Maybe it will be better tomorrow*, I told myself. It wasn't.

The next day, I continued my search for more.

I bought five workbooks on dissociation and derealization and mental breakdowns and eagerly awaited their arrival in the mail. One told me to focus on the present. Another told me to count the things in front of me to bring me back to reality. *Lamp. Couch. Fuck you.*

I bought so many books, desperately searching for answers—books on depression, on anxiety, on anything vaguely mental health–related. One book helped—a book by a Buddhist woman named Pema Chödrön about her husband leaving her, *When Things Fall Apart*. I found it helpful mostly because it was not hopeful—life sucks; you learn to feel the things and then you move on. The only way out of the forest is through it; there are no shortcuts, no helicopters coming to rescue you. I thought Buddhism was more flowery than this. It was comforting that it turns out it is not.

Okay, so socializing didn't reenergize me. Maybe my other passion—my career—could. So I attempted to get back to work. I sat in an airy cafe in a gentrified section of the city and tried to write. I stared at my computer screen. Nothing came to me. I responded to two emails. Then the panic hit. I leapt up from the wooden chair as if it was electrified and ran outside. I called my mom, crying, my breath convulsing, saying I was forever disabled, that I couldn't go on like this, that if I couldn't write I might as well die. She told me to relax—to focus on my own mental health before my work. I told her I should check myself into a mental hospital. She said that's probably a bad idea—they're usually horrible.

My mom also insisted I do a lot of four, seven, eight breaths, and I obliged. This did calm me down a bit—if only because they reminded me that my mom was there, just one city away—her presence in my breath a comfort.

My parents were always there for me, a phone call or a visit away, but did not understand exactly how bad things were in those days. I still don't know if this is because I kept some of the worst from them, or because they were really too scared to understand how much their child was suffering, or because it was impossible for anyone (them, my therapist, my friends) to really understand how close I felt to death, how scared I was—of life, of a car backfiring, of the knots that would not go away in my stomach, of myself—nearly every waking moment.

What my parents told me in those early days of recovery that helped me the most was that what I was experiencing was relatively normal, something they'd seen before as psychologists. Not good, but not uncommon. My dad was like, "So, you're going through a hard time. And eventually it will get better. There's no rush." "Yeah," I'd say. I know. But I still wished that was not the case.

In hindsight, I could have chosen other forms of therapy. Cognitive behavioral or dialectical behavioral therapy might have helped me a bit quicker—they're both very goal-oriented, about changing your patterns of thinking and your reactions to triggers. That takes less time than something like psychoanalysis, which is about really exploding your whole brain and putting it back together again—going on a self-directed journey through *everything*, from your current stressors to your family dynamics to your dreams, to find connections and tie them up into a cohesive picture. That can take years.

As slow as analysis was, it allowed me to reframe how I thought about my life, sometimes bit by bit, and sometimes all at once. I remember, about two years after my breakdown, Dennis asking me a question: Are you afraid of cumming? I was taken aback. No! I love cumming! Why would he ask me such a thing? And then, I started applying that question to everything in my life as a kind of metaphor. Cumming as the ultimate form of release, cumming as an embrace of pleasure in its purest form, cumming as a surrender of control. And I started realizing it fit as a framework for so many things in my life: There was, of course, Charlottesville, which had completely overwhelmed my circuitry. The excitement of the protest, of kicking a bunch of Nazis out of town, of coming together with thousands of people, and then the terror of all that immediately being pierced by the screeching of tires, the loud metal bangs of car against flesh. Going from immense joy to immense fear. Charlottesville seemed to have wired two neural pathways—excitement and danger—firmly together. So anytime I became excited, I would think of death. Not consciously think of it, but my brain would sense it, smell it. That fit in the framework.

Sure, the cumming thing was a particularly Freudian way of framing the problem; maybe another kind of therapist would've told me that I was simply afraid of anything that activated my PTSD, or told me that my nervous system was deregulated. But the framing worked. It enabled me to see that much of my life was governed by a fear that excitement and even happiness were dangerous.

Most obviously there was me being a 9/11 kid—a beautiful, blue fall day, a day I actually remember thinking, as I walked from the Chambers Street subway station in downtown Manhattan to my middle school, that I was ready to come to terms with being gay or bi or whatever, that maybe it wouldn't ruin my thirteen-year-old life. Life might be good!

And then, in Spanish class an hour later, the deep rumble. My notebook falling on the floor. A kid at the window of the classroom saying, "Holy shit, something exploded in the World Trade Center." Twenty minutes of tenseness; trying to get back to normalcy, trying to get back to the lesson plan, probably just a boiler explosion or something, someone said. And then the classroom door opened and my friend Melissa's mom was there, tears streaming down her cheeks, telling Melissa it was time to go. And then the announcement on the PA to get down to the cafeteria. I remember thinking Melissa's mom was overreacting. I remember when I bumped into my best friend, Jamie, as hundreds of us quickly filed down the stairs, and him telling me it was a plane, and that a second one just hit, that he saw it go into the building, and thinking, *That's a funny coincidence.* Last fragments of innocence—grabbing on to them like my life depended on it.

And then in the cafeteria, realizing my little Motorola cell phone wouldn't work, that I couldn't reach my parents. And then my friend Henry's mom running in, yelling at the principal, telling her she was taking her kid and his friends out of the school, even if there was a shelter-in-place order from the mayor, that we weren't far away enough from the towers—three short blocks. And then being out on the street with that mom and eight of us kids, looking up at the gaping hole, the fire, little black things, bodies in suits, floating quickly downward. *Don't look at that. Look forward. Toward where you're walking.* Except there too there were people, in suits, with blood on their heads and dust all over them. And then *whoosh*—several floors of the top of one of the towers slid down it like an avalanche. I still cannot describe what that looked like. Everyone kept saying "it was like a movie." Because ten stories of concrete and steel and bodies and glass falling toward you does not look real, or because to realize it was real would be to acknowledge what was happening to you. Last fragments of innocence—grabbing on to them like my life depended on it.

We ran.

At my friend's apartment a few more blocks north we watched on television as the second tower collapsed. It appeared to fall in the direction of our school. For an hour or so I thought everyone I knew was dead.

I felt . . . I didn't feel. I felt nothing. My eyes were above me, watching me, directing my actions—put your hand here, put your foot here, sit down on the floor in front of Jamie now. Two hours, maybe, my parents showed up. They'd biked down from work, pushing past all the people streaming in the opposite direction. Physically pushing to get through. The cell phones didn't work. They'd thought I was dead too. But then there they were. And then that's when I started to feel things—when I saw their eyes. My dad, his floppy mop of brown hair and scruffy face usually projecting something like hippieish calm. But his eyes. As they rushed up the stairs toward my friend's apartment, I saw them. They looked bloodshot. His pupils small. Like they were zoomed out. And my mom's hug. I'd never had a hug like that. So hard it hurt. That's when I felt things.

But we weren't sure we were out of danger yet. No time for those emotions. So I pushed it all down again. And my eyes floated back above me. I was no longer me, but a character in a video game I controlled. It hurt, but it worked.

So, there was that. Yes, excitement and fear, wired together.

That day had taught me a skill I'd perfect over the coming years—taking something that scared me, that made me uncomfortable, that threatened my stability, and boxing it up as best I could. Those things didn't have to be as dramatic as 9/11, but the process was nonetheless the same: Realizing I was gay, or queer, or whatever (I did not yet know the words "trans" or "nonbinary" in eighth or ninth grade) was, in many ways, realizing that my desire, what excited me, would forever be directly linked to danger—estrangement from friends, physical danger from bigots, maybe fucked career choices. My happiness meant pushing through things that scared the shit out of me. Outside my high school, at the top of the block where we would meet up after classes were out for the day, a winter day, gray. I was fifteen. I told Jamie I was gay. He didn't yell at me. But it changed things. A little coldness. That's what being myself, following what I want and need in the world, got me, I guessed—only bad things. So back in the box it went.

Charlottesville was the instigator of my breakdown, but through breakdown, I found so many other things I needed to address. If I wanted to be able to cum in that metaphorical, psychoanalytic sense, to feel pure joy, to lose control, to actualize my desire, I would need to address it all.

Uggghhhhh, I told Dennis at a session maybe three years into my recovery. You were right. You were right about the cumming thing, you were right about how I'd need to talk about *all of it*—the gender stuff and the childhood stuff and whatever else came up—because it was all linked. That there was no getting better from Charlottesville without getting better from everything else too. Fine. Yes. That was right.

He smiled again, this time not his usual sympathetic smirk, but a smile of, I think, happiness. Happiness maybe because I was finally getting it—there was finally a sign of some serious progress. But also, maybe, smiling because, after many sessions of me complaining about him not understanding, I had finally told him he was fucking right.

| | | | | |

Acknowledging that this was going to be a long and arduous process, that it was no quick matter of repairing my nervous system from the destruction of one event, also enabled me to realize I needed more. If it was going to take years, I needed to find things in the interim that made me feel better, so that while I worked on my brain, I didn't want to die all the time.

So I began to explore other interventions.

Maybe three months after my mental breakdown, I went to a yoga class. At a small studio in South Philadelphia, a very nice young woman instructed me and about six other people to form into various shapes. This felt good. At my next session, I realized I was the youngest person there by several decades. I wondered if it was strange to the sixty-year-old women to see this younger, gender-confused, wide-eyed, and scared-looking person walk in. But I liked it there more than any other yoga I'd tried—because that studio specialized in getting into *very* deep poses. Which, I learned, helped me—in several classes, when I got into certain positions, especially ones involving my hips and thighs, I began to sense tears forming in my eyes; the deeper I got, the more emotional I felt. No specific emotions or memories rose to the surface, but nonetheless I could sense a form of release. The few studies done on yoga and trauma seem to suggest it's helpful for PTSD.[1] Researchers think this is because trauma dysregulates your amygdala, basically your brain's "smoke detector,"[2] causing it to go off all the time—and yoga and breath work and the like can bring this back in check. In that moment, I did not care about its scientific efficacy, though. I was just starting to learn a valuable lesson about healing: follow whatever makes you feel better, no matter what it is.

And with that in mind, I began to throw whatever I could think of at the wall to see what stuck. An acquaintance mentioned acupuncture, so I tried that. I sat in a dark room, and a friendly woman with frizzy hair came in and readied about sixteen tiny, bendy needles, and then stuck them one by one into my skin, from my feet, up my legs, into my chest, and finally into my ears and face. As soon as the first one went in, I felt a calm overtake me, as if the needle had a direct line to my nervous system and told it to calm the hell down. Which, it turns out, might be true: studies have shown that acupuncture can help regulate your parasympathetic nervous system (basically, the thing that tells your brain and body to calm down).[3]

Every session put me into a kind of dream state—half-awake and half-asleep—thoughts colliding in slow motion. I could never remember the thoughts after a session ended, which to me was proof that some subconscious repair work was being done without my conscious energy being needed. After forty-five minutes, the needles were removed. I felt slightly better. Not *good* by any means. But maybe a point or two lower on the Richter scale. Not unbroken, but more willing to accept my current brokenness. Not as effective as Klonopin, but at least not addictive.

But still, these things were not enough. I was still in this terrible haze, not fully feeling anything. I was exhausted from processing my own thoughts, so much so that it was hard at times for me to move. So I spent hours a day in bed—watching TV, scrolling, thinking about the future I sacrificed—that I'd no longer be a writer, that I simply no longer had the energy. I consoled myself with the fact that many people, countless people, spend much of their time trying to survive—that there were plenty of others whose main work in life is the work of getting better, of not dying in this fucked-up world that's trying to kill them. This was not much consolation, though. I did not wish to be part of this group if I could help it.

I told myself there is nothing wrong with being disabled—and this is undoubtedly true. In a just society, my mental breakdown would not have led me to desperation. I, and everyone else so burdened by the world, would have the care and time needed to heal. In a better world, I would not feel like a lack of productivity equated to the death of my life. But we do not live in such a society, so the weight of the idea that my career could be over, that life as I knew it could be over, terrified me.

The pain was so physical at times, in my chest and my legs and my stomach, that I felt constantly and vaguely ill. In the months after my breakdown, I went to the doctor at least five times—shortness of breath, muscle cramps, fatigue. *Maybe I have chronic fatigue syndrome, or maybe I have chronic Lyme disease*, I thought. I wanted so badly for there to be an explanation that ticked all the boxes—a category I fit neatly into that explained what felt so unexplainable. But of course, the doctor, and then the doctors, plural, told me there was nothing wrong with me. Which, in some sense, was true. I was just crazy.

I worked to accept my fate—that this would take several or many years to figure out, like my therapist said. And I worked to make myself feel better in the interim with yoga and acupuncture and anything else I could find. But then there was this little itch, this nagging in my head: What if Dennis was wrong? What if there really *was* a faster way out?

There, in books and TV shows and doctors' offices and memes online, was a plot already prewritten, one that promised to get me better much more quickly than analysis and bodywork: a diagnosis.

In the story of diagnosis, history, trauma, childhood, gender, belief—none of that mattered. Diagnosis was a much simpler kind of story—no complete disassembly and rebuilding of one's brain needed. In the book of diagnosis, one had something—a disorder of some kind—and there was a cure to it.

After many years of me being resistant to this kind of thinking, the simplicity of diagnosis began to be appealing. I had struggled for months and months to repair my life, and I had become sick of my own story; sick of my excavating and explicating my history and traumas. I just wanted to be better. When I told Dennis this, that maybe I was just bipolar, or had major depressive disorder, or something else, he seemed a bit skeptical. But he didn't outright tell me I was wrong.

And everyone else was telling me I was right. "Sounds like you have depression and could be helped by medication," my primary care doctor told me. "I used to be so crazy, but then I realized I was bipolar II and got on meds and now I'm better," a friend in Philadelphia said. This tracked with everything I'd seen online too—the thousands of tweets and posts over the years of strangers saying things like "this drug saved my life," and "there's no shame in relying on medication." TV ads seemed to know I was diagnosis-curious too. I remember lying on the hardwood floor, perfectly motionless, in my dark apartment in Philadelphia and staring at the television as it played an ad I'd seen a thousand times—a woman wandered around her blue-lit suburban home with a look of immense distress on her face, until something called a selective serotonin reuptake inhibitor made her a good mom again and also turned the lighting in her house back to a normal, yellowish-white color.

I used to roll my eyes at commercials like that. But in my near-catatonic state, I thought, *Hey, maybe I'm like that woman. Maybe whatever house-brightening chemical she's on can help me too.*

What finally convinced me, six months after my breakdown, was the day my parents came to town.

It was Passover, and some people I didn't know particularly well were having a dinner in the Philadelphia suburbs. It was spring, but it was cold and dark in this way that made me feel four hundred times worse—like I could not even have warmth; like God couldn't even do me that favor.

I drove with my parents to this house I'd never been to, and we milled about and made pleasantries and discussed intergenerational trauma and Palestine and all the other things lefty Jews do when they meet. And then, at a certain point, during dinner, sitting there with uneaten matzoh and underseasoned meats in front of me, that sense of being separated from my body became particularly acute. Perhaps it was because of the dissonance—here I was with my parents, with some friends, having what should have been a lovely meal, and instead I felt horrid, a sense of dread in every limb and organ in my body. I was not having a panic attack, I was not triggered by anything; this, it seemed, had just become my natural state. A state of death. A state of ghostliness. That moment—more than Charlottesville itself, or the day in Oakland I went insane—was the day I most wanted to die. Because if a lovely and fine time with nothing notable about it felt so deeply *wrong*, then what else was there? If my mood was this bad in a moment that should have brought me happiness, what hope did I have?

The dinner kept going. I did not know if I could make it all the way through. Somehow, I did. Thank God. Thank Hashem. But the feeling was still there. As I traveled back to my apartment with my parents. As we opened the door. As they talked to me in my kitchen. Everything was cold and dark; the bright lights of the kitchen felt somehow gray as they bathed my body. This was worse than a panic attack. This was the end of life.

I had hoped my parents' presence at least would warm me. But they seemed so far away—even when they were standing right next to me. Like everything they said was coming through two tin cans connected by wire. I wanted so badly to feel what normal humans feel when their parents hug them—safety, love. Instead, as they hugged me and said goodbye, I felt nothing or, somehow, worse than nothing. I had become a shell of a human.

I realized that even though I was more stable than I had been six months ago—more able to function on a daily basis, to sit at my computer and type words and earn money; more able to see friends without crying and writhing on the floor—I also felt worse. Being in the throes of a mental breakdown had at least provided me with a new set of challenges to face every day. But this was something scarier: Nothingness. A void.

A few days after my parents' visit, I googled "psychiatrist near me," found one a few blocks away with good-enough ratings, and called her. And a few days after that, I walked to her office and sat down in a plush, white chair, and started to speak about all that had happened to me—Charlottesville, 9/11, my breakdown, the void I lived in. I was so accustomed to this process—talking talking talking—and I thought that's what I was supposed to do. Not here, apparently. After five minutes, she interrupted me.

"This is all pretty typical," she said. "You have depression. Don't worry. We can do something about it."

She was the first person to tell me anything like that. I cried more at this premise—the idea that I had an obvious problem, and that there was something equally obvious to fix it. I knew it. Dennis was wrong. My parents were wrong. There was nothing complex about my brain and my situation. It was just chemical. The psychiatrist spent the next thirty minutes speaking to me. I barely talked. She told me that while scientists aren't exactly sure of the causes of depression, that it's definitely a disease that can be cured, or at least managed, with the right medication. I asked her a few questions about those medications, and she calmly answered them: Yes, it's safe. No, the side effects are minimal. Not that I really cared about those side effects. She could've told me that I risked growing a horn out of my forehead, and I would've been happy to take whatever pills she prescribed. I just needed something.

She told me to go to a pharmacy a few blocks away to pick up my new medication.

An hour after I first met with her, I was handed a white bag with a yellow bottle filled with orange capsules containing beige little dots not much bigger than poppy seeds. This, I was told, was Effexor, an antidepressant. I stood in a parking lot in South Philadelphia, in a spring sunshine that felt physically painful to me, evidence of how different I was from it; how far away I was from warmth. I opened the bottle, took out a pill, swallowed it with a swig of Diet Coke. And as the various chemicals flowed down my throat with a bubbly scratchiness, I felt something that I had not felt in what felt like forever—hope.

The first day I took Effexor, generic name venlafaxine, I imagined my brain to be a dehydrated land, a lush forest-turned-desert, its flowers wilted, parched, shriveled, hoping for sustenance even as they knew they would likely die. And then, boom, a rainstorm, life falling from the heavens, the flowers immediately perking up, becoming plump, reaching upward, toward the sky, hoping to soak in every last drop.

It was as if I could actually *feel* the neurons in my brain changing after the first dose. I remember walking downstairs from my bedroom in Philadelphia, and as I descended into the living room, sensing something move in the back of my head, near my neck, something come alive.

I felt, mostly, an immense sense of relief. I had discovered the cure. I had been wary of antidepressants for years. The idea that a little pill could cure you seemed too simplistic to me—it made much more sense to me that the brain was infinitely complex, and that depression was not something that could be boiled down to a few neurotransmitters. But now I was ready to be a true believer. I had a chemical imbalance, and this chemical was going to fix it.

WHY WE LOVE SSRIS

As soon as I popped that first Effexor, I joined a very large and rapidly growing group of people attempting to alleviate their psychic pain through prescription medication. Since Prozac, the first major SSRI, was brought to market in 1986, the amount of antidepressants Americans consume has increased nearly every year, rising by 15 percent between 2015 and 2019 alone,[4] and by almost 40 percent among teens. Every year, about 17.5 million Americans are diagnosed with depression, and nearly 60 percent of them are prescribed an antidepressant.[5] As of 2018, one in eight Americans was taking some form of antidepressant.[6]

My initial skepticism of the drugs was based partly in my belief in psychotherapy—one I'd grown up with thanks to my psychologist parents. It seemed more logical to me that people's problems were material and external, rather than internal and chemical. People were depressed or anxious because their jobs or relationships were bad, or because they'd experienced traumas in their lives, not because they had a disease in their brains. How could a pill rectify a bad boss, or a bad boyfriend? How could a pill help people heal from near-death experiences, or abuse?

My reluctance was also based in what I observed around me: I'd seen a lot of people take these drugs and not really get better. Friends would constantly get on them, then get off them. And the ones who stayed on them often didn't seem any happier. In fact, they often seemed *less* able to deal with their lives. I remember in college one of my roommates deciding to stop taking her SSRI, one she'd been taking since childhood, and then one night her crying to her mom on the phone so loudly I could hear it from my room. Later, she told me that she hadn't been able to cry, or to process her anger at her family, while on the drugs. She was too numb. She was happy to be off them.

That seems true at a societal level too: Every year more and more Americans take psychiatric medication,[7] yet few of us appear to have alleviated our pain. From 1999 to 2020, the number of people who died via suicide, drugs, or alcohol *tripled*, from about 60,000 to 186,000.[8] Rates of depression and anxiety have increased too. And the same is true in much of the Western world: in Australia, Canada, and several European countries, more than one in ten people are on an antidepressant.[9] Yet depression is increasing in those countries—the number of people registered as "depressed" with their primary care doctors in England, for example, doubled between 2013 and 2023.[10] I thought it logical that if the drugs worked, and so many people were on them, then the amount of misery society experienced, or at least the number of people killing themselves, would decrease too.

But in my crisis state, I was willing to ignore these doubts. I wanted a solution—one that was less amorphous and long-range than psychoanalysis or acupuncture or meditation. And one that was more permanent than popping a Klonopin. I did not have years. Medication promised to remedy my problems in a matter of weeks.

I spent the first week on Effexor in a stupor. My stomach hurt. I was nauseous and dizzy. I felt high, but not in a good way, as if I was on the most boring drug imaginable—which, I guess, I was. My brain was still adjusting, so I was, in a literal sense, high on a drug.

But then, I remember, about two weeks after starting, walking from my house to the gym I'd always go to, about twenty blocks away, and sensing a slight buoyancy in my step. It's not that I felt *good*—I still had that head-floating-above-the-clouds sensation every day; there was still a rock of dread lodged in my stomach. Not healed. Not better. Still angry and confused. But I felt . . . protected, I guess. Like there was a thin barrier between my very extreme feelings of doom and death and fear and the logical part of my brain. I could kind of separate myself from those feelings in brief moments. I had a bit more space; wiggle room.

What, I guessed, was happening was that the antidepressants were working.

The theory of every modern antidepressant, whether Prozac (fluoxetine) or Lexapro (escitalopram) or Zoloft (sertraline) is pretty simple: The drugs flood a serotonin-deprived brain with serotonin. They're called SSRIs, selective serotonin reuptake inhibitors, because they, in theory, bind to the nerves that usually reabsorb your serotonin and block them, so that the serotonin is forced to stay in your brain, and thus give you a little happiness boost.[11]

If you have sex, or go for a run, or do any other happiness-inducing thing, your brain rewards you with serotonin. And then, after a while, that serotonin is reabsorbed, ready to be deployed for the next happiness-inducing activity. Well, in theory, SSRIs work by limiting some of that reabsorption, so that a brain that has less available serotonin in it than it should keeps some of that serotonin floating around. The drug I was on, Effexor, was an SNRI, a serotonin and norepinephrine reuptake inhibitor, nearly the same as an SSRI except that in addition to serotonin, it also worked, in theory, to prevent the reabsorption of another neurotransmitter called norepinephrine, one that specifically dictates how our brains and bodies respond to stress.

In theory. Everything in theory.

Because, it turns out, despite this theory being exceedingly popular, no one can really agree on whether this is how antidepressants actually work. Many scientists don't even agree that serotonin is primarily responsible for happiness, or a lack of for it a lack of happiness.[12] Most of what we know about SSRIs comes not directly from science, but from advertisements, and a mainstream media that is wont to take the pronouncements of pharmaceutical companies at face value, and tout their most recent inventions as miracles, silver bullets, until enough evidence comes out, often years later, that they're not.

When I thought Effexor was my silver bullet, or really, when I deeply wanted to believe that Effexor was my silver bullet, because it felt like nothing else would be, because it felt like there was no other option, I was willing to ignore all this doubt. The alternative, that my brain would indeed have to be repaired over years and years, was a thought too depressing for me to accept. So I kept faith that antidepressants would work, that the bottomless well I had fallen into would be given a bottom by the drugs. And, for a time, whether because of the chemical itself, or because of my intense belief in it, or both, they seemed to work as advertised.

And then, after a few months on Effexor, something scary happened: I began to feel stupid. I remember sitting at my desk and attempting to write an article—to use all my brain's capabilities to synthesize information and criticism into something coherent—and feeling like I couldn't do it. The words wouldn't come. The thin barrier that blocked me from fully feeling the most intense feelings also apparently blocked the part of my brain that could translate complex thoughts into words on a page. The neurons weren't clashing into one another fast enough.

I told myself that this was okay, that the benefits—less intense panic, a bit less dread every second of the day—outweighed whatever the costs might be. But then the costs kept adding up.

At a therapy session with Dennis one day, I assumed I would, as I usually did those days, start sobbing about my trauma. We talked about Charlottesville—he asked me to go over the day in detail again and talk him through what was still scaring me. And I obliged. Except now, I couldn't quite feel the things I was talking about. The details were there, but they were detached from their usual emotional intensities. This, despite how it may sound, felt bad. I *wanted* to cry. Crying felt cathartic. And now the tears wouldn't come. They too were behind some thin barrier. An emotional condom.

I began to wonder: How could I sort through my traumas if I couldn't feel them?

A few months after starting Effexor, I drove from Philadelphia to New York to visit my family. I love driving. I love the exhilaration of going fast; I love how it requires your full attention; I love that it's a skill you can always get better at. That afternoon, I gunned my little turbocharged stick-shift hatchback up the highway, weaving between cars, trying to find the stretches of road where I could really let loose. And I felt nothing. Slightly worried, I tried to amp up the experience a bit more. I put on a heavy metal song, "Here to Stay" by Korn, I'd heard hundreds of times before. The crunchy bass began, then the distorted and hard guitars, and finally the guttural screams. This is where I'd begin to feel it, normally, like the first drop on a roller-coaster after a long and slow ascent. But I didn't feel it. I felt, still, nothing. No goosebumps at the chorus, no eye-widening at the breakdown, no elation at the song's chaotic yet wrapped-in-a-bow-perfect resolution.

Not being able to write was concerning. Not being able to feel my emotions in therapy was too. But this was terrifying. If one of the things that brought me the most joy in life—driving fast while listening to metal—was now muted to the point of pointlessness, then what were the antidepressants doing? I felt trapped. I couldn't figure out what was worse: a life without Effexor, and thus with intense panic and dread, or a life without joy.

But I decided to stay on them. I convinced myself the alternative of experiencing life the way I'd experienced it before the drugs would be too destabilizing. I convinced myself the side effects would lessen. They didn't. After six months on the drug, I'd gained twenty-five pounds. I not only felt slower mentally, but physically, literally—my average speed on the gym's treadmill was down by about 20 percent. I researched the side effects on countless Internet forums, hoping to find solutions. Instead, I found mostly excuses: "What's worse, being fat or killing yourself?" "Sure I feel a little dumb, but I'd rather be dumb and happy than smart and suicidal!" The posts about sex, or lack thereof, scared me the most. It turns out up to 60 percent of people experience sexual dysfunction on SSRIs—something no doctor had told me.[13] I'd seen this was common on the Internet forums, but it was memed as if it was funny—like no babe sorry I can't cum I'm on SSRIs, haha. This was not funny to me. I liked sex! And it sucked, deeply, to realize I was one of the people this side effect applied to.

One day, I invited a man from an app over to my house. He was hot—tall and muscular but in a natural-looking, not gym-bro manner.

He passionately kissed me and pushed me onto my bed. We fucked. He looked into my eyes. I felt . . . again . . . nothing. I knew theoretically it was pleasurable, but nothing in my body told me so. My orgasm took forever and required *so* much effort from both the hot guy and myself. Like unlocking some kind of insanely complex safe.

I was no longer in crisis, but I instead just felt anhedonic—nothing had pain, but nothing had pleasure either. When I did some more Internet searching, I found that this too was a common side effect. Common enough to have its own name—tardive dysphoria, a kind of perma-deadening.[14] Doctors never told me about that either.

Yet I was not convinced that getting off the antidepressants was a good idea. I was terrified of the prospect. They helped me cope. They helped me not fall deeper.

So my life moved on. I went through a breakup. I kept doing the little work I could. About a year after my mental breakdown, I decided to do something I'd always wanted to do: I moved to New Orleans. I'd been there several times before and had loved it. I had friends there. Dennis told me we could keep talking over the phone or via video chat, and at this point I felt stable enough to take the risk of not being in his physical presence. But most of all, I wanted to move because I needed excitement, and New Orleans seemed like one of the most exciting places on earth. There were always parties and carnivals and festivals and parades. While I'd always dreamed of living there, the antidepressants gave me all the more reason: my life, no matter what I did, contained no excitement. Maybe New Orleans would fix the SSRI side effects that nothing else could.

It didn't.

One night, during the two-month-long stretch leading up to Mardi

Gras, when the entire city is basically constantly partying, after one of the countless parades, I walked through residential neighborhoods with a dozen or so friends, at around three a.m., doing lines of coke off our credit cards. The stuff was good. Like, really good. Best cocaine I'd ever done—in the shape of a rock but shaved down it became soft and melty like warm snow. I kept wanting more and more. Another block. Another swig of a beer from a paper bag. Another bump. Another. Another. It was never enough. Because my brain wouldn't let it be enough—there was that thin barrier again. Protecting me from deep pain, but deep everything else too. At realizing that, one emotion did get through: sadness. What is the point of life if one cannot have fun walking around New Orleans doing drugs with friends? What is there to look forward to if life's most pleasurable activities no longer feel pleasurable?

A visit from my parents was what had convinced me to get onto the meds. And another visit from them was what finally convinced me to get off them.

Erin, my best friend whom I'd survived Charlottesville with, had moved down to New Orleans too. And we took my parents out to central Louisiana, into the most rural swamp. I knew of an environmentalist tour company out there that I'd encountered in my reporting on a big oil spill a decade prior. I'd loved riding on their little motorboat back then. I wanted to show my mom and dad just how different the South was from where I grew up. The alien landscape, of water and green algae and weeds and bending trees with moss dangling for dozens of feet down like the cursed hair of some humungous creature; birds, dozens of them at a time, as big as small dogs, flying through the sky; fish, also as big as small dogs, jumping up above the water's surface and hitting our boat; frogs croaking in the distance and our very attractive tour guide telling us how he could shoot them from the boat if he wanted, that he loves making his mother, who lives in a cabin in the swamp, a frog salad (*Marry me*, I thought).

I was in love with this place. Something in me told me it was wondrous. One of the most bizarre landscapes I'd ever seen. Yet, again, it felt like nothing. Like a whisper instead of a scream. Like flat seltzer. Being there. With my family, my best friend, in this insane landscape, and feeling nothing. I nearly began to cry. Except I couldn't cry. That too had been muted by the Effexor.

That's when I accepted I'd need to come off antidepressants.

It took me a while, but I began to see antidepressants less as a cure, and more like Klonopin—a way to feel less pain, but not a solution to it. But unlike Klonopin, antidepressants were constant. When I was on them, there was no off-switch. Every second of my day was affected by this thing that put a barrier between me and the world, and between me and my deepest emotions. In that way, they had one other horrible side effect: they lessened my ability to actually figure out what was going on with me, to reach into my brain and sort through my traumas and my identity and all the rest.

Antidepressants made me feel better, at least temporarily, but when I was on them, I could no longer plunge deep into the abyss of my brain and my past. The drugs gave the endless well of pain I'd been trapped in a bottom. But, I began to wonder, what if the well wasn't a well, but a tunnel; something with another side—something I *needed* to go through in order to emerge into my future? If that was the case, then antidepressants weren't a cure, they were a blockage to my own healing.

Perhaps the biggest problem with antidepressants is the expectations we have for them. We have been sold these drugs as cures, when in reality they are modulators of pain, grief, and trauma. They do not necessarily end depression, they do not necessarily cure anything. They are drugs like any other. Like ibuprofen or heroin, they do not solve pain, but they can make it somewhat manageable. But because we are told that antidepressants, and psychiatric medication in general, are somehow different, I think we put an unearned faith in them. We get so focused on soothing the pain that we forget to look for its true causes, and work on solving them.

"You have this 'check engine' light on, because your car is about to fall apart," someone I interviewed about antidepressants once told me. "And someone comes up and is like, 'I have this great solution.' And they just turn off the light. And meanwhile your car is smoking and on fire."[15]

Eventually, it became clear that if I really wanted to get better, I would need to stop focusing on just feeling more stable, on turning off the "check engine" light, and instead focus on what my brain, my body, was trying to tell me. I was justifiably exhausted from all the work I'd done to piece my life together; the work I'd done to link all the disparate parts of my past into a cohesive whole—the trauma and the gender and the relationship dynamics and all the rest; but that didn't mean I was done.

I went back on all the antidepressant forums I'd become a frequent reader of and began to find people who were in the same situation— people who were less rosy about the drugs and more concerned with the dulling effects. So many of them said that their doctors and friends and everyone else warned them not to get off the drugs. That doing so was like telling a cancer patient to stop chemo. Yet many of these people persisted in taking themselves off the drugs. In order to do so, without the permission and thus the advice of their doctors, they had to experiment with what worked best. And many of them found that getting off antidepressants is a bitch. There was a plethora of advice, but most of it boiled down to: do it very slowly.

So, one morning in New Orleans, I took out the bottle of Effexor from my bathroom cabinet, opened one of the orange capsules, removed a few beads of the drug, about 10 percent, reclosed it, and swallowed. Ten percent. Seemed like a small-enough tweak to my brain chemistry . . . how bad could it be?

The first sign something was wrong were the brain zaps. I'd be walking through my apartment and all of a sudden feel, like, a . . . *zzzp* . . . in my head. Static and noise. Like turning off an old TV or computer monitor. *Zzzp*. I'd take a step, and then the next step would feel like it happened in an alternate dimension. Like my life had skipped a millisecond. It was an unnerving sensation, and one completely new to me. When I looked online, and asked friends who had been on antidepressants, they explained they'd experienced the exact same thing. Like a misfiring piston, except in your brain.

These went on for about a week. But, mostly, I was okay. Unnerved. But okay.

So I kept lowering my dose of the drug, bead by bead. I'd read online this was the way to go—slowly. As slow as possible. Studies back this up—the closer you get to zero on an antidepressant, the more the withdrawal affects you. The concentration in your brain exponentially decreases with every halving of the drug.[16] So I was cautious. 75 milligrams to 50, 50 to 25, 25 to 20, to 15, to 10 to 7 to 5 to 4 . . .

Already, even with my dose lowered just slightly, I was feeling a bit more like myself, like that thin barrier protecting me from my emotions and also from everything that made life worth living was growing thinner by the day. Soon, I thought excitedly, it'd be gone for good.

And then, one morning, all of sudden, I woke up in a panic. I had the feeling I was being chased by some unseen creature. It wasn't dissimilar to that day in Oakland. I thought I was past this. My heart thumping, I felt physically like I needed to run. *Fast.* As fast as I could. If I sat still, I thought I might die. I paced and paced, convinced my breakdown was coming back, convinced that I'd just erased more than a year's worth of progress. Eventually, when I did sit still, a sense of doom like nothing I'd ever experienced before overtook me, like I could see into the future and it was hell. On fire. The whole world on fire. This was not a normal panic. It was something scarier.

I took half a Klonopin. The rest of the day was shaky, but okay.

The next morning, with the Klonopin worn off, the doom and the panic were back. I was losing it again. And this thought was more terrifying than anything. Cumulatively, between the chemical withdrawal from the antidepressants and the resultant thought that I was falling backward, back to square one, I felt perhaps worse than I ever had.

I gave up. Went back up to the original dose of Effexor.

I stayed on Internet forums called things like Surviving Antidepressants like it was my job. Hours a day combing trying to find the solution to my Effexor problem. Some people, after much experimentation, found they'd had an easier time getting off Effexor if they first switched to a different antidepressant. The theory was that because Effexor had a short half-life of about twelve hours, the withdrawal from it goes too quickly. Lexapro's half-life is thirtyish hours. Zoloft's is somewhere between twenty-two and thirty-six. But one stands out from the pack: Prozac, aka fluoxetine, which takes four to six *days*.[17] So some very creative people suffering from very bad withdrawal had come up with the "Prozac bridge" and posted their success with it online. It involved tapering off Effexor (or other antidepressants with a short half-life), while tapering onto Prozac, and then eventually tapering off that. The idea is that the shock to your system, your neurotransmitters, is lessened by the slow pace of the chemical's departure from your bloodstream.

I talked to my doctor about it. She'd never heard of it. No one I talked to had ever heard of it except the random people online who told me to do it. But she obliged. Prescribed me Prozac. And, thankfully, it worked.

Over a period of two weeks I went up on the Prozac as I went down on the Effexor. I was anxious when I stopped taking the last Effexor, but the Prozac seemed to provide enough of a buffer—no more doom and panic. And then, after a few weeks of stability on the Prozac, I began going down on that too. And everything was fine. Until I hit zero. The withdrawal wasn't as bad as with the Effexor, but I'd still get horrible anxiety spells and strange physical symptoms like the brain zaps.

I didn't want to get back on the lowest-available dose of Prozac, so I began dissolving the pills in water, measuring out a tiny dose, milligram by milligram, each morning with a milliliter dropper. I've attempted to get off the final milligram of the drug for the past year or so. Every time I do, after a few days, the panic comes back. I can't tell if it's a return of my normal anxiety. Or withdrawal symptoms. Both, probably.

But for a brief window, before I inevitably decide I am not yet stable enough to go through this process and decide to get back on the drug, I feel just slightly more like me. Embodied, clearheaded, or just alive to the fullest extent possible. I miss that me. I'm not sure I'll ever fully have that person back. And I'm not sure I'll ever know how much these drugs are to blame for that.

That's the compromise I make, I guess. A compromise a lot of us make. A little sacrifice of me-ness, of excitement, of cumming and getting goosebumps from hearing music, for a little more stability. A little haze, a little floaty-ness, in exchange for a little normalcy. One can only go so far down the rabbit hole until the depths feel unsustainable, a true blackness in which it is easy to become convinced there is no way out, forward or backward, up or down. Sometimes, even if you really do need to push through to the other side, even if the only way to out is through, the pushing gets too exhausting.

THE PURPOSE OF DEPRESSION

There are timelines and conditions on the amount of sadness you're allowed to feel before doctors begin deeming it a problem in need of solving. The *DSM* gives people a year to grieve a death. If you grieve for longer than that, you can be diagnosed with "prolonged grief disorder."[18] Government campaigns tell us to break the stigma of depression, which in one way makes sense—we don't want people to fear acknowledging they're sad; but in another almost feels like a stigmatization itself, the implication that none of us *should* be depressed, that if we are, we must act as quickly as possible to rescue ourselves from this state.

We speak of depression as if it was cancer, something that no one should live through, something that you cannot live with—it must be excised or zapped away as a tumor.

But what if depression isn't a disease, but a productive state, a state less like cancer and more like grief? The cure for getting over the death of a loved one is not to cure oneself of grief, but to grieve! By thinking through your attachment to their loss, you process that loss so that you can eventually move on. What if depression functions similarly—a logical response to external stressors that must be felt fully in order to fully process? What if depression is trying to tell us something, or many things?

As I continued through recovery, as months became a year and then more, this view of depression began to make more sense to me. I thought back to the very beginning of my breakdown, my parents sitting across from me in their apartment, telling me that I'd get through this, not offering me a quick solution, but instead insisting that the despair I was experiencing was an okay thing to experience. I thought back to Dennis saying over and over again, session after session, that we'd work through it together, and that eventually I'd get better. And suddenly, the meaning of these words changed: My parents and Dennis weren't telling me they didn't know what to do; they weren't trying to provide cold comfort to someone whose problems they didn't understand. They were telling me this *was* the thing to do, that I needed to feel the despair and grief and all the rest.

Once I settled on this understanding of depression and recovery—that it is not a disease but a modality through which meaning is made, through which progress is made, a necessary thing—it became easier to handle. I began to trust my brain more. I began to accept that, even if it feels bad, my mind knows what it is doing—it is working through vast problems of my identity, my past, and my relation to a cruel and violent world. It is asking: How can you exist, and how do you want to exist?

So, eventually, two years or so after my mental breakdown, I stopped thrashing around and asking, *Why why why isn't this over?* I stopped searching for quick fixes. Which is not to say I stopped asking for help. I still needed the Klonopin and the kratom and various other drugs. I still needed therapy and friends and sometimes acupuncture and yoga. But I changed what I was asking for from these things. I was no longer asking for salvation. I was asking for a bit of space. I was no longer expecting a cure; I was just looking for breathing room so that my brain could do what it needed to do. Instead of thinking there was some theoretical "better" I was trying to reach, I accepted that all of it—the depression, the dissociation, the panic—was inevitable, that it was my brain's and my body's way of sorting through my past and my traumas. This was a big change, because I was no longer working against myself. Therapy, drugs, meditation, yoga—they all became tools not to arrest my intense despair and grief, but to assist them, to move them forward, to get me deeper.

I began to find solace in writers and thinkers who've theorized depression as a fruitful state, one that can produce new thoughts, perspectives, ways of relating to yourself and others, growth.

"Some periods of our growth are so confusing that we don't even recognize that growth is what is happening. We may feel hostile or angry or weepy and hysterical, or we may feel depressed," Alice Walker wrote. "It would never occur to us, unless we stumbled on a book or a person who explained it to us, that we were in fact in the process of change, of actually becoming larger, spiritually, than we were before."[19]

For the writer Carina del Valle Schorske, depression was like the "devil's tuning fork, pointing toward the poisoned river running beneath the surface of our society."[20] She found that her state made her more aware of others' suffering. It reoriented her life.

None of this recontextualization took the pain of depression away, but it gave the pain a purpose, and thus helped me stomach it. It helped me realize that what I was going through was necessary. Of course I was depressed! I was nearly killed! Twice! I was processing the trauma of that, and the various other traumas it had triggered. And on top of that, I was questioning my place in life—my gender, my identity, my purpose. What other way was there to be?

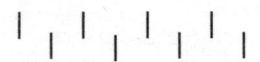

As I reframed my recovery, my sessions with Dennis changed too, because I began to see therapy as a tool to help further the grieving rather than to cure it. I think this is the use of therapy, at least good therapy: to have a guide at those depths. The worst kinds of therapy—the ones that attempt to reframe all your thoughts as positive, or attempt to simply change your reactions to your stress—are ways of pulling you out of the hole, or creating a false bottom, so that you have a sense of security. The best kinds of therapy, in my experience, allow you to go deeper safely. And this is what Dennis helped with. I began to view him less as someone to get advice from, less as someone to bounce emotions off of (though sometimes I would do those things too), and more as a kind of chaperone leading me through my own brain. He couldn't solve anything for me, but he could tell me what tools to use when we got to tricky parts of the terrain, and assure me that there was nothing deadly up ahead. And in that way, he kept me from giving up in the middle, from settling down when I hadn't made it all the way through yet.

Eventually, I got better at doing this on my own too—at letting my psyche go places I was scared of. I would take long baths and feel this immense darkness within me, stomach pangs of pain that would nearly double me over. I would take these baths *with that purpose*. To feel as deeply as I could. And then scream into a towel afterward. I would take walks at night, sensing a frightening yet awe-inspiring aloneness. I would lie in bed and sob. I started setting a goal for myself of five to ten minutes of stillness each day. Not meditation, not a nap, just sitting or lying down and feeling what I felt.

And in these depths I discovered more about myself than I ever thought possible—I found the foundations of my grief, over the death of a fellow demonstrator in Charlottesville, at the childhood that was robbed from me by the September 11 attacks; I felt the anger of having to grow up too fast because of those attacks. I felt the jealousy toward others who got to experience normal childhoods.

I felt a sadness about the brokenness of my family; a good family, much more stable than many—but one still deeply hurt by the murder of their ancestors during the Holocaust; one afraid to let anything, any person, me, my brother, go, from its grasp, because that prospect subconsciously felt just like my grandma letting go of her mother's hand in a concentration camp. I felt it all. I communed with the dead, with my ancestors, saw their faces when I closed my eyes. I realized how much my pain was connected to theirs—both in a very specific sense (the perpetrators of the two terror attacks I had been at the center of had little in common, the small sliver of their overlapping Venn diagram being an intense hatred of Jews) and in a more broad one, in that all human pain is connected. If we all hurt, then that means none of us are alone.

And through this plunge down deep, I changed. I became more steadfast in what I believed both about the world and myself. I felt more solid. And in that solidity, amorphousness and nuance emerged—because it takes confidence, it takes steadfastness to stomach the gray areas, I think. I stopped asking to be known, and instead promised myself to know myself more. My gender, my identity, my body, my desire, my politics, my everything. I would joke with my therapist that PTSD made me trans, a joke I did not really even understand until recently. But now it makes perfect sense: I needed to break down the walls in my psyche to awaken to who I really was.

I do not know if all of this would have been impossible without guides, but it certainly would have been much harder. Without a therapist (first, traditional psychoanalytic; then, years later, the less traditional somatic), I would not have had someone to let me know that my grief, my anger, my fear would not break me. As I healed, I began to feel incredibly grateful for my privilege, my support systems, my community, and my family and friends. Having enough support, time, and money to plumb the depths is rare these days. Perhaps it is not surprising that antidepressants have become the preferred modality of treating mental health problems—not only because putting someone on pills is cheaper than years of therapy, but because every other modality requires *so much more*. It requires allowing people the time and space to explore their own minds, to process their own grief.

Maybe that is a secret purpose of the current structure of our world—not only to overwork us and wring capital out of our every pore, but to fill our days with stress and work and mundanity so that we do not have the time and space to figure out how we really feel, so that we cannot have five minutes or five years, however long it takes, to understand what is truly going on; to understand that our struggles do not lie solely within us, that we are not broken, that our despair is not a matter of brain chemicals but a matter of osmosis—us absorbing the psychic violence of capitalism. While there is nothing inherently radical about meditation, or self-care, or baths, or taking a Klonopin and allowing yourself peace for a night, or staying up all night blowing lines of coke and writing in your diary, or just sitting still for five minutes and allowing yourself to feel, feel, really feel, in your gut and in your bones, the true reality of your life—I believe there is potentiality in that: if we were allowed the time and space to think, to grieve, to explore our own psyches, we could not only find ourselves, but find our enemies.

5

A TENUOUS STABILITY

HOW ONE ACHIEVES STABILITY;
THE VERY AMERICAN URGE TO MAKE EVERYONE
STABLE AND NORMAL; SELLING STABILITY

Everywhere I turned, it appeared that people were in a similar place to me—equally confused about their way forward, equally confused about how to process their traumas and build a life that felt worth living as the world around them felt increasingly unlivable.

I began querying my friends, and realized that most of them were in therapy, or on mental health medications like SSRIs, or self-medicating with drugs of all kinds, or (frequently) all of the above. I began to have more conversations with them about these things—why they felt so trapped, why they felt they were just treading water and trying to make it through the day. And nearly everyone I talked to seemed to be experiencing these existential crises. It didn't matter if they were struggling financially and directionless, or rich and blessed with a good career (or wealthy parents)—they all couldn't figure out how to deal with a constant sense of grief.

These conversations convinced me to change the kind of writing and journalism I was doing. Before my breakdown, I'd written more directly about politics and gentrification and capitalism and social justice movements. But now it seemed clear that so many people in the world already agreed with what I was writing, but still felt utterly stuck. Few needed to be convinced that the world needed to be changed, that global warming and inequality and racism were big problems. No one needed another article to tell them that the world was falling apart. Instead, people seemed to want affirmation that they weren't alone in feeling depressed or crazed. And they wanted to know what to do about that—how to not burn out or kill themselves, how to simply survive.

As I started writing more about our internal worlds, I began to receive emails and DMs from people who wanted to tell their stories. Their circumstances were varied; not all of them had big, capital-T traumas like I did in Charlottesville. But all of them seemed to have the same question: Why do I feel so stuck, and how do I become unstuck?

Melissa was one of those people.

Out of all those whom I'd gotten in touch with about depression and grief and ennui, Melissa was the one I wanted to learn about most. Not because her story was particularly unique or dramatic (indeed, her story was all too common), but because she was really willing to go there; to plumb the depths. Usually, in my conversations with friends, or in the messages I'd receive online, there was a stopping point—a point at which people seemed to clam up. But Melissa was willing to keep going.

Melissa had no context for how good her life was—she didn't hear the term "upper middle class" until she was older. She had a good home: tan with a front porch and a back deck, on a cul-de-sac in a suburb of Madison, Wisconsin, called Middleton. Lush, with a big yard, with one particular tree, a really big one, that Melissa would climb as a child. Her parents had worked hard for this place. Both were lawyers. They'd moved away from the region, to California, but then moved back, as many did, because they missed the life there, in the Midwest. Every family on her street is still there. Generations in the same place. Her siblings, a brother and a sister, older just by a few years, and she would play out back—the playset built by hand by her father. The backyard was more than a yard; it led to a prairie. A hill at its back.

Melissa had lots of friends. She was popular, not in the Cool Girl sense, but in the Girl Who Everyone Gets Along With sense. She danced, played golf with a team, was a part of 4-H.

Hard, then, to pinpoint where, exactly, things went wrong. Or why.

One day, early on in high school, Melissa was in her parents' kitchen. She opened up the medicine cabinet, next to the stove, next to the salt and pepper, and found a prescription bottle with her name on it, for something called sertraline. Zoloft. Melissa had never taken it. Or at least had never taken it intentionally. Did not even know what it was.

That was the day she found out she'd been on antidepressants since she was a child, since she was nine or ten, since fourth grade.

Looking back, she knows there was something off with her, but she doesn't know what—which emotional states were about her, or her family, her surroundings, her brain, and which were the medication, its side effects, its intended effects.

"It's really hard for me to know what was what, because I've never not been medicated," Melissa told me. "I always feel like I'm making up how bad I feel because I've always been told that it's all in my head. I've never considered that I've actually had a lot of situational challenges that are the reason I struggled—that maybe I don't have a chemical imbalance, but that my life was hard."

Melissa is now in her early thirties. She lives in a nice apartment in Chicago, close to downtown. She has a new baby. A husband. A cat. A good job. She reads a lot. She's pretty happy. And she's still on antidepressants. She doesn't want to be. But she's not sure she'll ever get off them; she's not sure she can.

It all started with separation anxiety. Common for kids. But Melissa's was bad. She has a memory of being very young, maybe four, and her parents telling her they were going to dinner, and Melissa taking a piece of paper, drawing a huge storm with lightning bolts on it, attempting to show them how scared she felt. When she transferred schools in fourth grade, she was dragged, literally, kicking and screaming, into the building.

It's around then that the obsessive thoughts started. *If I get hit by a car, my parents won't go somewhere*, she thought. She couldn't stop imagining her family dying. She began counting her steps. She became terrified of throwing up—she was convinced that if she hit the ground with her right foot on the sixth step, she'd barf. She couldn't pass garbage cans because she was afraid she'd puke in one. One day, she was so distraught that a school counselor locked Melissa in her office. Melissa was thrashing around, crying, and the counselor attempted to stop her, and broke Melissa's crucifix necklace, the one she was given at her First Communion.

Maybe that day, or a day around then, Melissa can't remember exactly, she ran away from school. Cops went looking for her. Her dad found her. She remembers walking with him, passing a stray dog on her way home.

And that's when the appointments started.

"I saw four or five doctors. Vague memories of being in old buildings. Playing games with these people. I don't think I ever told them anything, talked at all, or saw them more than once," she said. "For such a little child to have such huge emotions. That was my only way to express it. I don't think any of that was heard in the way it needed to be. I don't know if that's anyone's fault. But I can still feel what it felt like to be dragged into the school by strangers, physically holding my thrashing body."

At some point, a few years after she began seeing the doctors, things got a little better. She ended up liking her new school. She was more stable. But the anxiety was still there, the obsessive-compulsive tendencies. And at the beginning of high school, it worsened again. Melissa felt too scared to go on field trips—she was afraid of being on buses, afraid of being away from a home base. Kind of an agoraphobia. She told her music teacher and he said he'd experienced it too. That made her feel less alone. But still scared, still trapped in her own body. So, at some point, early on in high school, at fourteen or fifteen, she can remember going to yet another doctor's office. Having one appointment. Being prescribed a new drug, paroxetine, aka Paxil—another antidepressant, an SSRI. Her sixth year being on an antidepressant in her short life.

No one asked her how she felt taking the new drug, nor explained to her why she was switched from one to another. No one told her what it was supposed to do to her, or what she was supposed to feel like on it. But quickly, Melissa began to feel something more terrifying than even the worst of her panic attacks and the worst of her compulsions—nothingness.

"I don't know why that was first prescribed to me," Melissa told me. "I know it was early high school. I can remember another doctor's office space that I went to. I don't remember why. I have almost clearer memories from childhood than from then. But I remember how I felt when I was on it. Those were some of the worst years of my life."

Melissa had no other appointments with the doctor; she just kept taking the medicine. And the nothingness was constant. She felt not-alive. Like a ghost of herself. It scared the hell out of her.

"It's one of the harder things to describe, to describe nothing," she said. "It's easier to explain why self-harm helped."

After months of this terrifying void, Melissa found a solution, if it can be called that, that helped her feel alive again. She would go to her room after school. There was a big, vintage stereo there with two cassette tape slots. In one slot, Melissa would hide rags and a razor. And a few times a month, she'd take them out. She'd cut her wrists until she saw blood. Then soak up the blood with the rags. That was the goal for her—to see red.

"It was this very real need to be reminded that I was alive," she told me.

She kept cutting. The scars piled up. She wore ballet stockings on her arms. Chunky bracelets. "You figure out how to hide it, but I bled through a few times."

A teacher noticed and told her mom. Her mom asked her about it. Melissa was able to convince her it wasn't true. Somehow this was enough to keep her private ritual going without further interruption for years—on and off until Melissa was in her thirties. She still sometimes gets the urge. But now when she does, she texts her husband and tells him she wants to hurt herself, and that's enough of a pressure valve to stop her from actually doing it.

At no point did anyone ask why Melissa felt the need to do this. At no point did anyone question whether it could be related to the medication she was on.

It wasn't until the early 2000s, after several people across the country committed suicide, murder, or other violent acts shortly after starting Paxil, that the drug came with a warning label that stated it increased the risk of suicide among teens.[1] It wasn't until 2015 that a major study concluded that the original data that GlaxoSmithKline used to justify the drug was faulty.[2] The reanalysis concluded Paxil was unsafe for adolescents, period[3]; that it did little to curb their depression but led to increased self-harm, heart conditions, and other serious problems.

"I'm very resentful that I was on Paxil in high school," Melissa told me. "I read about Paxil's effect on young teens a decade after the fact and found out I wasn't alone in feeling nothing. But I was alone when I was living it. I still have scars on me from that—real and emotional."

With no one asking her what was up, no one suspecting that the drug was partially to blame, Melissa kept feeling unalive and alone; unalive but living—getting all A's, dancing, smoking weed with her brother, James. She loved English class. She found books with characters that reminded her of herself, that had the same emotions, or lack thereof. She wrote her honors essay on *Catcher in the Rye*.

And she kept cutting.

"It felt like I needed to relieve pressure from my body. If it leaked out, I could get rid of some of the feeling of nothing," she said. "Like bloodletting back in the day. Bloodletting for the purpose of getting out some sort of demon that was in me."

Melissa relays all this to me on a sunny day in Chicago. We are in a park in the center of the city. It's warm. Ducks waddle by. Melissa loves ducks. Her husband bought her some old duck decoys for her thirtieth birthday.

When we first meet, she's pregnant and happy about it. She has a stable job at a big university. We drink flavored seltzers and sit on lawn chairs. She looks well, full of life. But she hasn't been off medication since childhood. Even though she wants to be. She really, really wants to know what life is like off meds. But she's terrified of what will happen if she quits. So every day she reluctantly takes a dose of another antidepressant, duloxetine, aka Cymbalta, always wondering how, exactly, her life ended up like this, and what it would have been like if things had gone a little differently—if instead of assuming she needed the drugs, people had asked her how she felt, and why.

"I used to be a believer," she tells me. "I used to say all the time, 'You wouldn't deny a diabetic their insulin. So why wouldn't you take your meds?' Well, what if I'm not a fucking diabetic?"

THE INVENTION OF CHEMICAL IMBALANCE

The idea that we can achieve stability, happiness, a normal life via the use of medications is a relatively recent one. The psychopharmaceutical industry as we know it—a few corporations creating novel chemicals in an attempt to soothe or cure mental illness—did not exist until the 1950s. The idea that we know what chemicals control these things—stability, happiness, normalcy—is even more recent. The idea that serotonin is primarily responsible even more recent still. Modern antidepressants came to market less than forty years ago.[4]

Amazing, then, how much popularity antidepressants, and mental health medications writ large, have obtained in their short period of existence. How quickly we have adopted not only an entirely new class of drugs, but an entirely new way of thinking about the brain, and an entirely new way of thinking about human functioning, about what makes us able to live happy, or at least normal, lives.

At least 50 million people in the US take psychiatric medication.[5] One in seven takes an antidepressant. More than 15 million Americans have been on antidepressants for over five years, a rate that's doubled since 2010, and tripled since 2000.[6] The number of teens on an antidepressant rose by 40 percent between 2015 and 2019. The US is not an anomaly—14 percent of people in Iceland, 10.6 percent of people in Australia, 10.3 percent of people in Portugal, 10 percent of people in England take an antidepressant.[7] They are some of the world's most popular drugs. There were more escitalopram (aka Lexapro) prescriptions in the United States in 2020 than there were prescriptions of amoxicillin. It was the fifteenth most prescribed drug. Bupropion (Wellbutrin), another antidepressant, was the eighteenth most popular. Fluoxetine (Prozac) the twenty-fifth.[8]

Much has been made of the prescription drug industry's influence on doctors when it comes to opioids like OxyContin—funding lavish trips around the world, giving them free samples of drugs they want to promote, offering high-paid speaking gigs—but less attention has been given to the industry's influence when it comes to drugs that are considered less harmful, like antidepressants. Drug manufacturers are by far the largest lobbying group in the US, spending $283 million in 2023 to influence politicians, $120 million more than the second-biggest lobbying group (electronics manufacturers; insurance corporations, including health insurers, are third).[9] Pharmaceutical companies also spend $6.68 billion a year[10] in the United States on advertisements directly to consumers to showcase their drugs.

What the industry is promoting in their influence campaigns and direct consumer outreach is not only a specific drug, but a specific view of the brain, and of depression and mental illness writ large, one in which mental health issues can be fixed through neuron tinkering, and therefore can be mediated with their inventions.

"While the cause is unknown, depression may be related to an imbalance of natural chemicals between nerve cells in the brain," one popular commercial has asserted. "Prescription Zoloft works to correct this imbalance."[11]

This strategy has worked, giving Americans the impression that chemical imbalance is the main cause of depression, rather than, say, trauma or life circumstance. A survey of 262 college students in 2007, for example, found that nearly 85 percent thought chemical imbalances were primarily responsible for depression.[12] That survey also found that the primary source people intuited this information from was not scientific textbooks, nor doctors, but television.

The problem is, no one really knows if any of this is true. Even the most ardently pro-prescription-drug psychiatrists admit that the chemical imbalance view of the brain is overly simplistic.

"It's mostly a discredited theory," Michael Thase, a psychiatry professor at the University of Pennsylvania, once told me. "There's not any good evidence that depression in and of itself is caused by deficiencies or deficits" of serotonin or other neurotransmitters.[13] Thase is a very prominent psychiatrist—and one who has been paid by the prescription drug industry. If someone like Thase doesn't believe the chemical imbalance theory holds much weight, the fact that so many of us do suggests that what we as the public know about antidepressants and mental health medications, in general, is less about science and more about the creation and selling of an effective narrative.

Which is not to say that prescription drugs help no one's mental health. I've taken several prescription drugs throughout my life. At points, they've helped me. But the billions of dollars the industry spends every year has had a totalizing effect on mental health care across the world—it's funneled money away from other interventions like psychotherapy, it's changed how mental health is researched at universities and other institutions, and, perhaps most damagingly, it's given the general public the impression that there is only one way to address their mental health; that their problems are not due to their life's circumstances or their past traumas, but solely dependent on the balance of chemicals in their brain. And that's left many, many people, including Melissa, feeling trapped.

Melissa's apartment; two bedrooms, old, parquet floors in good condition, midcentury modern furniture—the real, vintage kind, not the cheap knockoffs. The duck decoys sit atop a shelf with books called things like *Recipes for a Sacred Life* and *Notes on a Nervous Planet*. Melissa holds a black-and-white cat like a baby in her arms as we chat.

It's the second time we've met and she's emotional—she hasn't been able to talk to many people about her past. She's reticent to reveal what she feels about the medications she's been on because she doesn't want to seem crazy. But it feels good to get it off her chest.

From the time she was prescribed Paxil until now, she's never not been on a prescription medication. She's tried something like ten different ones. At the end of high school, she switched to escitalopram (Lexapro). Then there was Zoloft again. And then bupropion (Wellbutrin)—an "atypical" antidepressant that often makes people feel more energy. She was put on that to counter the effects of the SSRIs, because she was always sleepy. But she never knew if it was because of her brain or the medication. Then gabapentin, an anticonvulsant that's often used off-label to treat anxiety. Then amitriptyline, an old-school antidepressant called a tricyclic that's been around since the 1950s. (The mechanism of action of tricyclics is different from that of SSRIs, but both work to increase the available levels of serotonin in the brain.)

"It was always the promise of, 'This will help your current medication work,'" she said. "There was always the promise of feeling better if I tried something else. But I don't ever remember feeling wildly different from medication to medication. But they're never gonna take someone who has been on medication for years off if they're doing well on the surface—they're gonna say, 'This is clearly working', if you're getting all A's."

And Melissa was getting all A's. She went off to college, not too far away—a Catholic university in Minnesota. She studied comparative literature with a focus on German and English, and minored in communications and journalism. Her life as the good, if oft-troubled, child, continued.

Freshman and sophomore year she felt relatively stable, "tenuously stable" as she calls it—anytime she's stable that's how it feels. Tenuous. But that was better than high school.

And then, more trouble started. Her brother, James, got into harder drugs. He did heroin sometimes. Sometimes with a mutual friend of his and Melissa's.

On Valentine's Day of her sophomore year of college, Melissa woke up to seventeen missed calls. The mutual friend, she was told, had overdosed on heroin and died.

The death shattered that tenuous stability Melissa had reached.

"It was a very clear example again of how people didn't want to be around my big emotions," she said. "I was still dating my high school boyfriend, and he told me over the phone that he didn't want to hear me cry anymore."

Melissa didn't know where to turn. Her brother's life was dark before the death. It was darker after. Melissa felt she had to be the grown-up. She felt she had to be the one to communicate with her parents, and monitor her brother.

"There was no support system that was able to handle my emotions," she said. "If your friend dies, and your brother wants to die, you're going to have some big emotions."

With few outlets for her grief and her confusion, Melissa began drinking a lot, and blacking out on weekends. She slept around a lot, not in a way that felt fun and freeing, but in a kind of sad stupor—escapist and chaotic.

"I spent years wondering how I would kill myself if my brother succeeded in killing himself," she said. "It's my story, but part of me feels like it's his story and not mine. The fact that I had to figure out how I would die if he did—that shows to me how much I wasn't living my own story."

Somewhere in there, during college, during the period she felt as if she were drowning, Melissa was prescribed lorazepam (brand-name Ativan), a benzo like the Klonopin I've relied on. She and her boyfriend in college would crush it up and snort it. But Melissa never developed an addiction to it, partly because she was aware that she could go overboard easily.

And then, eventually, again, things improved. Melissa's life settled. She graduated. Began working. But there was still something, a stubborn something, always there. So she kept switching meds, seeing new doctors, hoping one would finally provide the fix.

A few years ago she went from Lexapro back to Zoloft. It didn't seem to make much of a difference. But she kept taking it, mostly because she didn't know what else to do.

Her life was stable enough for her to feel like she could travel on her own, and that she did—going all around Europe. But then it all seemed to hit again. As she was seeing a musical—*Les Mis*—in London, sitting in the audience, she suddenly felt that weird anxiety tingle. Her arms went numb. She felt "not right." After years of feeling tenuously stable, the thought of losing it all again caused her to panic.

"I was so paralyzed by the idea that this could come back," she said. "I was so afraid. The feeling of, *Well, maybe this time, I don't come out of it*: to the present day, that is probably the source of my worst fears."

So she went back to a psychiatrist yet again. She was told to switch from Zoloft to Cymbalta (duloxetine). The doctor told her she could simply stop taking one pill cold turkey, and then immediately switch to the other (there's a growing recognition people need much more time than this to quit SSRIs[14]). A few days later, the withdrawal from the Zoloft hit.

"I was lying on my couch, crying hysterically, squirming in my body," she said. "I called my parents saying I felt like I was dying. I was ready for it to be hard. But to feel like I was dying, that's the only way I can describe it. It was unbearable. And that made the prospect of ever getting off medication again even more frightening."

After a few weeks of terror and mental paralysis, Melissa began to acclimate to the new medication. She decided to stay on it.

Then the pandemic hit. She became a bit agoraphobic again. She was prescribed Klonopin. She took it every day for a few months. And then she knew she'd have to get off it so that she could have a baby.

The withdrawal for that was bad too, though, surprisingly to herself, not as bad as from SSRIs. She was nauseous. She felt a deep fog all around her. The only thing that eased the symptoms was weed. Her brother had introduced her to it in the prairie behind their house when she was a teen, in a big concrete drainage pipe. It'd always been helpful. The withdrawal from the benzos was still tough, but manageable.

"I did it and got through it, but it's never part of the discussion when you get on medication—like how to get off of it or what your life will look like after it," she said. "If you're just having a hard time, it's really easy to be prescribed medication, and really hard to get off it."

That fact still makes Melissa angry.

She knows each drug was supposed to help her, but she's not sure they ever did. She knows that the people—her parents, her teachers, the doctors—who got her on the meds had good intentions. But she still feels resentment. Her life has been like a scientific experiment without a control group. There's no way of isolating the variables. With a carousel of drugs, but no therapy, no one asking her what was going on, it's impossible for her to know why she felt the way she did, and what ultimately helped.

Nonetheless, she's attempted to move on. She found a therapist she actually liked. She began to plan a family, and as she did, began to feel stronger, and less like she was going to go back, more stable and less tenuously so.

"I thought, *How am I going to prepare this vessel?*" she told me. "*How can I be a good home to someone when I'm not a good home to myself?* Then I got pregnant faster than I thought and I had to figure it out."

Six months after my first trip to Chicago, Melissa is sitting with a baby in her lap, William—he's cooing in the background. She's talking to me on the phone from Chicago.

Before William was born, Melissa, like she always has, assumed everything would go wrong. That she'd have a crippling postpartum depression; that she would crack under the pressure. She assumed she'd end up in a straitjacket somewhere. Carted off for failing to be a sane-enough mother. None of that happened.

"The definitions that were given to me as a kid have just stuck with me," she said. "I've just never given myself the space to be okay, to be anything else than what I thought I am. So this is the best surprise I could get."

Melissa wonders how much energy she's wasted and continues to waste waiting for something bad to happen. She doesn't want the worry of "being happy to stop me from being happy."

But mostly, she feels like she's moved on, no longer defines herself as anything that fits in the *DSM*. Those diagnoses may have served her at some point, but she also feels like they've held her back, like rather than describing her, she became them. She had to find an identity outside psychiatric labels.

Recently, her therapist told her she was ready to leave therapy. Not quite ready to be completely on her own, Melissa went down to one session every other week. And she's still taking the duloxetine, not because she really knows it's helping, but because she is scared of what could happen if she tried to get off it.

Still, some days, she feels like she's waiting for the other shoe to drop. Or, as she put it, like she's at the edge of a cliff, and one day she will just fall off it.

"I'm still there in many ways," she says. "But I at least feel like I've set up camp here, gotten comfortable on the cliff's edge, if that makes sense."

I tell her it does. I feel the exact same way.

SELLING THE IDEA OF STABILITY

Pharmaceutical advertising is not a new phenomenon. For as long as mind-altering pills have existed, so have marketing budgets to convince doctors and patients to use those pills. But until a few decades ago, the narrative used to sell us these innovations was much different, and perhaps more honest.

A 1969 ad for Butisol, a barbiturate (a class of now-banned drugs that were predecessors to things like Klonopin) shows a blond woman with a wide smile and a checkered dress; a stove behind her; a small child in a Native American war bonnet at her feet, tying rope around the mother's legs as if she's the child's captive. On the left, large text: "NOW SHE CAN COPE. THANKS TO BUTISOL."[15]

"When the stress is situational—environmental pressure, worry over illness—the treatment often calls for an anxiety-allaying agent which has a prompt and predictable calming action and is remarkably well tolerated," the ad, from a medical journal targeting doctors, proclaimed. There was no claim that Butisol solved an inherent chemical problem. Instead, the ad, and others like it, seemed to suggest that drugs were necessary because life was stressful and overwhelming at times.

Another ad, for Miltown, shows another stressed mother. This time the bold type reads "Syndromes of the Sixties: The battered parent syndrome." It continues:

> *Some say it's unrealistic to educate a woman and then expect her to be content with the Cub Scouts as an intellectual outlet. Or to grant that she is socially, politically and culturally equal, while continuing to demand domestic and biological subservience. Or to expect her to shoulder the guilt burden of this child-centered age without unraveling around the emotional edges. Or to compete with her husband's job for his time and involvement. But whatever the cause, the consequences—anxiety, tension, insomnia, functional disorders—fill waiting rooms.*[16]

What's striking about the ad, beyond its overwhelming sexism, is where it places the blame for the predicament women face in modern life: not on their brains and the chemicals within them, but on the demands of the society they live in. This is a common theme among drug ads in the 1950s and '60s—yes, they're misogynist, and often racist too, but they showcase a time before we collectively decided (or were convinced) that our problems, the things drugs are meant to rectify, are primarily internal.

Another ad shows another woman, this time looking tired and grasping her chest as she leans over a pile of dirty dishes: "Why is this woman tired? Because she is physically tired? If so, you'd only prescribe her rest. No, it must be that she is mentally 'done in'—crushed under a load of dull, routine duties that leave them in a state of mental and emotional fatigue."[17] The solution: Dexedrine—a very pure amphetamine (it's essentially speed sold in pill form)—the market precursor to Adderall, Ritalin, and nearly every other drug prescribed for ADHD.

And my personal favorite, at least from an art-direction standpoint: an ad for Serax, aka oxazepam, an early benzo, which reads: "Beset by the seemingly insurmountable problems of raising a young family, and confined to the home most of the time, her symptoms reflect a sense of inadequacy and isolation. Your reassurance and guidance may have helped some, but not enough. Serax (oxazepam) cannot change her environment, of course, but it can help relieve anxiety, tension, agitation and irritability, thus strengthening her ability to cope with day-to-day problems." The accompanying photo shows a housewife trapped in a jail cell, its bars made of brooms and mops.[18]

There's no talk of a chemical imbalance, no mention of diagnosis. The causality lies in the external—kids, husbands, work, the drudgery of everyday life, of housewife life, of American ennui—not the internal, not the mind. They're surprisingly politically forthright—tapping into the anxiousness of the American condition.

How, then, just a few decades later, did we come to a popular conceptualization of mental health, in both the medical and popular imaginations, as the exact opposite—one in which well-being is an *internal* state, not the result of external stressors; one in which drugs do not help with the uncontrollable aspects of life, but the uncontrollable aspects of one's own mind?

The story we have been told of prescription drugs is that science discovered a chemical theory for how the brain works, and drugs were developed to complement that theory: Medical breakthroughs allowed us to understand that neurotransmitters, mostly serotonin and dopamine, were responsible for a host of maladies, from depression to schizophrenia, and drugs were produced to modify those neurotransmitters. But psychiatric drugs have existed for decades longer than our chemical explanations for their efficacy. The chemical model of the brain was not a scientific innovation that led to new treatment modalities, but a narrative innovation that justified the continued and increased use of already existing ones. So why was that new narrative necessary?

For much of American history, institutionalization and psychotherapy were the primary modes of psychiatric care. By 1955, half of all hospital beds in the US were for mental patients.[19] But the conditions of these asylums were often bleak, and that, combined with the federal government's desire to spend less on psychiatric care, led to a period of deinstitutionalization starting in the 1960s.[20] As science historian Anne Harrington documents in her book *Mind Fixers*, this relatively abrupt switch to deinstitutionalization caused an abrupt switch for prescription drug manufacturers too. Tranquilizers meant to sedate those in institutions were now less needed; instead, there was a new and larger market they could tackle—everyone else.

So prescription drug companies got to work searching for and buying up the rights to "minor tranquilizers"—pills that would calm people down without putting them into a near-vegetative state. Ten years after the 1950 invention of Miltown, more than a *billion* pills of meprobamate had been sold to Americans. Fifty tons of meprobamate were being produced each month, and even that wasn't enough to keep up with demand.

These drugs not only represented a medical revolution, they represented a narrative one: With each new pill sold, the psychoanalytic model of mental health, popular since the mid-1800s and championed by people like Sigmund Freud, and the mainstay of most psychiatric schools until the 1950s, was losing favor to a more mechanistic view of the brain. As early prescription drug advertising suggests, the medical establishment and Americans still believed that their mental health problems could be caused by everyday, external stressors. But now the solution being proposed was not to explore or attempt to fix those stressors through something like psychoanalysis, but to chemically mediate it.

It's hard to overstate how large a shift this was: theorists and practitioners like Freud wanted you to get to the bottom of why you were feeling anxious. That took time, effort, money, and an honest look at your life's circumstances. By contrast, the new chemical model promised to remedy what psychoanalysis had attempted to remedy in years in a matter of minutes. With happiness, or at least functioning normalcy, a swallow away, the *why* of mental distress no longer mattered.

The drugs were part and parcel of a new vision of American living. As drug historian David Herzberg writes, "Like suburban houses, new cars, and washing machines, medicine became part of a new consumerist 'American dream' that reconfigured conceptions of what a good middle-class life—what happiness itself—ought to be like."[21]

And, like every aspect of this new American Dream, the unstated point of it all was profit: New housing developments jump-started the postwar economy, new appliances jump-started American manufacturing, and new drugs spawned an entire new industry, one with better profit margins certainly than psychoanalysis, but also better profit margins than virtually any other sector. Manufacturing in the late 1950s returned on average 10 percent profit, but for pharmaceutical companies, the rate was 20 percent, and for those who made tranquilizers, it was even higher—35 to 55 percent.[22]

But drug manufacturers faced a roadblock in their quest for market dominance and narrative control: most mental health practitioners were still psychologists wedded to the teachings of Freud and his contemporaries. To sell these new drugs, and this new way of thinking about the brain, a new army of people were needed who saw the brain not as a complex and semi-unknowable site of trauma and identity-processing, but as a relatively simple chemical machine. Enter the psychiatrist. In 1957, there were only 695 members of the association that represented mental health professionals. A decade later, that number had doubled.[23] Today, there are 45,000 psychiatrists in America.[24]

PHARMACOLOGICAL OVERPROMISES

The history of psychopharmacology since its industrialization in the early and mid-1900s is one of grand and overstated claims about the ability of medication to fix the human brain, and even the human condition, followed by widespread belief in those claims by the press and the public, followed by a lot of backtracking.

Only a few years after the tranquilizer Miltown became so popular that Milton Berle, one of America's most popular comedians, joked he would change his name to Miltown Berle, and told Elvis during a talk show that "you don't want a girl, you want a Miltown,"[25] the drug's sales came crashing down. It turned out Miltown, and the other tranquilizers like it, weren't so safe and effective after all. For one, they were extremely addictive, and many thousands of people became dependent on them. Those prescribed Miltown also seemed to die at higher rates, researchers found.[26] To top it all off, double-blind placebo-controlled trials found that Miltown did not really quell anxiety in any meaningful way for prolonged periods of time, or at least not any better than its predecessors, barbiturates.[27]

Facing a mounting backlash against tranquilizers like Miltown, drug companies began to focus on a newer class of drugs—benzodiazepines. Sales of Miltown plummeted; sales of benzos skyrocketed, backed by the same claims of safety and efficacy as their now passé predecessors.[28] By the late 1960s, one of the first benzos to market, Valium, was the most prescribed drug in the United States. "Reduce psychic tension . . . usually without complications," one Valium advertisement, accompanied by a terrifying extreme close-up of someone's face in an angry glare with teeth bared, claimed.[29] Newer benzos followed—Klonopin, Xanax. But all worked in essentially the same way, pushing your brain to release a neurotransmitter called GABA that slows down the human nervous system.[30]

Unsurprisingly, after another few years of the press and the public and the psychiatric profession trusting in and touting this new class of pills, a backlash again began. It turned out Valium and other benzos were addictive too, just like Miltown. And it turned out that patients who stopped taking the drugs could experience withdrawals as severe as those associated with any illicit substance. In 1975, the relatively new Drug Enforcement Administration placed Valium on its list of controlled substances. The party was over. And drug companies would have to go back to the drawing board, just like they did after barbiturates, just like they did after Miltown.

It would take them more than ten years, but in the mid-1980s, the industry came back swinging with a new pitch: Unlike the pills of the past, the industry said, these wouldn't be addictive; they wouldn't cause withdrawal if you stopped taking them. In fact, the industry claimed,[31] they'd revised their entire theory of how drugs work: it wasn't that people were stressed and depressed because they hated their lives and wives and children and jobs and thus needed something to take the edge off, it was because a subset of the population had different brain chemistry, a brain chemistry that gave them an inherent *need* for chemical alteration, a brain chemistry that would make it irresponsible not to medicate them. As the common saying came to be: you wouldn't deny a diabetic their insulin. Why would you deny the depressive this newest class of drug?[32] Why wouldn't you give them an SSRI?

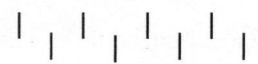

| | | | |

In 1987, Prozac, the first-ever selective serotonin reuptake inhibitor, came to market. It was heralded as a revolutionary advance in the field of psychiatry, and medicine writ large. But the real revolution had occurred in the preceding years, as psychiatrists, scientists, prescription drug companies, and universities touted their new biochemical understanding of the brain.

"It now appears virtually certain that problems in the brain's chemical functions, rather than purely psychological or emotional upset, underlie much mental illness," the *Washington Post*, citing the scientific director of the National Institute of Mental Health, confidently told its readers in 1982.³³

It would be one thing if this change was purely theoretical, left on the pages of research journals, but theory—especially theory that can cut costs and make some people a lot of money—can change everything.

When the third edition of the *Diagnostic and Statistical Manual of Mental Disorders (DSM)*, the psychiatric profession's bible, was released in 1980, it signaled a sea change in the way the psychiatric profession thought of mental illness. Gone was nearly all the psychoanalytic language about family and life dynamics. In its place was a new language that supported a biological understanding of mental illness.³⁴ That same year, Congress passed the Bayh-Dole Act, which for the first time allowed researchers, including at universities that received federal funding, to patent their medical discoveries, and then sell those medical discoveries to pharmaceutical companies.³⁵ And simultaneously, nonprofits like the National Alliance on Mental Illness lobbied for federal funds to be directed toward research that promoted the same biological view of the brain and mental illness as the *DSM* (the majority of NAMI's funding comes from the pharmaceutical industry).³⁵

This new, chemical model of the brain, and its attendant research priorities, jibed well with governments in the throes of austerity. In the US, states and the federal government had slashed funds to mental institutions, which were expensive to run and staff, so that by 1980 the number of Americans in these institutions had declined from a peak of 559,000 to 154,000.³⁷ The same was true in other countries: in the UK, the number of beds available in hospitals for people struggling with mental health declined from nearly 70,000 in the 1980s to under 20,000 in 2017.³⁸ Who needed a team of doctors and nurses and psychologists and social workers working on them when they could simply take a pill?

And take a pill or two people did: Prozac was an instant bestseller. "The antidepressant drug Prozac has been lifting the spirits of millions of Americans and thousands of Eli Lilly shareholders," the *New York Times* wrote in 1994.[39] By then, six million people had started taking the drug in the US. The discourse surrounding it was relentlessly positive too. Books like *Listening to Prozac* touted the pills' amazing efficacy, and became bestsellers. The mainstream media wrote over and over again that this was the pharmacological revolution that promised to end mental illness as we knew it.

In 2021, nearly 5 million Americans were prescribed Prozac.[40] But now there are many other antidepressants to choose from as well. More than 8 million Americans take Zoloft.[41] Another 7 million–plus take Lexapro.[42] Today, at least 37 million people take antidepressants in the United States.[43] Antidepressant prescriptions have ballooned in virtually every European country as well—between 1995 and 2011, the number of people on antidepressants in the UK doubled[44]; in Portugal, between 2000 and 2020 the use of antidepressants *tripled* (Portugal has the highest rate of antidepressant use anywhere in the world).[45]

The one problem, though, is that the scientific revolution these new drugs were meant to be based on, the one touted through the 1980s and '90s by scientists, popular authors, the press, doctors, and pharmaceutical companies, never really happened.

In 2013, Steven Hyman, a director of the National Institute of Mental Health (about as mainstream as one can get in the field of psychiatric science in the United States), wrote a scathing article in a medical journal that argued that new antidepressants were no more effective than the ones discovered in the 1950s.[46] In it, Hyman stated it plainly: despite decades of claims that psychiatry had figured out the working of the human brain, "the molecular and cellular underpinnings of psychiatric disorders remain unknown."

While Hyman was perhaps the most prominent scientist to challenge the supposedly steadfast science of chemical imbalance, other researchers had been sounding the alarm for decades, nearly right from the start of the supposed pharmacological revolution. One of the first to question the efficacy of SSRIs was Irving Kirsch, who in 1998 was a psychology professor at the University of Connecticut. By analyzing nineteen studies of antidepressants, Kirsch concluded that 75 percent of the efficacy of SSRIs could be explained not by chemical changes in the brain, but by the placebo effect.[47] In further research, Kirsch found something even more alarming: by using the Freedom of Information Act to force the FDA to turn over unpublished studies on antidepressants, he found that nearly half of all the studies conducted by pharmaceutical companies were left unpublished, and that when those studies were included in analyses, the efficacy of SSRIs looked minimal at best. Kirsch had found evidence that drug companies hid studies that suggested their drugs didn't work, and only released the studies that showed their drugs had some effect.[48]

"My guess is that, twenty years from now, people will look back at prescribing antidepressants the way we now look at things like bloodletting," Kirsch told me.[49]

Kirsch's research proved controversial, but he's still no radical, antiscience nut. He's now the associate director of the Program in Placebo Studies at Harvard Medical School.

Recently, large-scale studies have added to the pile of evidence that antidepressants may not be nearly as effective as promised: A study examining the health outcomes of over 17 million people diagnosed with depression found that those prescribed antidepressants fared no better than those not given any medication over a ten-year period.[50] And a 2022 study questioned whether boosting serotonin, the main mechanism of action for SSRIs, could even theoretically help with depression. The researchers found no correlation between the neurotransmitter and depression at all.[51]

At the same time, further research began to paint a troubling picture of the myriad side effects of SSRIs. One study found that 60 percent of people taking antidepressants experienced sexual dysfunction.[52] Other studies have found that the majority of people who take the drugs then feel like they can't get off them without experiencing extreme emotional dysregulation.[53] And one study of rats given Prozac might point to the reason why: after being treated with the drug for a few weeks, the rats' brains downregulated their own serotonin receptors, suggesting it's possible that our brains become accustomed to the new flood of serotonin provided by these drugs, and then stop being able to produce as much of it without them.[54]

It's hard to parse all the information about psychopharmaceuticals. It seems for every study avowing their efficacy, another suggests they're near worthless. It's also hard for me to discount people's personal experience. I have many friends who feel their lives were saved by the drug. And many others, including me, who feel their lives were deeply and negatively affected by them. But the one fact that seems obvious and clear is that these drugs, at a societal level, are not enough. During the period of the most recent scientific and pharmacological revolution, suicides have kept increasing, drug overdoses have kept increasing, and "deaths of despair" of all forms skyrocketed. Between 1996 and 2015, the number of Americans taking antidepressants doubled.[55]

Between 2000 and 2020, the suicide rate in the country increased by 30 percent.[56]

Yet even as nearly every indicator of societal misery—depression, suicide, alcoholism, drug addiction—rises, SSRIs and other psychiatric medications are still considered the gold standard of mental health care. Without sufficient evidence, we've put a lot of faith into these drugs, much like we did in the 1950s with Miltown, and then the 1960s with benzos.

To be sure, a large part of the reason that doctors, researchers, and the general public continue to support these lackluster chemical revolutions is because pharmaceutical lobbying and advertising work. But I think there's also something else at play: by insisting that these drugs are effective, we're also insisting on a chemical, internal model of mental health—a model that suggests we can fix our problems nearly completely on our own. It's no coincidence that SSRIs skyrocketed in popularity around the same time Reaganomics in the US and Thatcherism in the UK had completely slashed governmental support in nearly every facet of society. SSRIs were not only part of a scientific revolution, but a neoliberal economic revolution, supported by the same forces that pushed sick people out of hospital beds and onto the streets, that pushed workers out of unions, that told average people that being poor was their own fault, and that they should "pull themselves up by their bootstraps." By switching from a psychosocial understanding of human emotion to a chemical one, we've effectively placed the blame for the despair modern life causes on individuals, and let those responsible for the despair—namely, our governments—completely off the hook.

So perhaps asking whether antidepressants, or any other mental health medication, is effective, is too small a question. Perhaps a better one would be: Why are we all so depressed in the first place?

Answering that question is what brought me to Denver one snowy evening. Because this is where James, Melissa's brother, lives.

Down a suburban street lined with one-story houses, boxed in by commercial strips of chain stores, sits James's house. James sits here this evening in his oversize lounge chair, drinking whiskey with his humongous dog, Piper, white and brown and goofy and sweet, at his feet. The whiskey is stored in a bottle that looks like one that a Saint Bernard would carry in an old cartoon while it rescues someone off a mountain, which James finds charming. James isn't home much. He rents out his house to families visiting their kids at a nearby university when he's away, which is more often than not.

He'd rather be in his camper, which is parked out front. He takes it across the country with Piper every chance he gets. To Palm Springs. To Michigan's Upper Peninsula. To Wisconsin to see his family that still lives there. To visit Melissa in Chicago, or their older sister in Virginia. If he could, he'd be on the road all the time, working remotely at his job at a large Internet provider.

"Hunt. Fish. Walk. Sit. Drink beer," he tells me. "I don't have shit to worry about, I guess. I don't have things to do. I think that goes back to being a kid. My earliest memories are taking care of my family, and Melissa in particular. . . . I was always trying to put out these fires. Between my mom and Melissa. My mom and my dad. My dad and the waitress that he was rude to. In fourth grade, I'd wake up every day at five in the morning and watch cartoons by myself and make pancakes and waffles for the family before school, which I guess is kind of a weird thing for a kid to do, but looking back, it was about calming the chaos in the morning and having that time to myself. I relished that."

He still does relish that time now, in his midthirties; successful enough monetarily to afford this house and renovate it with his own hands, hard wood, and solid furnishings; successful enough, stable enough, to know exactly how he wants to live. With a reddish mess of hair in a bun. A T-shirt on. A glass of whiskey in his hand. And, many days, a dose of LSD in his system.

Most of James's time is alone, but not lonely. There's a difference, he says, between solitude and isolation.

He's good now, he tells me. He wasn't always. He still drinks too much. Chews tobacco too much. Wishes he could be a bit less obsessive about his projects, about his life. But he likes his life now, and he didn't always.

James gets mad when I ask him what went wrong, how their—his and Melissa's—white-picket-fence childhood could produce two children who for so long were on such shaky ground. Not because he's reticent to talk about his upbringing, but because, as he correctly ascertains from my white-picket-fence question, we have different politics. I tell him about mine: I believe this country does not provide enough for people, that it forces us into boxes of isolation, that we are often required to live lives of meaninglessness, and that this often leads us to states like depression. He identifies as a libertarian. He doesn't want to impugn an entire country because of his childhood. To him, this is the struggle everyone goes through: to find independence; to free oneself from the pressures of one's family; to figure out which cocktail of meds and drugs, and which style of life, you best respond to.

"When you're a child, you're supposed to be free, you're supposed to be pure," he says. "I think that most kids have to take on more than they should."

That's his read of the situation. And on this, we agree.

As a kid, James liked shooting hoops, often alone, outside his family's home, on that cul-de-sac. His dad was often too tired after work to play catch with him. He wasn't really a jock, nor a nerd. He got his first computer when he was twelve. But he also hung out with the football guys. He got along with nearly everyone, like Melissa did, though he didn't have many close friends, largely because most of his neighbors went to a different school than him. There were few kids on the block to play with.

"For the most part, I had a good life," he says.

But then, seemingly randomly, he began feeling like he wanted to die.

When he was young, like ten, nine, eight, seven, he would do things like look at the corner of his bedside table and think about smashing his face into it. He would take the cover plates off electrical outlets and shock himself. He would build little piles out of tissue paper and place them on a lamp, then try to fall asleep, hoping to die in a fire before he woke up.

He didn't tell anyone about this; he didn't feel like he could. Melissa's fear, her rage, her obsessiveness were so outward that James says he didn't feel like he had the space for his own.

"All her shit was so explosive and visible," he says. "And I was so under the radar."

And then, just as suddenly as the thoughts appeared, they receded. James's high school years were relatively stable. He did the normal high school things. He tried alcohol. Bacardi the first time, stolen out of a bottle held by his older sister, when he was fifteen. He threw up. But he liked it, wanted to try it again.

He smoked weed. He liked weed a lot. A lot a lot. His brain often feels like a movie reel but each frame is a different scene, he says. Weed just slows that down a little. He tried to help Melissa with weed too. Gave her some for the first time in that drainage pipe out back to calm her down.

"You gotta find your own reward out of life," he'd tell her. "You gotta get what you can out of it, accept what you can't."

The advice didn't seem to help.

James graduated high school. Went to a public college in Minnesota. His sisters went to private school. "I was gonna be the cheap kid," he says.

He studied engineering. He was supposed to be an engineer. Follow in his father's footsteps.

He's not sure why, or how, but that's when it all started back up again. The weed, the drinking, then the cocaine, the heroin. The antidepressants that ruined his life and then saved it, and the antipsychotics too. And the suicide attempts.

Piper licks my hand. James pours us another glass of whiskey and re-ups his chewing tobacco. If I want to hear about it, James tells me, tonight has to be the night, before the alcohol and the acid wear off, before he locks it away again.

Freshman year of college, James began feeling suicidally depressed. He went to a school counselor. He was prescribed Prozac.

"That's what started my descent into the rabbit hole of pharmaceuticals," James tells me.

The Prozac didn't seem to do much of anything. James remained depressed. The suicidal thoughts got worse. But the counselor who had prescribed the Prozac did not follow up with James, nor recommend any kind of therapy or intervention beyond the medication.

So one day, freshman year, James took a few dozen Tylenol PMs in an attempt to kill himself. It did not work.

So he went on living. He smoked a lot of weed every day, blowing through five or six grand his freshman year. By junior year, James was living in an apartment with a fellow engineering student and a few other friends. One day, his roommate's younger sister came up to see a concert nearby. She and James ended up hooking up. It turned out she was into heroin. They began seeing each other sporadically. And eventually, he shot up with her—not a full dose, but a rinse, spraying water on a used spoon to get the leftover heroin off, then boiling that up. The girl took a filter out of the butt of a cigarette, used that to filter out any sediment, and drew the liquid up through a syringe.

"It was okay. . . . It was great, I guess, I love pretty much any drug," James says. "I remember I wanted to use because she always said I never knew what it felt like. I wanted to take that away from her. We cried a bunch about the relationship. It was whatever."

James never got deep into the stuff. That was the only time he shot up. But sometimes, he'd buy some heroin off a friend, tap out a little on his dresser, snort it, and go to the school library and try to study.

"I didn't really worry about overdosing because I didn't do that much, but I was also kind of suicidal, so I didn't care that much. I wanted to get high and not worry about it."

The girlfriend, Emily, even though she was using, worried about James using too.

James called her once, told her he was high. She called James's parents. Four hours later his dad was there to pick him up from school. James went home. Back to Wisconsin, to where he and Melissa grew up.

He planned on going back to college, but never did. A month later, that friend, the mutual of Melissa's, the one James had used heroin with several times before, overdosed and died.

"I could have been right there with him," James says. "I had no business trying to go to college."

James stopped using heroin when he was home. But he continued feeling depressed, listless, purposeless. He spent his days trying to find weed. He'd drink bottles of Robitussin for the dextromethorphan, a drug that, yes, relieves coughs, but also causes a trippy and out-of-body experience. (I experimented with it when I was a teenager and it's quite powerful.)

"Four dollars could get you a bottle and get you real fucked up," James says.

But one day, he took it too far, drove his mom's minivan to a parking lot and drank half a liter of cough syrup. His mom came to pick him up. He ended up in the hospital. They had to insert a catheter because he couldn't pee. His stomach had to be detoxed with charcoal. That was the low point.

I ask James what was going on, why he felt bad enough to attempt to end his life, to get on heroin, to overdose on cough medicine, to end up back home.

"I don't know," he says. "I can't pinpoint anything. There was no big trauma. There were a lot of little things. Taking care of my sister and my mom and always being worried. Always trying to keep the peace. My friend recently told me I'm really good at making people feel comfortable. I'm not sure that's a compliment."

It was obvious to everyone, including himself, that James was struggling, but the solution was less clear. He went to a psychiatrist. His parents paid thousands of dollars to get a battery of tests done to figure out what his condition could be. The psychiatrist prescribed him a litany of pills—sleeping meds, Trazodone, several antidepressants. By the time he was twenty-two, he'd been diagnosed as schizophrenic. Which confused James. He never had delusions or hallucinations. He was just doing a lot of drugs—weed, cough medicine, alcohol. That fucked with his mental health, but the schizophrenia diagnosis and subsequent medication—several antipsychotics, including aripiprazole (Abilify)—felt ill-fitting.

"I felt fucking crazy," he says. "They were no good. Nothing did nothing."

The meds made him feel dissociated, floating above his life. He felt unmotivated, would barely leave the house. He developed tardive dyskinesia—a side effect of certain psychiatric drugs. His legs would kick uncontrollably.

"I would have rather drank another liter of Robitussin than whatever the doctor was giving me," he says.

His life a mess, the prescribed medication not working, the other substances not helping, James tried to end it once more, taking an overdose of his mom's prescription sleeping pills. That was the last straw for James. He needed serious help. He went to a psych ward, and then to an in-patient rehab in Milwaukee for two weeks.

There, he had therapy—real therapy, not just seeing someone for a few minutes until they prescribed a drug—for the first time.

"All of the therapy helped," he says. "It's helped me be where I am now. I regret the psychiatrists, but not the therapists. Who knows where

I'd be, what my life would be like, if I hadn't gone down that crazy prescription drug rabbit hole."

James's experience with psychopharmacology turned him off to the whole idea of meds. So, from the time he was twenty-five until he was thirty-two, he stayed off the stuff.

"Fifty years ago we were doing lobotomies," he says. "I'm curious and afraid of what we'll understand brain-wise, pharmaceutical-wise, fifty years from now."

He slowly got his life together. He got a job, first an internship, and then a real job, working in tech. He never finished college, never got an engineering degree, but he's successful, working as a database administrator. He got married. Moved to Colorado. Got divorced. Saw many therapists. Started feeling more confident in his own life. What he wanted. What he needed.

"I'll give you an analogy, as an engineer," he says. "I might be able to put together a computer, but no one person can design a computer. It's based on past successes. Past inventions. It's the same with therapy. A constant building-upon of past knowledge."

After James's divorce, he felt a bit obsessive. He ruminated for too long on everything—the position of a rug on his hardwood floors, his past life and mistakes. He wasn't nearly as bad as in his early twenties, but he thought his life could be a bit easier, a bit less emotionally charged.

So he saw a nurse practitioner who prescribed yet another antidepressant, this time escitalopram (Lexapro). James was surprised by how quickly it helped ease the obsessive thoughts. For the past two years, he's taken it consistently, first at a low dose, and now at a higher one.

"There'll be times where I forget to take it for two or three days, and

I almost get scared where I'll go," he says. "I feel this fear. I don't wanna go back there."

He's grateful for the SSRI, happy he's found one prescription drug that hasn't sent him into a tailspin. But he likes other drugs too. Weed helps calm him down a bit. Acid and shrooms help with his depression. He takes acid several times a month.

"It's a reset of some sort," he tells me. "I didn't do it for a few months recently, and I was completely useless. It helps jump-start me, helps me enjoy the things I enjoy doing."

He still drinks nearly every day. That he wants to cut back on.

"I trip more than ninety-nine percent of the world, but that's not an issue," he says. "That makes me a better person, it helps me contribute to the world. Drinking does not."

He makes sure not to keep downers like painkillers in the house. He knows he'd enjoy them too much. He's found a substance routine that works, and he wants to stick to it.

The second day I meet James, on a cold and sunny morning, Piper greets me at the door. James is drinking strong coffee. He seems in a good mood, relaxed in pajamas, with his hair in a bun. He used to never wear it in a bun because once, when he was a teen, while dining at the local country club in Wisconsin, his dad said it made his nose look too big. It made James furious. Now he doesn't care anymore about what his dad thinks. Or about what psychiatrists think, or really what anyone thinks. His life isn't perfect, but it's his, and it works.

Since I began interviewing Melissa and James, they'd begun talking to each other about their mental health too. Melissa shared her cliff metaphor with her brother—that she felt on solid ground, but that the cliff was always right there. James said he gets that too. He says for him it manifests as a fear of heights. You're standing at the edge of a cliff, or a building, or whatever, and you realize how easy it would be to go over. How close you can be to death.

"You just gotta get comfortable and stay away from the edge," he says. "That's an attitude you have to have to stay on solid ground. For me, now, that means taking my Lexapro, trying to eat healthier, being around people that make me feel good about myself, trying to be dependable for myself and others. All that maintenance stuff."

Life isn't always easy. James sometimes feels like he can't juggle everything—the house, his job. Mundane errands like grocery shopping sometimes fill him with dread. It's just all too much, this life. He has vague thoughts of suicide sometimes, but nothing specific. Given the stressors of the world, given what he and his sister and so many others he knows have gone through, he assumes these thoughts are pretty common. At least he's now managing them.

"That's the story of the white picket fence, I guess," he tells me. "Everyone has the fucking same story everywhere you go."

That does seem true. The same story, everywhere you go. For him, for Melissa, for me and Lucas and countless friends of mine and so many others: We're all just struggling to make it through. Sometimes the drugs help with that. But we all know, it seems, regardless of where we live, regardless of our genders and politics and identities and jobs and stations in life, that, beneath the chemical placidity, there is still something, or many things, that feel off.

6

THE STABILITY TRAP

THE PERSONAL LIMITS OF A STABLE LIFE; WHY WE ALL SEARCH FOR BOXES TO FIT IN; DIAGNOSIS AND PSYCHIATRY AS TOOLS OF EMOTIONAL LIMITATION

After seeing James in Colorado, I kept thinking about what he and Melissa had said about being on the edge of a cliff—feeling like even when you're stable, there's always a threat a few feet away; that you could lose it all at any moment. It stuck with me, I realized, because I'd felt that way my entire life. Long before Charlottesville, long before my breakdown.

I, like Melissa, had resigned myself to always knowing the cliff was right there, but at least wanting a bit more comfort—to, as she put it, "set up camp" at the cliff's edge. That, to me, for so many years, was my goal: a tent, a box, to fit in; not so that I could confront my fears a few feet away from me, but so that I could remove them from view. When I yelled at Dennis to tell me what was wrong with me, when I pleaded with doctors to diagnose me, what I was saying was that I was sick of searching for answers, sick of sorting through my traumas and identity and all the rest. I didn't want to do the hard work; I wanted to be happy *while* being repressed.

And everywhere I looked, it seemed people agreed with me that this was a good idea. The collective message of a thousand TikToks and tweets and TV commercials was that exploring the *why* of my sorry state was unimportant; that as long as I had the right label and its corresponding medication, I did not need to spend years breaking down and reconstructing my psyche, my identity, my life.

That's how diagnosis had always functioned in my life. It's why, a year after 9/11, I began searching for a label that would define me—so that I would not have to actually work through the trauma of that day, so that I could be happy boxing it up and labeling it and tucking it away in a corner of my brain.

Looking back, I think my parents could see me doing this—see the effort I was putting into my own repression. That's why, a year after September 11, at fourteen, my parents put me in therapy for the first time. Her name was Talia. She was nice. Israeli; big curly hair; she'd sit cross-legged in her big chair and calmly ask me how I was doing and laugh at my jokes and nod along with my nascent politics—"America is so fucked up. Can you believe Bush is bombing Iraq?" But try as she might, she could never get me to address the cliff—the trauma caused by 9/11, my sexuality and gender confusion, the way those things combined to turn me into a dissociative being, floating through the world.

Working through it all piece by piece seemed too hard. I just wanted it to go away.

If I'd been honest with Talia, I'd have told her that I walked through the world with a deep discomfort with my very being. That walking down the hallway at school made me panic, that even sitting in my room alone, it felt as if my skin was too tight, or my body somehow misshapen. Later, I'd find a term for this—"dysphoria." My discomfort wasn't based on bullying or name-calling. Instead, it was largely intuited—somewhere in my psyche knowing that I had to act a certain way to make it through the day emotionally unscathed: masculine, straight, though it was more complex than that; a thousand micromovements and intonations and words and phrases and styles of dress I'd subconsciously picked up from the teens around me, repeating them every second of the day like I was making my way through the world's longest dance routine. I don't know what would happen if I had stepped out of line, but I saw what happened to the more flamboyant kids, the weirdos, so I didn't dare find out.

It's hard to know what I would've been like as a teenager had 9/11 not happened. Though it and my queerness were obviously two separate struggles, the trauma of that day and my subsequent reaction—namely, trying as hard as I could to just move on and not thinking about it—had given me a kind of blueprint for how to deal with my fear and my anxiety and my dread: suppress, suppress, suppress.

By asking me to work through this all, my parents and their preferred method of psychological healing—seeing a therapist—became threats to my effective strategy of boxing it all up. I did not want help processing, I wanted help with packing it all in until I couldn't feel anymore.

So one day in tenth grade I came home from school and told my parents that I needed ADHD medication. We fought, but eventually they relented.

A week or so later I sat across from a gregarious Jamaican woman in her garden-level West Village home office filled with warm-hued rugs and candles and antique dark wood furniture. I thought the session would be similar to my therapy sessions—her pressing me to divulge my trauma, to dig deep into my brain and unearth what was causing me such discomfort. But as soon as I opened my mouth to tell her about my various traumas and difficulties, she interrupted: None of that was necessary, she said with a big smile. She knew just the meds for me.

First was Ritalin, which made me feel queasy. So then we tried Adderall, which made me feel a bit spacey. I wanted to try yet another amphetamine. But a few months after I first met her, the psychiatrist suddenly packed up shop and told me she was moving out west. So I switched to a different psychiatrist, a white guy with a more somber demeanor and a colder-feeling office, who nonetheless had no problem prescribing me amphetamines immediately, and lots of them. I told him the side effects of the Ritalin and Adderall, and he immediately suggested Dexedrine, the same kind of speed housewives took in the 1950s.

I loved it. With a diagnosis of ADHD and a prescription for speed, I had all the help I needed to suppress everything for the foreseeable future.

I remember my first day on amphetamines. Sitting in tenth-grade biology. Staring at the leg of a table in front of me. The teacher's voice faded away. My peripheral vision was gone, and with that came an immense joy. With my vision narrowed to a pinpoint, all the other thoughts in my head—that million-step routine of micromovements I'd spent years perfecting to stay safe, the walls I'd put up to protect myself from the trauma of 9/11—were suddenly beyond my scope. The amphetamines worked as they were supposed to; they quieted down the noise in my head so that I could intensely focus. It didn't matter that what I was focusing on was the leg of a table. The point, for me, wasn't to get better at school. It was to get better at blocking out the noise, or what I thought of as noise.

Outside school a few weeks later, at three p.m., at the top of "the hill," which is what we called the corner of Sixty-First Street and Tenth Avenue, I waited for my best friend, Amanda. I was so excited to tell her that I'd found the solution to all my problems in the form of this diagnosis and pill.

Except she spoke first: "You're so quiet now," she said. "I miss the other you."

The noise I was so keen to block out? It turns out there was a lot of important stuff in there.

I stayed in this state for five years, and I was, I guess, kind of happy. It didn't matter that my grades kept falling, or that the amphetamines made it hard to eat to the point I developed something like an eating disorder and lost an unhealthy amount of weight, or that my other interests—guitar, which I'd been intensely passionate about since I was a toddler—fell by the wayside. It didn't matter that I'd spend hours in compulsive loops, organizing my Mac desktop icon by icon for two days straight, or fixing one sentence on a school paper over and over again until three a.m. None of that mattered. Because the drugs kept me within a tiny box in my own brain, and in that box I felt so, so safe. I wanted to remain in there forever.

Until one day, when, I think, something in me knew, even if I could not put words to it, that this was not sustainable. That what brought me comfort was a trap; that I could not live life boxed up forever.

One of the last nights of my first year of college. I was in my dorm room at my mediocre liberal arts school, door closed, alone, staring into the mirror above the college-issued cheap wood dresser. I'd been up for thirty-six hours straight. In one of those compulsive loops, staring at my computer for hours on end, not doing work, not eating. I looked like shit. I weighed thirty pounds less than I should have. I smelled bad from a lack of sleep and a lack of movement and a lack of fresh air. My hair was thinning and my cheeks were gaunt. I don't know why it was that moment that I decided I'd had enough. Perhaps it's because, looking into the mirror, I could tell I was dying—not necessarily physically, but in every other way that really mattered.

So I opened the top drawer of that dresser and fished out my bottle of Dexedrine. I walked to the shared bathroom at the end of the hallway and threw every single pill down the toilet. I remember feeling proud, and then feeling guilty for giving the fish at the other end of the sewage system so much speed. And then I promptly entered into my first mental breakdown.

If my ADHD diagnosis and the amphetamines it provided were the wall with which I'd blocked my vision of the parts of the psyche I was too afraid to address, what I'd effectively done by stopping cold turkey was blow up the wall and let all the trauma I had, all the questions, roll over my brain like a tidal wave. It probably would have been better to take it down piece by piece: withdraw from the meds slowly, go back to therapy—but something just told me I needed to be done with it.

Without the comfort of a drug-induced mental safe space, my brain's circuitry was suddenly overwhelmed. I had panic attacks daily. I would wake up from nightmares in my sophomore-year dorm room and think I was still dreaming—the fires from my sleep following me throughout the day. The only thing preventing me from full psychosis was knowing that I was experiencing psychosis, knowing that the amphetamine withdrawal was doing this to me, that it wasn't, exactly, real. I was not in reality, but I at least could tell this was the case, and thus remained at least tenuously tethered.

I wasn't only in withdrawal chemically, but psycho-spiritually: after a decade or more creating safety by putting up walls in my psyche, I now rabidly searched for new ones to replace what I'd lost. I went back to Talia, my therapist from high school. I called her on the phone from college and told her how insane I felt. I wanted her to diagnose me as psychotic, or schizophrenic, or bipolar, which she refused to do. She, like every therapist in my life—including my parents and, later, Dennis—has assured me that I would be okay, that feeling insane was not the end of my life, and that I would, eventually, be able to work through it all. It took me a while to accept that, that the tearing down of walls did not necessitate a rebuilding of new ones. I think I'm still learning that. It's a practice.

Over the next year, my thoughts began to race less. The panic attacks subsided. By the two-year mark, I felt mostly like myself again. A different self, but a stable one. I did not take any medication to get there. I stopped going to therapy. My brain just needed time to adjust to its new, drug-free state. And, slowly, it did.

By my senior year of college, I was well enough to do my work, and to find an internship at a local public radio station in western Massachusetts—my first journalism experience. The news director there, a fortysomething man named Fred, who had a gravelly voice and stubble and smoked a lot of cigarettes, took me under his wing and taught me everything I know about reporting. More important, Fred was the first person in my life to basically tell me to get it together—that yes, life was hard, but that I should still expect a lot from myself. I'd walk into his small office with floors and walls in a condition that reminded you how underfunded public journalism is in this country, and he'd take a look at a story I'd written on his computer, and press backspace for an entire minute until I was left with a blank page. "You can do better than that," he'd say. One day, as I walked from my car toward the office in torn-up shorts and an oversize polo I'd taken from my dad's closet, Fred caught up with me. "Hey," he said, giving me the once-over. "You should dress like you respect yourself." Coming from anyone else this perhaps would have offended me, but I loved it. Because it meant he respected me. It meant he thought that I could really make something of myself. It meant he thought I had a future. So I began to believe I did too.

I stayed another year after graduation in that small New England town, working at the radio station, learning to take responsibility for myself, learning to make money. I spent a lot of time alone. Which, for once, I loved. On my days off I'd bike around the leafy rail trails from town to town. No destination. Just biking and thinking.

After my yearlong fellowship at the radio station was up, I packed up my belongings and moved back to my hometown, back in with my parents in Manhattan. I decided to go to journalism school. I began writing a lot—essays, reporting. I graduated. I worked at prestigious internships. I got my first real journalism job. I dated more, someone serious—like nearly-getting-engaged serious. That ended. Which was sad. But not destabilizing, because life was good. I moved to Philly. I wrote a book about gentrification. There were bad days and a few panic attacks when things felt overwhelming, but I felt generally . . . normal, like life was a straight line from point A to B to C and beyond. A good six or seven years of stability.

Which is why that morning in Oakland, the morning I went insane all over again, took me by surprise.

I should have learned my lesson by then. That putting up barriers to prevent myself from feeling things I did not want to feel would lead me back here. After Charlottesville, I realized that even without amphetamines or an ADHD diagnosis, I still hadn't worked through all that scared me. The stuff—gender, sexuality, trauma, family history—was still sitting there, unsorted. Yet it still took me years after Charlottesville to accept that that's what I'd have to do, that I could not simply box it up again. Which is not to say I jettisoned diagnosis or medication completely, but that I began to view them differently—as tools to help me work through my trauma, not tools to help me suppress it.

In 2021, I moved out of New Orleans and back to New York once again. I wanted to be around family during the pandemic. I wanted to feel at home. But with everything going on—the total disruption of the world by the virus, the fear that caused, I was having a bit of a hard time, mainly with doing work. So I went back to a psychiatrist for the first time in years.

I met Dr. Jim on Zoom, and immediately liked him, mostly because he seemed much less resoundingly confident in the power of drugs to cure me than every other psychiatrist I'd seen. Medications weren't necessarily necessary for me, but, he said, if I wanted my life to feel a little easier during this emotionally taxing time, then we could experiment with some things. There was no talk of a cure, no proclamations that I had a disorder.

Dr. Jim prescribed me half of the lowest manufactured dose of Abilify (aripiprazole), an antipsychotic, on the theory that it would help reduce my nervous system's hairpin trigger. The change was very subtle, but it seemed to work—I still had panic attacks, I still would get overactivated and dissociate, but now in a slightly muted way. He also put me back on ADHD meds, this time Adderall, and at a much, much lower dose. And he prescribed only enough to be taken three or four days a week.

The other thing I liked about Dr. Jim is that we never once discussed diagnosis. I'd see him once every few months, and we'd talk about how I was feeling, and whether the narcotics were still effectively modulating those feelings, and that was it. This might seem like just a semantic difference in psychiatric styles, but for me it was huge: I finally had found someone who let me have it both ways—who acknowledged that sometimes you do need to set up a tent on the side of a cliff and take a breather, but that you cannot stay there forever; that you still have actual work to do to confront the things scaring you.

And because of this, I began to no longer crave a diagnosis or simple explanation for my emotional states. After a few years, I finally stopped asking Dennis whether I was manic or depressed or both or something else entirely. I worked on accepting that I just have a lot of emotions, and that sometimes those emotions feel bad, and that that's okay.

That doesn't mean I stopped yearning for more stability. The hardest days, the days I really do wish there was a cure in the form of diagnosis and pill, are the ones on which being happy triggers me. Like, for example, about a year ago, at a Mets game with the warm sun shining down on me and friends surrounding me and a beer in hand. My nervous system suddenly realizing I wasn't on guard; that I wasn't being hypervigilant to any possible threats. Some automatic process in me pushing me into panic and then dissociation. My brain thinking this was the only way for me to be safe. I wish shit like that didn't happen.

But I now have a different goal. I no longer want immediate relief on these days. I now try to accept that the bad and scary stuff is just part of life. The only way out is through—true. But it's more than that: It's learning that there is no true out. No ending. No final boss. No paradise at which to arrive, fully healed. Life just keeps going, sometimes good and sometimes bad.

So much discussion of trauma misses the fact that there's no going back. So much of the discourse I've seen on healing from trauma presupposes the end goal is to be as you once were, before the trauma. This, I've come to believe, is impossible. But it is in there, in refusing to go backward, that real growth comes through. As the psychoanalyst Avgi Saketopoulou writes, trauma breaks down old structures, and through that, it can "put something new in motion."[1] You can become a different person. A stronger one. By diagnosing away all our problems, we effectively let go of the opportunity to grow through our trauma, to take lessons from it rather than to hide from it.

The fact that there was no going back to my pre-breakdown state used to terrify me. It no longer does. I am a different person. My life is in some ways harder than it once was—without the safety of a box, I experience life with less protection. I have more emotions; I sometimes feel less able to cope and must give myself more time to be unproductive, to convalesce and process my pain. But the flip side of that is that I also feel more real—more able to experience pure joy, more passionate about my work and the reasons I do it, more able to fall in love.

It's tempting in a world filled with pain and stress to push it all down, to get comfy in our tents at the edge of a cliff, to label every emotion we are scared of and try to rid ourselves of it or numb ourselves to it. But that, to me, is a form of giving up. The fact that we are more diagnosed and labeled and medicated than ever, and also, statistically, more isolated,[2] less sexually active,[3] and more afraid of one another than in any time in recent memory, is no coincidence: we've numbed ourselves to pain and, in doing so, numbed ourselves to everything else too.

A BRIEF HISTORY OF DIAGNOSIS

To see how diagnosis operates today, it's useful to see how it's always operated—as a tool of political and social control. No disorder better showcases this than schizophrenia. In 1935, the *New York Times* claimed that schizophrenia was a "mild form of insanity" often seen in artistic and literary types—those who had a hard time functioning in the real world but were capable of flowery writing and "grandiloquence."[4] For much of its early history, schizophrenia was thought of as a disorder that mainly affected white, upper-class people. As the psychiatrist Jonathan Metzl describes in his book *The Protest Psychosis*, many literary references to the disorder in the mid-1900s described housewives who were simply neurotic. It was an odd turn for the disorder, because just a decade earlier, schizophrenia and its diagnostic precursor dementia praecox were mostly used to stir up fear about dangerous immigrants and Black people lurking among American whites.

Practically every mention of dementia praecox in major American newspapers between 1910 and 1930 referenced the term in relation to anxieties about "Negroes," immigrants, criminals, or "subnormals," Metzl writes. White Americans worried that new influxes of immigrants, supposedly biologically disposed to dementia praecox, would go on murder sprees. The diagnosis had no basis in science. Instead, it helped a deeply racist society justify its racism with a scientific sheen. The early 1900s were just a few decades after the end of slavery, and many white Americans feared the prospect of integration. And, at the same time, the country was seeing a huge influx of immigrants, especially from Europe. Dementia praecox functioned as a way to separate good, upstanding Americans from the people much of the country was frightened of.

People began calling for trained alienists to evaluate each new steamship full of immigrants for dementia praecox.[5] Papers like the *New York Times* reported, with urgency, eugenic talking points about how letting the mentally ill procreate would lead to more crime and chaos in the country.[6] Prominent scientists suggested sterilizing and segregating "defective stocks" of humans so that they could not procreate. These ideas about mental illness would go on to directly influence the Nazi regime in Germany.[7]

According to Metzl, the very invention of the word "schizophrenia" was meant to destigmatize the same symptoms associated with dementia praecox so that they could safely be diagnosed in white people—the "mild" and nonbiological schizophrenia for respectable white people, dementia praecox for everyone else. "In sharp contrast to dementia praecox, schizophrenia often implied an illness not of the black body, but of the white mind," Metzl writes.

This false separation stood strong for a few years, but by the 1960s, the idea of schizophrenia had drastically changed yet again: as Black Americans increasingly organized, protested, and fought for their civil rights, doctors and scientists came together to link their struggle back to schizophrenia. In 1968, two doctors published a paper in which they argued that the civil rights movement was a form of "protest psychosis"—that Black people, and Black men in particular, had developed a mental illness that prevented them from living in racial harmony with whites, and caused them to act violently.[8] The idea was reminiscent of a diagnosis from a century earlier, drapetomania—a theory that slaves ran away from and rebelled against their conditions not because their conditions were inhumane, but because they were experiencing mania or psychosis.[9]

The idea that schizophrenia was to blame for the racial reckoning of the sixties wasn't fringe: dozens of prominent scientists and practitioners published papers with similar claims. The FBI "diagnosed" Malcolm X with "prepsychotic paranoid schizophrenia" in classified documents. They did the same to other civil rights leaders. The makers of the tranquilizer Haldol began advertising to doctors with an ad that depicted an "assaultive" and "belligerent" Black man staring out at the viewer, fist clenched in a not-so-subtle reference to the Black Power symbol.[10] In the 1970s, the makers of Thorazine, who just two decades earlier had created advertisements that suggested the drug was meant mostly to calm down white housewives, now advertised their drug to tame "primitive" problems using "Western psychiatry." The ads were not subtle either: they featured images of African tribal masks, African art, and traditional walking sticks.[11]

Though the more jarring and obvious racism has now disappeared from psychiatry, we're still living in the shadow of this racist psychiatric system: today, Black people are 2.4 times more likely to be diagnosed with schizophrenia as white people.[12]

But the discriminatory diagnostics of psychiatry are not limited to schizophrenia. Queer people are more often diagnosed with ADHD, depression, and anxiety. Trans people are more often diagnosed with psychotic disorders.[13] Seventy-five percent of BPD (borderline personality disorder) diagnoses are in women.[14] If we believe the biomedical model of mental health, we must believe that these populations are inherently more diseased than their straight, cisgender, male, or white counterparts.

What seems more likely is that the conditions one lives in, or the conditions a group lives in, make their mental health worse in specific ways. In short, the world is crazy-making for everyone, but it's significantly more crazy-making for the oppressed. We know that the stresses of poverty, of racism, of housing discrimination all contribute to mental health outcomes. So, while Black people may be unfairly overdiagnosed with schizophrenia, it also seems logical that societal oppression may make Black people more prone to mental health issues. Similarly, trans people may experience more symptoms of psychosis not because they are genetically predisposed to it, but because societal oppression drives us trans people crazy.

The radical Black psychiatrist Frantz Fanon wrote extensively about how expressions of mental distress were specific to oppressed populations, arguing that North Africans who attempted to assimilate in France faced a wide variety of physical and mental ailments that were caused by the racism and colonialism of the French,[15] but that these symptoms were dismissed by French doctors. Fanon called this "North African syndrome."

If we can agree that the vast differences in diagnosis from population to population are not biochemical (and I hope we can, lest we become eugenicists), and thus agree that different populations experience different forms of pain and oppression that present symptomatically distinctly, then we must ask: How is any disorder much different from something like "North African syndrome"? Why would any diagnosis *not* be politically, socially, racially contextual?

It may help an individual to say "I have ADHD," which is, in a way, a way to say, "I feel crazy/malformed/maladapted in this specific way that looks like the specific way that some other people feel." But without a materialist understanding of why we all feel this way, or these ways, we are bound to internalize the oppression of our society, to blame ourselves, or others, for distress, and erase its true causes.

It wasn't always this way. We used to have a counternarrative to the dominant diagnostic one, a narrative in which people were seen as affected by the world around them as opposed to solely being victims of their own chemistry, a narrative that attempted to give people agency over their own emotions, illnesses, maladaptations, and neuroses, and thus agency over the world. In fact, I would argue that this more nuanced, less chemical narrative has been the most popular one throughout history. The idea that your outside world, your family history and your traumas, are primarily responsible for your mental state was not a fringe idea until the popularization of psychiatry in the middle of the twentieth century.[16]

But this understanding of mental health began to be lost under the ever-growing dominance of psychiatry, and the ever-growing reliance on medications to alleviate what some saw as social conditions. As this pharmaceutical-industry-based dominance rose, a radical movement that attempted to recontextualize mental health as part and parcel of capitalist society was born.

In 1971, a US-based group called the Radical Therapist Collective published a manifesto that posited that the predominant way of understanding the brain was essentially a form of victim blaming, that psychiatry and psychology viewed those who struggled to adapt to society as "'sick' people who need 'treatment' rather than oppressed people who must be liberated. . . . A 'struggle for mental health' is bullshit unless it involves changing this society which turns us into machines, alienates us from one another and our work, and binds us into racist, sexist, and imperialist practices," the collective wrote.[17]

Around the same time, psychiatric survivor collectives were springing up across the US and in Europe. Groups like the Insane Liberation Front (ILF) on the West Coast of the US and the Mental Patients Liberation Front on the East Coast protested against common psychiatric practices.

"We are beginning to get it together—beginning to see that our problems are not individual, not due to personal inadequacies but are a result of living in an oppressive society," the ILF's manifesto stated.[18]

In Germany in 1987, the Socialist Patients' Collective (SPK) published *Turn Illness Into a Weapon*, a manifesto in which they argued that illnesses both physical and mental were a necessary part of capitalism—something that could not be eliminated without the elimination of the economic system that caused poverty and struggle. They wrote that illness worked as an "inner prison," meant to limit the ability of people to fight against the system, and that if people *did* fight against their illnesses, and the cause of their illnesses (work, isolation, racism, sexism), those inner prisons would be replaced with literal prisons.

Which, it turns out, is exactly what happened: the German government declared the SPK a criminal organization and jailed one of its founders, the Heidelberg University physician Wolfgang Huber.

To these radicals, mental health liberation was linked to every other struggle—for civil rights, against the patriarchy, for an end to war and imperialism. When people stood up against racism or sexism or capitalism, they were deemed crazy. When people simply could not live under the conditions of racism, sexism, and capitalism, they were deemed ill and in need of medication or institutionalization.[19] To this mental health movement, illness itself—what we deemed sick and what we deemed well—was a necessary form of capitalist control. There was no societal liberation without the liberation of people deemed sick.

These ideas were radical, but they weren't unpopular: Prominent civil rights leaders like Stokely Carmichael attended antipsychiatry conferences. Prominent thinkers across the political spectrum, from popular left-leaning theorist Michel Foucault to the libertarian Thomas Szasz, argued in bestselling books that psychiatry was a way to repress and oppress anyone who dared deviate from capitalist norms.

The fact that the inherent politicalness of diagnosis is *not* incredibly obvious in this day and age, that so many people today consider ADHD, depression, any diagnosis to be an inherent chemical condition and not contextual to our world, which requires us to be constantly well enough to work, is a testament to the wild success of the pharmaceutical industry's advertising and lobbying campaign over the past four or so decades. Their narrative was not the only narrative, but it's the one that won. And that was not inevitable. It required billions in research, influence, and advertising to convince the world over that there was one true framework for mental health.

None of this makes medications inherently evil, but it does make them inherently political.

I know many people helped by mental health medication, and many people harmed by it, but I know no one who is helped by a system that treats all of our ailments as individual phenomena, a system that denies the collective and material basis of our struggles. This system is deeply isolating—it forces people into a constant search for labels to explicate their distress when the real answers are right in front of them. With a mask of scientific truth we have created a religion that hides our chains, that hides our pain behind false chemical certainty.

I woke up today and popped an Adderall so that I could work at a computer for ten hours. I took half an Abilify because right now, with the constant work I have to do to process my past near-death experiences while also just living my life, my days are often stressful enough that something minor will trigger my fight-or-flight response. But I refuse to call my inability to sit still for ten hours without medication ADHD. And I refuse to call my overwhelm depression or bipolar disorder or psychosis or anything else. In this refusal, I am staking a claim: my problems are based in the real world, not my brain. My problems are not unique to me, but consequences of a violent world that every single one of us experiences to greater and lesser extents. By saying that, by de-diagnosing, I'm saying: we're all in this together.

ESCAPING DIAGNOSIS

By refusing to put a name or a box around my mental problems, I've ended up feeling a lot more attached to the rest of the world, and a lot less on my own. By viewing my anxiety and panic attacks and dissociation as a symptom of violence—in my case, the violence of Charlottesville and 9/11—I can then relate it to others. Lucas's ennui because of growing up gay in the South; Melissa's lack of support (except support in the form of SSRIs) as she struggled to find herself and find her footing; James's depression; the people on the streets of Vancouver and Philadelphia, there because the government had completely given up on them—all of us are in vastly different circumstances, but we've all turned to some form of drug to cope, because, in my opinion, we are all facing different tentacles of the same beast.

In the past few years, countless friends have told me they feel similarly, that they'd rather view their problems as based in the real world instead of defining them within psychiatry's strict rubric. And they've found alternate modalities outside of or in addition to medication that help them.

I met Maddie in Philadelphia, when we were both working in an activist group to pressure the federal government to stop deportations of migrants. When I talked to them about mental health, I realized their story of diagnosis was similar to mine. When Maddie was in college, they knew they needed mental health help. They began to see psychiatrists, but each seemed to have a completely different understanding of their distress, and thus a completely different diagnosis for them. Maddie saw each psychiatrist for fifteen minutes or maybe half an hour. None seemed to have a good grasp of what they needed.

That made them want to take mental health care into their own hands. So they went online, to Facebook, and began finding dozens of groups dedicated to mental health. In some, Internet strangers would post lists like, "Here's thirty symptoms; if you have ten of them, you have this disorder." In another group, people would post memes about passive suicidal ideation.

The Internet was the only place Maddie felt they had real support. But slowly, the language they were picking up online creeped into their real life. They'd find out about a diagnosis through a Facebook group and bring it to a psychiatrist, and then the psychiatrist would affirm that diagnosis and hand out medication for it. OCD. Anxiety. Depression. Bipolar. BPD. CPTSD. ADHD.

Maddie was put on medications that never seemed to help. Celexa, an antidepressant. Wellbutrin, another antidepressant. Xanax, a benzodiazepine.

"Because the Internet was the only space I could even talk about my feelings, everything ended up being framed through mental illness," Maddie said. "So I ended up with a whole list of diagnoses. It wasn't until later that I realized, *Wait, maybe I'm just carrying a lot of trauma, and maybe I just have emotions like everyone else, and maybe the world is just a bad place.*"

Online, everything was connected to mental illness. It felt deterministic. A bad day was a sign of clinical depression. A bad relationship a sign of BPD.

"You have this condition, you can't help it," the language went, Maddie said. Which helped them feel less guilt about their mental health, but also made it feel like nothing could ever change. People would even shame group members who suggested that they were starting to feel better. The point was not healing. The point was definition.

"When we've got all of these different labels, you end up with oppression Olympics and infighting because people don't always have the perspective of being able to see what and who is harming them—the actual causes of our pain," Maddie said. "It's like, I know I feel bad, and I know I feel alone, but I don't know why, so I fight with the people around me. We're in this very individualistic culture, so we're coming up with hyperindividualistic solutions. It's easier to grapple with it being your own brain because it's something I have control over. I don't have control over a society making me sick. I don't have control over the fact that we're being failed by the psychiatric system. But I have control over my own brain, and control over the people around me."

Eventually, Maddie began to feel like each diagnosis explained less and less, and that the online spaces they took part in were actively making their mental health worse. They'd see things like people who had recently experienced sexual assault blaming themselves for not trusting people anymore, calling it a symptom of their borderline personality disorder.

"Coping mechanisms were called a personality disorder," they said. That began to make them feel anger toward the communities they'd once relied on.

It all changed, Maddie said, when they realized they could take agency over their own life. So they simply undiagnosed themselves with everything they'd been told they suffered from. They found a therapist they actually liked who didn't focus on labels. They found social support networks and friends that didn't try to define their various struggles. And they began working on their issues—anxiety, fear of abandonment, codependency—one by one, until they improved.

"I had to realize it was okay and possible to heal," they said. "I had to realize that I could get better."

I'd heard from a friend of a friend about a similar trajectory: finding solace in diagnosis, then realizing that that diagnosis was becoming a hindrance to healing. Maude had struggled with an eating disorder for a long time. By her early thirties, she'd decided to do something about it. She began seeing a therapist who specialized in eating disorder recovery. The therapist assigned workbooks and homework for Maude to do. Maude also found herself delving deep into online ED recovery content on Instagram and TikTok.

Her whole life started to revolve around getting better—every TikTok and Instagram post was about "recovery" or "being mentally ill girls" or "BPD."

"In ED recovery, you often hear about how your brain is a pie chart, and thinking about food and planning your eating takes up so much of that pie chart so you can't think of anything else," Maude said. "But in recovery, it felt like recovery itself filled in that pie chart. It started to make me feel like I had nothing else in my life."

The entire Internet felt geared to self-diagnosis. *Five things girlies with an eating disorder know. Five signs your relationships are toxic. This is how you know you're borderline.* Maude's experience tracked with the rise of mental health content on the Internet writ large—it's become increasingly common for young people to come to understandings of their struggles through TikTok and Instagram, leading to a rapid rise in self-diagnosis that's worried doctors and other mental health experts.[20]

Maude, even as she developed a better relationship with food, began to feel like she was inexorably broken because of this deluge of online content.

"I was in this period of rebuilding my identity and my relationships without the really fucked-up coping mechanisms I had used in the past," she said. "But I replaced all those coping mechanisms—all the things I was using to not feel the pain—with diagnosis, a whole new identity based on all this content."

It made her feel completely stuck. Like she wasn't fixing the right things. Like there was always more she could be doing.

"After dealing with the depression, then I'll deal with the ADHD," she told herself. "I was diagnosis-stacking. There's an endless list of things I could fix."

Maude had a job *at* Instagram at the time. And part of her job was to be regularly in contact with mental health influencers. But she realized that they too seemed stuck between presenting themselves as either forever broken, or miraculously and completely cured.

"We'd work with recovery influencers and then a few weeks later they'd start posting suicidal content, or even kill themselves," Maude said.

The deluge of mental health media made Maude not trust herself, her own brain, her own relationships. She was convinced everything was gaslighting, that every relationship was toxic. It was a self-reinforcing system. The more she consumed the content, the less the real world felt safe, and thus the more time she wanted to spend online, compulsively searching for the next thing wrong with her.

As she began to realize this, she vowed to change her relationship to the Internet, and the diagnosis culture that was so prominent on it.

She deleted apps from her phone. She felt less connected to the amorphous online "community" she had spent years building, but she also began to feel much more sane. She decided to quit her job at Instagram.

"Is it worth the risk of the damage it can do to your brain to have access to these communities?" Maude asked herself. "For me, it's not.

Now that I don't work at Instagram anymore, I'm like, let's fucking burn the Internet down."

| | | | | | | | |

My friend Britt's story reminded me of my own too. We grew up very differently, and our traumas were very different, yet we'd both somehow ended up in this place of trying to contain those traumas within diagnoses and their attendant medications. And then, as I did, Britt realized he felt trapped.

Growing up in Athens, Georgia, Britt was relatively well-off. When he was a kid, his dad made six figures as an administrator at the University of Georgia. But then things began going downhill quickly: when Britt was fourteen, his dad was diagnosed with frontotemporal dementia. He lost his job and became homebound. Suddenly, the family had to rely on Britt's mom's income. She worked three jobs just to get by.

Britt and his brother's life were quickly consumed with the stress of a sick parent and living without much money. At the same time, Britt was, like many young teens, beginning to go on Tumblr, the blogging website. And there he became immediately immersed in a world of mental health content. Everyone online talked about how they were depressed, or anxious, or had a disorder. People made jokes and memes about it. People congratulated one another for getting out of bed, and told them to not blame themselves for their chemical imbalances.

"'You wouldn't get mad at a cancer patient; why would you get mad at someone with depression?' Stuff like that," Britt told me.

As Britt went through high school, he rarely talked about his dad and the state of his family. But he did find comfort in the Internet, where it seemed that *everyone* was struggling with depression or some other mental health problem. And he began to adopt the Internet's language of mental health. He started to feel like he wasn't circumstantially depressed, but a *person with depression*, and that there was nothing he could do about it—that depression and its symptoms were lifelong struggles.

"It wasn't even a badge of honor, it was a badge of existence online," Britt told me. "To bastardize Descartes, it was like, 'I am depressed therefore I am.'"

This all left Britt feeling like there wasn't much he could do about his mental health.

Britt went off to college, and he noticed that Tumblr-style language had begun to creep into the real world too. Everyone was claiming to have some kind of niche disorder. Which was curious to Britt, because it seemed obvious that if everyone felt sick, then there was something bigger going on, beyond individual sickness.

"If everyone I know has depression and anxiety then it can't be an illness," Britt thought. "Because if everyone has it, then it's normal. We'd just have to recalibrate where normal is."

At the same time, Britt was still struggling a bit with his own mental health. He had his first big panic attack right before his first spring break. Back home, he went to see his primary care doctor. After meeting for less than thirty minutes, Britt was prescribed Lexapro and Xanax.

"I'd heard about Lexapro because of the Internet communities I was on," Britt said. "On the Internet there was a glorification of being on medicine, and of considering everything a chemical imbalance."

Again, no one asked him about the context of his anxiety and depression—specifically the fact that his dad was dying.

Britt stayed on the Lexapro for three years. It helped quell some of his anxiety, but also made him feel "dead to the world." He realized he couldn't cry when his dad died. "I didn't feel positive or negative emotion about pretty much anything in my life for, like, three years."

One day, Britt's friend proposed doing molly (aka MDMA), which people can't do if they're on SSRIs. So Britt quit cold turkey. He felt "insane" for a month, but after that was basically fine.

"I was just mad that they'd drugged me and were like, 'Okay, you should be fine now. We fixed whatever problem you had.'"

After his experience with diagnosis culture and medication, Britt began searching for other explanations for his, and everyone else's, distress. He studied psychoanalysis in school. He became skeptical of the chemical imbalance model.

"Chemical imbalance is really well received because it naturalizes all of this," he said. "You say, 'It's not my fault and there's nothing I can do about it. I don't have to do any soul-searching, because the medicine will fix me.'"

The more psychoanalytic theory Britt read, the more he was convinced that there was no "normal" search after, that there was no "good" state of mental health to be in.

"It's really sad to me that people only think they can be happy on these cocktails of drugs," he said. "We're never going to get better putting our faith in corporations that are more beholden to shareholders than to our actual health."

Britt now spends a lot of time thinking about the solution to this. After college, he pursued a PhD to further his study of a psychoanalytic model of the human psyche. He wants to encourage people to stop thinking of themselves as completely autonomous, their mental health simply a matter of their own individual brain chemistry.

"The first step would be to understand that what we are being given now is already politicized—this individualistic way of thinking about our mental health is political, it's not neutral," Britt said. "To de-diagnose is to say that it's not just you. It's the entire world. It's the entire structure of our world, of capitalism. It's that our society is structured so that we can't be happy. But that's a really scary thought for a lot of people."

FINDING SPACE OUTSIDE DIAGNOSIS

For decades, disability theorists have posited that what qualifies someone as disabled in a capitalist society is not an inherent biological or physical truth, but their relationship to productivity—their ability to work and produce profit for someone else. Philosophers like Michel Foucault have argued that mental health functions in the same way—that which is deemed normal and abnormal is not a function of biology, but a function of social control.

Foucault believed that to uncover this social basis of madness would be to ask for revolution—that if people were to realize their sicknesses did not lie within their own bodies and minds, but in the pens of scientists and psychiatrists and lawmakers, they would not stand for the laws and practices that made them feel alienated and ailed.

The philosopher Hubert Dreyfus, summing up Foucault's view of mental illness, wrote, "Social contradictions cause alienation, alienation causes defenses, defenses cause brain malfunction, and brain malfunction causes abnormal behavior."

The inequality, violence, and power dynamics of our society cause us to feel deeply alienated from the world, from our fellow man, and from ourselves, and thus we form neuroses—defense mechanisms against this deep alienation—which are then defined as illnesses by arms of state power (the psychiatric and psychological establishment, corporate-backed scientific institutions, and so on).[21]

In Foucault's words: "It is not because one is ill that one is alienated, but insofar as one is alienated that one is ill."[22]

These foundational critiques of mental illness are all but lost today. Even in progressive circles, when we talk of mental illness we most often use words and frameworks developed by the mainstream psychiatric and psychological institutions. We are not alienated, we have clinical depression. We are not lonely, we have social anxiety. We are not traumatized by the violence inherent to our capitalist world, we are bipolar, or have borderline personality disorder, or any of the 298 diagnoses listed in the *DSM*.[23]

Our inability to see our brains as anything other than lists of disorders and imbalances disables us from discussing what is being done to us, what we are being *made* to feel by the world we live in. How we discuss our mental health and the way we deal with it creates a politic, and that current politic is one of individualism, self-blame, and a constant search for pharmacological cure.

If we were to speak of mental health in *externalizing* terms, in words that enable us to see who and what was at fault for our deteriorating mental states, we could do something about what ails us.

But we are, of course, discouraged at every turn from doing this, because there are people who benefit not only from our alienation, but from our inability to experience or explain that alienation as such. This lack of definitional and explanatory power over our own mental states serves to further increase our estrangement from our own minds and bodies, and from one another.

"Debilitating alienation is the result of being thrown into a world of preexisting meanings as one incapable of meaning making," philosopher Kelly Oliver writes in *The Colonization of Psychic Space*. "And the greatest pain of this alienation comes from the fact that even the meaning of one's own body has been already defined."

This lack of ability to make one's own meaning, to define oneself and express oneself as one sees fit, to Oliver, and to the groundbreaking and radical philosophers her work is based on, is an inherent part of capitalism and colonialism. Summing up Frantz Fanon's work on colonized people in Africa, Oliver writes: "Along with economic imperialism that divides the world into 'haves' and 'have nots,' colonization brings with it affective imperialism that divides the world into the civilized, those who have control over emotions, and the barbaric, those who don't. Fanon's work suggests that there is a transfer of affect in the colonial situation, that the white colonizers inject or deposit their anger into the colonized, who are then forced to expel it in self-destructive ways...."

Though Fanon was writing specifically about the European colonization of Algeria, his lessons can be applied to racist, capitalist societies the world over. Today, we see the underclasses in the United States and other Western nations experiencing these kinds of injections of anger—forced to withstand the violence of capitalism to the point that they break, by carrying out either external or internal violence.

Violence, suicide, deaths of despair are all logical conclusions to the internalization of brutality so many of us experience. But less obvious is how this brutality affects us on a day-to-day basis. Even if we do not become suicidal or enact violence upon others, most of us carry with us the loneliness and despair of our world, and blame ourselves for it.

In this world, in which we are all each individually asked to carry the burden of society's ever-increasing violence, it is no wonder that we need to be medicated to survive; it is no wonder that we must constantly search for therapeutic answers and self-improvement regimens. We are all in pain, but refuse to recognize the collective reasons for it, so all continue our lonely journeys to okayness.

But if the problem becomes clear—that we are all individualizing and pathologizing societal violence—then the solution becomes clear too. We need to collectively address what is making us distressed—racism, sexism, classism, being overworked and underpaid, living in places where community is hard to come by.

Those, of course, are big asks. So perhaps there is a first step, a precursor: to find the space within our own psyches, and within our own lives, to actually name what is distressing us—to search for the time and the resources to stop internalizing our oppression, and to begin to externalize it.

INTERLUDE THREE
Fear of Freedom / Freedom from Fear

Five years after Charlottesville, five years after my mental breakdown, I'd achieved a tenuous stability, yet I still did not feel fully alive. It's like I was on low-power mode—protected from expending too much energy, but consequentially left half-functioning. This kept me secure, but also meant that beauty, excitement, sex were not compatible with my brain. It was no small feat that I'd achieved this, yet I knew there was a next step—the process of becoming alive. So from there, from this place of okayness, I began my search for more—for a form of healing that would not just bring me to stasis, but allow me to experience the outer edges of human emotion.

    I wasn't sure where to start. There was no road map for how to jump-start one into aliveness. But I'd heard from a friend that something called somatic therapy had helped her. I knew basically nothing about it, only that it focused more on the body and its feelings and resetting the nervous system than on thinking through one's traumas. And though I was skeptical of a more . . . some would say modern, some would say hippieish and woo-woo . . . approach to therapy, I was also definitely sick of thinking through my problems every week. It felt as if I'd reached the limit of what my conscious mind was able to tell me in psychoanalysis. So I was willing to try it.

A week before the fifth anniversary of Charlottesville, I logged on to my first online video session with a somatic therapist named Rebecca. After a bit of chitchat about my problems, we got down to business, and business was, at first, very awkward. Rebecca, with a tie-dye wall tapestry behind her and flowy yoga pants on, asked me to pick a few people or things I could think of—anchors, she called them—in case I got triggered. I picked my dad for his calm rationality; my friend Michael for his relaxing chill-out-everything-will-be-fine attitude; and my dog, Remi, the big and sweet pit bull whom I could always count on, to feel grounded.

Then Rebecca asked me to go back to Charlottesville in my mind, and walk her through the day. And while I did this, she instructed me to interlace my thumbs and tap my hands on each side of my chest, one after the other. *Thump thump. Thump thump.* Tapping is based on traditional Chinese medicine—the idea is that you can calm down the nervous system as you work through traumatic events by hitting specific acupressure points. And studies suggest it really works at reducing cortisol and thus anxiety.[1]

"So we were walking away from the protest," *thump thump,* "and I heard the screech of the car . . ." I began laughing. It all felt a bit . . . silly. In contrast to the restrained intellectualism of psychoanalysis, this was a little too New Agey for me. Rebecca wasn't having it. She told me bluntly: "You're good at analyzing your emotions, but you're really bad at actually *feeling* them."

That, I guess, was true. Feeling anything at that point was hard for me. My mom would always tell me, quoting the famous line of Hebbian theory, that "neurons that fire together wire together." And Charlottesville seemed to have wired two neural pathways—excitement and danger—firmly together. Rebecca was challenging me to unwire these neural pathways. And to do that, I'd have to really feel. And to do that, I had to first feel safe, and that, apparently, is what the tapping was for.

I tried again: "We were walking away from the protest," *thump thump*, "and I heard the screech. . . ." I suddenly began crying, then sobbing, then nearly hyperventilating. In a millisecond, it all came flooding back—the terror, the confusion, all of it. Rebecca told me to think of my anchors. I did. This helped. She smirked. "Good," she said. I assume she wanted to say, "Told you so."

The following week, at the start of our next session, I realized I felt angry at Rebecca. Some subconscious part of me was scared by the efficacy of our previous session, and thus scared that this work could take away my coping mechanisms, which I felt were keeping me safe—the hypervigilance, the deadness. Without those things, I worried I'd somehow experience a breakdown all over again—that if I allowed too much excitement or freedom into my life, I'd also be inviting danger.

This is a central tenet of somatic therapy. In the perennially popular somatic-focused book *The Body Keeps the Score*, Bessel van der Kolk wrote that patients who'd experienced trauma learned to "shut down the brain areas that transmit the visceral feelings and emotions that accompany and define terror." Yet because those same areas of the brain are responsible for registering *all* emotions, the patients would begin to feel inhuman. "What we witnessed here was a tragic adaptation," he wrote. "In an effort to shut off terrifying sensations, they also deadened their capacity to feel fully alive."

This conundrum is central to a lot of more traditional psychoanalytic theory as well. It's what psychologist Donald Winnicott called in 1974 the "fear of breakdown." He wrote that infants experience a traumatic emotional response when the bond between mother and baby begins to change. But because they are too young to process this breakdown, they instead project it onto the future, and live in fear of a breakdown that has *already occurred*. And, he wrote, "There is no end unless the bottom of the trough has been reached, unless the thing feared has been experienced."[2]

That fear of breakdown had infected every part of my life—I was afraid to succeed, to be happy, to feel even a bit of excitement, to be a full person, because that meant I could lose control; it meant Charlottesville, or September 11, or any other Big Bad Thing, could happen again. The trick, then, the conundrum, of trauma is that you not only must heal, but convince yourself that healing won't kill you, that healing is not actually further injury.

I began to realize this catch-22 had been present in much of my life.

I told Rebecca about my childhood, about being raised by parents one generation removed from the Holocaust. I told her about things like my mom saying, "Careful, careful," as I biked down the bike path on the west side of Manhattan as a kid, afraid my carefreeness would lead to an accident. And how could she not feel that way, as a woman raised by two Holocaust survivors who saw their relatively calm Eastern European lives one day shattered, sent on trains to camps where they saw their entire families die, where they slept six to a bed, where any camaraderie they attempted was severely punished. (I remember my mom's mom's fake teeth, replacements since she was hit in the face with the butt of a Nazi's rifle as she tried to sneak a piece of bread across Auschwitz to a sick and dying friend.) How could my mom, or my grandparents, or anyone in my family accept happiness as a safe state? It seemed every time we let our guard down, something bad was bound to happen.

What Rebecca was proposing to me was that unless I could emotionally experience and process the trauma that already happened—in Charlottesville, during 9/11, in my family's past—that I'd always fear it happening again, and therefore be trapped in this conundrum of feeling stable, safe, and miserable.

So Rebecca and I worked each week to confront those past breakdowns in ways that didn't destabilize me. And nearly every session, I would sob—not as if experiencing the terrors of my past *again*, but as if experiencing them for the first time, because, emotionally, I was.

| | | | |

The more sessions I had with Rebecca the more I began to see fear of breakdown everywhere in the world. Most people I know have a sense of forebodingness about the future—global warming, the economy, all the things we took for granted as semi-stable, we now see as in a state of constant and dangerous flux. This bears out statistically—more Americans felt worried about the future than hopeful in 2024.³

But learning to reframe my own psyche in terms of fear of breakdown also began to allow me to see the world differently. Perhaps it's not only that the future seems bleak, perhaps it's also that we have learned to expect the future to be bleak by internalizing the breakdowns that have *already* occurred.

It's rational to think that breakdown is our natural state, because it is. Every step toward liberation met with police violence. Every dropping of one's guard met with sickness, joblessness, death. Our most basic needs like touch and love punished through law or through disease. We must always be "on." No wonder people turn to opiates and benzos to calm down this equation, or to dissociatives to remove themselves from it completely.

The psychoanalyst Thomas Ogden, in his 2014 journal article "Fear of Breakdown and the Unlived Life," argued that experiencing trauma renders patients unable to imagine joy and freedom in the present or future, because it unearths remembrance of how much pain exists in their pasts. "Such patients find it excruciatingly painful to feel alive—even to the extent of feeling pleasure in response to the sensation of the soft warmth of the sun on their skin," he wrote, "because it stirs the pain of recognition of how much of their life has been unlived."[4]

To greater and lesser extents, we are terrified of the feeling of pleasure, because to acknowledge that feeling would be to acknowledge our lives unlived. To acknowledge our desire would be to acknowledge how far we are from it. If we constantly live in breakdown, to hope for something better is to punish oneself.

This is one of the hardest parts of healing. You are not only working through the past, but through the future. You are unchaining yourself from what your brain and your body have already decided will happen, unchaining yourself from the story you have been drawn into. To change the narrative, when you know the breakdown that has already occurred, feels nearly impossible. If you know about the broken world you are healing into, and we all do, then how do you convince yourself anything can become better?

But if we internalize, to crib some stock-market jargon, that past performance is not indicative of future results, if we can create the space to process and feel the terribleness that has already happened in the world, then maybe we can open up the space for hope and begin to believe that the future is not the past; begin to believe that the future is possibly beautiful.

That, essentially, is what I was trying to do as I continued my recovery from breakdown—to will myself into believing that a future completely unlike my past was possible.

PART 3

REBIRTH

7

BECOMING ALIVE

FINDING A NEW LIFE; DRUGS AS TOOLS FOR
BREAKTHROUGH; THE HISTORY OF HALLUCINOGENS
AND DISSOCIATIVES; CAPITALIZING ON PEOPLE'S
QUEST FOR BREAKTHROUGH

A year and a half after that day in Oakland, the day my entire life collapsed, I am living in Philadelphia, with two roommates I do not really know and honestly have very little desire to know, in a shitty row house with those renovations so common these days—the gray and the laminate and cheap compressed wood that looks like plastic, or is plastic; the kind that makes life feel suicidally devoid of beauty.

And I feel stable but not good, able to live life but with no desire to live life if this is what life is like.

But at this point, I associate survival with this stability, and that stability with boringness, so I have made my life as boring as possible. I have stopped drinking; I have stopped doing cocaine. I have stopped going out most nights; I see friends once or twice a week. I see a therapist three times a week; I try to do some menial work, writing a few articles for news outlets, just enough to pay rent, but I have lost all ambition for anything except stability. Stability is my work now. I spend many hours a week watching Internet videos about yoga, or meditation, or aligning my chakras. I go to yoga once a week. I go to the gym. I hate my life.

So when a friend invites me to a party at a loft on the other side of the city one night and says she will be doing acid, I am both excited and terrified. I want so badly to leave my gray world, yet I am convinced that if I do, I will destabilize myself, fall back down down down, and have to totally start over again. My brain feels dead, but I am also at least physically alive, and I cannot take this fact for granted.

But something in me tells me to go, so I go.

I wear a black jean skirt with frayed edges and a ripped up T-shirt and a bright yellow windbreaker and a short, purple wig with bangs, my outfit willing my mind into party mode; it's giving off fake-it-till-you-make-it; the thing I'm faking is that I am a person who knows how to have fun, that my brain is capable of processing enjoyment.

I arrive at the party and walk up to my friend and she gives me half a tab of LSD. It's been at least five years since I've done it. I take it, dissolving it on my tongue, and wait. Thirty minutes pass. In that time, I am accosted by a random woman who likes my skirt and thinks that because I am dressed the way I am that I would not mind being touched by her. I also have a boring conversation with some man. I walk around the loft.

Everyone seems boring. I am bored. This was not the jump-start back to funness I had hoped for.

So I go back to my friend; I ask for the other half of the tab. She cautions me. She tells me to wait. It's strong, she says. I tell her to just give it to me, so she does. Whoops.

An hour later I am standing in a dark, small, empty park alone, somewhere near my house. It is winter and the trees look like skeletons. I do not see faces but the trunks somehow remind me of my ancestors. They are telepathically asking me to join them. The branches their hands and fingers, above me they whoosh around until they all blend together into a brown-and-gray ceiling, trapping me in this death box. I attempt to walk toward home but feel stuck, physically. My feet have sunk into the ground. Breathing becomes thinner and faster. Skin feels prickly and coarse. I am becoming a tree. I am becoming one with the earth. I have a terrifying thought: *This is death*. Not that I am dying, but that I have become death itself, that I will exist as death only, as a citizen of deathworld, even if my organs and blood are technically alive.

The panic is passing now and morphing rapidly into something that feels much worse—acceptance. *Let the earth take me*, I think. *Let me become a tree. Let me merge.*

And then, the moon.

It peers out between the swaying branches, its bright, blue rays illuminating what feels like just my body—like I am in a spotlight, or under a streetlamp. Which then I realize, in a brief moment of lucidity, is because I am under a streetlamp. It is not the moon. I do not know where the moon is. But nonetheless the effect is the same. The light is life. It blinds me.

The outside world vanishes.

My vision becomes internal.

My world is now red and pulsating. Coming into focus slowly I can see my brain. I am floating above it in this crimson, viscous sky; I can see my mind's grooves like the tributaries of a river. I zoom in. And to my surprise I can see the coffin I am trapped in. It's on a map, no, a timeline—I am stuck in the coffin, but I see there is life on either side of it, that this is not my final resting place.

I realize that my near-death experiences have placed me here, that I am death because I have nearly died (twice). Of course I live in deathworld. What other world could I live in?

And then the solution becomes so obvious that I almost feel embarrassed: I must walk out of the coffin, out of deathworld, toward the future. Eventually this will all be a memory if I just keep walking. But I must get as far away from deathworld as I possibly can, and fast. There is nothing for me here. I may feel trapped, but I am not trapped. I cannot give in to that feeling. I must fight it like I am fighting to survive, because I am. I must leave my ancestors and the trees and the branches and the dirt behind.

Okay, I say weakly.

My external vision returns. I am still in the park, but my feet feel lighter now. I realize I can move. Slowly, like I am relearning how to walk. But then my feet burst back to full function. Across the park I see my block and my house and I run toward it as fast as I can. I burst past the front door. My dog is waiting for me. While I was gone he has apparently turned into a lion. I am surprised by this. But also comforted, because he and his mane and his aura feel strong and secure. I hold on to him tightly and absorb his confidence. He tells me we'll walk out of this together.

Okay, I trust you, I say, and thank him.

I am still scared, but I feel resolute. Tomorrow I will begin my walk away from death.

I take a Klonopin to turn my brain off. Enough of this for now.

I awake suddenly the next morning with tears pouring down my cheeks, sobbing to the point of choking, as I rapidly come to the realization that I am finally and really and fully alive.

MAINSTREAMING PSYCHEDELICS

That acid trip was one of the scariest moments of my life. Yet it changed so much—by allowing me to see my brain from above, it let me see where I needed to go in the future in order to heal, and, in that way, it totally reoriented my life.

As I got more and more days of recovery from breakdown under my belt, I got more and more willing to experiment with things like LSD, in search of similar experiences of reawakening. It's not that the other modalities of healing weren't working—psychotherapy with Dennis was amazing at allowing me to understand all that led me here (and also at just ensuring I did not kill myself when I was at my worst); somatic therapy with Rebecca was amazing at making me less scared of my past, and thus at opening up space in my psyche to envision a future. But now I was stabilized, I was open, but I was also kind of empty. What I needed, I thought, was a spiritual awakening. Or several.

And, I'd kept reading, psychedelics and other drugs were showing a lot of promise in helping people envision different lives. A slew of new science has suggested that acid, ketamine, MDMA, psilocybin mushrooms, and other once shunned drugs may be really helpful in treating depression, PTSD, and myriad other problems of the brain.

A 2019 meta-analysis of eleven studies on LSD showed the drug significantly helped people with depression and anxiety and alcoholism.[1] A 2023 study suggested that even one dose of psilocybin (aka shrooms) can significantly improve people's depression.[2] And a 2021 study found that MDMA is "highly efficacious" in helping those who suffer from PTSD.[3]

Until recently, the science of how to treat brain disorders has been relatively stagnant. SSRIs, the main medication-based treatment for depression, anxiety, and PTSD, have remained largely the same since their introduction over thirty years ago, even as new iterations of the class of drug are introduced periodically. So the idea these still mostly illegal drugs can work better than their legal and widely prescribed counterparts has sparked optimism in the field, and in the media where seemingly every week there's a new story about the psychiatric miracles brought about by LSD, psilocybin, MDMA, and ketamine. The *New York Times* called MDMA a "balm for psyches scarred by war" in 2022.[4] The *New Yorker* wondered in 2024 whether psychedelics could heal the trauma of Ukrainians after Russia's invasion.[5]

But the psychedelic craze of today is very different from previous ones. This time, they're trying to go legit: rather than being researched as *drugs*, they're being researched as *medicines*—ones that can be used much like SSRIs. Gone are the proclamations of these substances as portals to a new world, as tools to increase human empathy and understanding. Gone is the image of LSD and shrooms as drugs that can help you turn on, tune in, and drop out—get weird and stop following the life prescribed to you by capitalism and normative society. Instead, the claims this time around are much more modest and individualistic: these substances aren't meant to liberate, they're meant to adjust, to make us well, to make us function within our extant society.

Researchers and the universities, nonprofits, and companies that support them have essentially attempted to depoliticize the drugs, to disassociate them from the hippies, the sixties, and the very prominent and groovy researchers of yesteryear like Timothy Leary, who argued psychedelics could not only help your brain, but could help save the world. As *Wired* magazine, summing up the feelings of the scientific field of psychedelic research writ large, bluntly put in their profile of the 2013 Psychedelic Science conference, "Timothy Leary really screwed things up for science."[6] But in their quest to mainstream these drugs, it's possible we're losing one of their best features: their ability to get us to think differently about our lives and our world, their ability to do what I wanted them to do—give my life new meaning.

White Westerners were very late to the psychedelics game. Indigenous tribes across the world have used drugs like psilocybin and salvia in spiritual or shamanistic rituals for thousands of years. Some research suggests that use of hallucinogens in Mesoamerica goes back at least five thousand years.[7] One very trippy mural from 500 BC in Teotihuacán, for example, depicts the Toltec rain god Tlaloc with dozens of what are assumed to be hallucinogenic mushrooms in the background[8] (you can still see this mural; just take an hour-long bus ride from the center of Mexico City). Evidence of people using psychedelics to get closer to God, to celebrate their lives, and as medicine for a wide array of physical problems has cropped up all across the Americas, Africa, and Europe.[9]

But it wasn't until 1957 that the white, Western world really began thinking about the drugs. That's when R. Gordon Wasson, a successful banker and amateur mycologist, traveled to Oaxaca and met with a Mazatec healer named Maria Sabina, and produced a photo-essay on the use of mushrooms in traditional ceremonies throughout the region. Much of the article was devoted to discussing Wasson's first trip, led by Maria Sabina.[10] He hallucinated mountains and rivers and "a woman in primitive costume, standing and staring across the water, enigmatic, beautiful, like a sculpture except that she breathed and was wearing woven colored garments. It seemed as though I was viewing a world of which I was not a part and with which I could not hope to establish contact. There I was, poised in space, a disembodied eye, invisible, incorporeal, seeing but not seen."

"They carry you there where God is," one Oaxaca resident told Wasson.

"He who does not imagine in . . . stronger and better light than his perishing mortal eye can see, does not imagine at all," wrote Wasson, quoting the poet William Blake. "But I can testify that the mushrooms make those visions accessible to a much larger number."[11]

The article opened a Pandora's box in the West—dozens of researchers and journalists traveled to Mexico. Hundreds of others who just wanted to experience a trip did too.[12] The Mazatec community despised the article—the tourism ruined their town, and many felt that Maria Sabina had sold out their culture to a bunch of ignorant white people. Her house was burned down. And eventually Maria Sabina and even Wasson agreed that the article had been a mistake.

"From the moment the foreigners arrived to search for God, the saint children lost their purity," Maria Sabina said. "They lost their force; the foreigners spoiled them. From now on they won't be any good. There's no remedy for it."

"A practice carried on in secret for three centuries or more has now been aerated," wrote Wasson. "And aeration spells the end."³

At the same time, lysergic acid diethylamide (aka LSD) was skyrocketing in popularity. In 1938, the chemist Albert Hofmann had discovered LSD accidentally as he experimented with finding novel chemical compounds for his employer, Sandoz Laboratories. He at first thought LSD was useless, but nonetheless five years later synthesized it again. And as the substance crystallized in the lab, Hofmann began feeling strange, and eventually began hallucinating. The experience fascinated Hofmann, and led him and dozens of other researchers to begin to experiment with the drug. Some of those researchers were funded by the CIA, which used LSD, often on prisoners and soldiers without their consent, in an attempt to find a new kind of psychological torture device or potential truth serum.[14]

By the 1960s, both acid and shrooms were circulating widely in the United States. To conservatives, the drugs were a scourge on society; to some on the left, they were proof that the government was attempting to kill social movements via hallucinogen-induced mind control; but to others, like Harvard psychologist Timothy Leary (who had also traveled to Mexico after Wasson's article), they were not only potentially helpful, but promised to change the future of humanity.

Leary began using LSD and psilocybin in experiments at Harvard, including one in which he gave prisoners who were scheduled to be freed mushrooms in an attempt to help them rethink their lives and reduce the chances they'd go back to committing crimes.[15]

But Leary's research became sloppy as he became more of an evangelist for the drugs (he would, for example, dose subjects with mushrooms while also being high on mushrooms himself), and in 1963 he was fired from Harvard.[16] That freed Leary up to become a full-time psychedelic preacher of sorts—giving TV and magazine interviews, leading trip sessions with big groups of hippies, and encouraging everyone in the country to "turn on, tune in, and drop out."

"You cannot do this alone in acts of isolated rebellion. Detaching yourself from the insanity of society requires group action," Leary once said. "As you drop out you will find that you do nothing which is not an act of beauty."[17]

To Leary and his followers, acid and shrooms were not simply tools of self-discovery. They were necessary parts of a larger, revolutionary machine. His words encouraged countless young people to leave their jobs, their families, and their hometowns behind. They headed to places like Haight-Ashbury in San Francisco, where they formed communes, participated in antiwar protests, and organized against racism and capitalism. Leary and his fellow travelers saw drugs as a way to foster hope, to push for the kinds of change that could be threatening to the order of the United States government.

But quickly, the dreams engendered by these drugs seemed to fade. Part of it was outright government repression of the era: Leary was jailed and fled the States. And the activist movements that provided so many with hope for a better future were sabotaged. The FBI, through its COINTELPRO program, surveilled and infiltrated civil rights organizations, antiwar organizations, and leftist groups.[18] They also used psychological warfare to turn the groups against themselves and one another. The actress Jean Seberg, for example, was followed around and wiretapped by the FBI because of her support of the Black Panthers. The FBI also spread rumors to the press that Seberg's unborn baby was the result of an affair with a member of the Black Panthers. Seberg was so distraught by the campaign that she attempted suicide, leading to the stillbirth of her baby.[19] The FBI also sent a letter to Martin Luther King Jr. in the voice of a nonexistent Black member of the civil rights movement, which called him a "filthy, abnormal beast" and threatened to expose him for infidelity if he did not kill himself.[20] They also attempted to drive the Left's more spiritual and substance-inclined members toward psychosis by sending them letters with "mystical, sinister" symbols like scorpions and cobras.[21]

Though obviously much of the "New Left" did not dabble in hallucinogens, in toto, this government repression worked to fracture the movement and spread immense fear that made it much harder to organize, and made it much harder to feel hopeful that they could actually change the world.

That's not to say that the psychedelically inclined branches of the movement were perfect before the government got involved. Indeed, a common critique of the druggier parts of the Left was that they were ultimately a hedonistic distraction from actual, material goals of liberation. But whether you blame the drug users themselves, or the government, or both, it quickly began to be obvious that the idealistic internal and external change that they were fighting for was not coming to fruition anytime soon.

When the writer Joan Didion visited San Francisco in 1967, she found a scene in chaos, in which amphetamines and heroin had begun to supplant LSD, in which children were being left unattended and even given drugs, in which no one seemed to know exactly why they were there, except to drop out.

"We were seeing something important. We were seeing the desperate attempt of a handful of pathetically unequipped children to create a community in a social vacuum. Once we had seen these children, we could no longer overlook the vacuum, no longer pretend that the society's atomization could be reversed," Didion wrote in her now famous essay "Slouching Towards Bethlehem." But, she said, "they are less in rebellion against the society than ignorant of it."[22]

By the 1980s, as we all know now, the feeling of a hopeful rebellion in the United States and many other countries had all but died. Many hippies had become yuppies. The "war on drugs," led by President Richard Nixon, and playing on the fears of the "silent majority" of white, suburban Americans who were afraid of everything from drugs to crime to people of color, was in full effect, leading to a quadrupling of imprisonment in the United States.[23] And the drugs had changed too. The eighties were not about hallucinogens and hope. They were about hard partying, and subsequently the country's drugs of choice became much harder—cocaine and heroin dominated the culture.

When hallucinogens returned to the public consciousness, they were no longer drugs of liberation, but drugs of personal modification. The point was no longer to envision a better world, but to envision a better, more productive self: In the 1960s and '70s, the new technologists of Silicon Valley became obsessed with LSD in particular. They saw the brain as a machine capable of upgrade and constant augmentation. Even figures once associated with the use of hallucinogens for the betterment of humankind got on board with this new techno-utopian project. Ken Kesey, the author of *One Flew Over the Cuckoo's Nest*, went from being a countercultural figure to a favorite cultural fixture among Silicon Valley acid pioneers.[24]

That's not to say the dream totally faded—there were, and are, still evangelists for the use of hallucinogens as tools to change the world.

Terence McKenna, probably the closest thing we have to a successor to Leary, published books and gave countless lectures about the possibilities engendered by the drugs throughout the 1980s and '90s. He once said that, "Psychedelics are illegal because they dissolve opinion structures and culturally lay down models of behavior and information processing. They open you up to the possibility that everything you know is wrong."[25]

McKenna believed psychedelics were inherently alienating, but that "what they alienate us from is preposterous, Earth-murdering, sexist, consumerist, shallow, trivial, inane, insane, and dangerous."[26] By purposefully alienating ourselves, McKenna believed, we could detach from the horror of our current world, and envision a new one.

But then Timothy Leary died in 1996. And Terence McKenna in 2000.

And with them so too did the idea of drugs as radical modifiers of the collective conscience.

When we think of the sixties now, it seems like such a distant memory, a blip of human hope in constant bleakness. Our memory of it as such, as an aberration, may be no accident. As the theorist Mark Fisher writes in his unfinished work "Acid Communism," it's possible this era of free thought posed such a threat to the current order of the world that it had to be repressed at all costs. It's less that the movement failed than that it represented something so potentially destabilizing to capitalism and to the state that it had to be quashed by any means necessary. And through that successful campaign of sabotage, we've been trained to see that era as an anomaly; and to see the idea of change writ large, of a world beyond capitalism, as unrealistic—what Fisher calls "capitalist realism."

"What if the counterculture was only a stumbling beginning, rather than the best that could be hoped for," he writes. "To recall these multiple forms of collectivity is less an act of remembering than of unforgetting, a counter-exorcism of the specter of a world which could be free."[27]

So what if we could reremember, or unforget, the lessons of the sixties and seventies? What if we could build on the sixties to create a culture of thought, of drug use, of mind expansion, of collectivity that changes the world? These seem like almost ignorant questions now. We've been so conditioned into a depressive capitalist realism that to think of a better world feels arrogant or childish.[28]

But the alternative is much scarier—to give in to this forced forgetting is to give in to the idea that the world is, essentially, doomed. No wonder so many are depressed, anxious, suicidal: it's not just that the world is hard and unfair, it's that we've been taught to think there's no way its hardness or unfairness will ever change. So what's the point?

Though I'm happy mainstream institutions are popularizing hallucinogens and other drugs as mental health treatments, I'm also a bit scared of what we will lose in that process. Being dosed with mushrooms by a doctor to cure depression is a much different experience than taking drugs within a community attempting to envision a brighter future.

Drugs are tools. They can help us modify our brains to better fit within our current societies, or they can help us see out of them, toward something new.

Even in these depressing times, every now and then, I get a glimpse of hope. Often, that hope is fostered by drugs—they allow me to see that a new reality is possible, and that it exists first in our minds, just waiting to be externalized. And it can feel almost embarrassing to allow myself to feel something we've been shamed away from feeling for so long. Cringe. But the more glimpses I get, the more used to it I get, the more I feel that one of the most important uses of drugs is to help continually foster the belief within yourself that something better is possible, and even imminent.

Three years after my mental breakdown, and about a year after that acid trip in Philadelphia that finally convinced me I was alive, I was living in New Orleans, in a nice, spacious house in a cute neighborhood. I had my trusty dog—the one I thought was a lion during that trip. And he still felt strong and secure and protective. I had a big backyard. I had more steady work—writing a newsletter I created for media workers, attempting to forge community and solidarity within a shitty industry. And I was living with two good friends, including Erin, the one who was with me in Charlottesville.

Life was, mostly, good. I did not feel 100 percent healed, or back to "normal." But I'd also at that point begun to practice giving up on returning to my prebreakdown self, began to realize there was perhaps no normal to return to. Life was new. And that was okay.

But there was still something critical missing—that energy, that sense of excitement, and it nagged at me. Something in my brain was still preventing me from getting too excited, from getting too happy—I still couldn't handle it. I was convinced I'd break down again if I let myself go. It was a frustrating experience—to know that your life is not being lived to its fullest, yet to run into a wall, to panic or dissociate or shut down every time you try to live it to its fullest.

But I kept trying new things to get that excitement back—blasting metal and emo music in an attempt to force my neurons out of their slumber; going to amusement parks in the hope that a roller-coaster would jolt me awake. Each of these things worked, temporarily, to make me feel a bit more alive. So too did cocaine.

One night alone in my room, I did more coke than I'd done since I was a teenager, since I was an addict. I did not have a plan. I did not exactly *desire* to rail line after line, yet I kept going. It was dangerous and stupid. But I kept going. The first ten minutes I just looked at my phone. Another line. The next ten minutes I looked at porn. Another line. By the end of the night, I was just pacing my room, my hands shaking, my teeth numb. Dangerous. Stupid. Especially to use alone. But there was a reason I'd kept going: this was the first time in *years* that I'd felt really and truly awake, my neurons firing on all cylinders. I wanted to yell at the top of my lungs. I wanted to say "woo-hoo" and run around the block. Instead, I just kept pacing, anxious because of the coke flowing through my system, but happy because I knew I was, for a brief moment, back. This, of course, would not be a sustainable solution to my deadness. But still, it was helpful—like the Klonopin back at the beginning of my breakdown, the cocaine helped remind me what I was fighting for: to be able to feel these things naturally again.

After that experience alone in my room, I began to grow increasingly frustrated. I'd seen what I'd been missing for so long—this feeling of being really and truly awake to the world and able to handle its joys. I'd seen the other side, touched it, and then been ricocheted back to this feeling of deadness.

The two things that got me through that period of deadness, the things that helped inch me closer and closer to the other side, closer to a future in which I'd want to live, were my best friend, Erin, and ketamine.

Erin was in Charlottesville with me in 2017. We marched together against the Nazis. Helped each other when we got a bit of the cops' tear gas in our eyes. Felt comfort in each other when the armed fascists were on the move. Celebrated when we felt like we'd won. Sat shaking together after we'd almost died.

Erin and I had barely known each other before Charlottesville, but we'd become inseparable since. If we weren't living in the same city, we were constantly texting. If we were in the same city, we were with each other daily—living together, watching TV, getting drunk, arguing.

I'd heard a lot on Internet forums and in pop psychology articles that bonding over trauma can be a bad thing—that people become too close, too dependent on one another, reinforce one another's worst tendencies and coping mechanisms. And to be sure, I could see that in our relationship at certain points. But mostly, our friendship felt, and still to this day feels, like having a buddy through the worst parts of one's life.

Erin and I seemed to go through the same things at the same times. When I was dissociated, she often was too. When I had a nightmare about Charlottesville, she often did the same night. Erin—slightly reserved and petite and pretty and blond but also very confident and willing to tell you you're an asshole if you're an asshole—was my rock. She gave me strength through those worst years.

Most important, we were both obsessed with Lady Gaga.

One night, at our house in New Orleans, to commemorate the release of Gaga's new album *Chromatica*, Erin and I decided to do a lot of ketamine, and to sit on the couch, and just listen.

We were not doing it with the express purpose of healing from our trauma, but I felt it couldn't hurt.

I took out a key. I put it in the bag. Put the powder on the key. The key to my nose. The ketamine burned. And the first song started. I got goosebumps from the first orchestral note. After only a few seconds, I began to feel I was entering a different world.

Gaga has said *Chromatica* is about healing from her own traumas, and with the ketamine, I could feel like I was on the journey with her. The music took on a heaviness, lyrically, but also aurally, like it had flooded into our house with a viscous goo. Like Erin and I were swimming in it (even though we were just lying on the floor and the couch).

Something told me to keep swimming into the music, further into the bass, to let it overtake me until I felt like I was drowning. But good drowning. Totally submerged. Disconnected from the atmosphere of daily existence. I now lived in *Chromatica* goo. Gaga's voice was a guide through the substance. She told me, in some subconscious way, where exactly to go.

And then the deep synths gave way to acoustic lightness, and I felt like I'd been lifted out of the syrup, and off the earth entirely. My body was still on the floor, but I was also above it. Two entities. Like a spirit leaving a corpse. I could see myself, I could see the room, and Erin, and the couch, and the dog, and the speakers, from six feet up.

And I could feel something in my stomach being pulled out, like a worm from my gut, a monster excavated. Someone was performing surgery on me. I did not hallucinate this—ketamine doesn't really make you see things. It makes you sense them. And this is what I sensed. *Get it out of me*, I thought. *Deliver me from this thing. Pull the creature out.*

I started sobering up. Exorcism-by-Gaga over. But I didn't feel done. I wanted another go in the goo.

So, more ketamine. Bitter and sweet. Pleasantly chemical. I loved the feeling of it dripping down my throat.

The second bump hit harder than the first. Again, I felt both up and down. Simultaneously on the floor and floating. Ketamine, dissociative that it is, did exactly that—it dissociated me from myself. But that is not a strong enough word for what was happening. My mind, it seemed, had literally left my body. They became two foreign objects, two magnets with their poles pushing them away from each other.

Three minutes later, I became convinced the music was speaking directly to me. Not in the sense that I was crazy enough to think Lady Gaga wrote the album for me (though maybe part of me thought that), but in the sense that I was amazed at the universality of the human experience; that the lyrics written about Gaga's recovery from a sexual assault could speak so perfectly to my recovery from something completely different; I was amazed that this music exists; that music, period, exists; I was amazed that we are allowed to have art; I was amazed that we are allowed to have life. Even if life sometimes sucks. What the fuck. Life. It was so goddamn cool. I loved art. I loved Lady Gaga. I loved Erin. And my dog. And the dirty rug I was lying on. And the air I was floating in and the syrup I was swimming in. I loved myself—my stomach and its pains, my shoulders and their aches, my heart and its palpitations. I realized that they were part and parcel. Everything was me. I was everything.

Wow.

As I sobered up the second time, I felt incredibly silly for how obvious these revelations were: that life and art and my body contain beauty, that I must move on from pain and experience pleasure, that I must practice self-acceptance of what will most likely forever cause me strife. But I nonetheless deeply appreciated these thoughts.

And that, I realized, is what I so appreciated about drugs like ketamine. It's not that they caused totally new thoughts. It's that they made ingesting those thoughts easier. In non-high life, it's easy to get stuck in a loop of waking up and working and drinking coffee and driving and seeing friends. I have these thoughts, largely the same ones I have on drugs, but they kind of bounce around the surface. There's no space to let them fully germinate. My brain is too busy doing other shit. Drugs helped me make space to plant those seeds and let them flourish—to really consider what the farthest reaches of my psyche was trying to tell me.

One more bump. The last song on the album, "Babylon," began playing. I was very high. This song has no deeper meaning. The lyrics did not attempt to do anything except be fun to dance to. Which in and of itself became meaning to me. Dance. Live. Slay. Be corny. Life is good and worth celebrating. In that moment, I wanted to leave all that other shit behind. Rip off the layers of gauze between my eyes and the world so that I could fully see again. No more protection. Full feeling. Of both pain and pleasure. Of everything.

And then the album was over.

Erin and I looked at each other. And we decided to start it again from track 1.

I thought back to one of the first nights after my breakdown, when I was really and truly convinced I was going to die. And I thought back to Bobbi holding me tightly on my bed as the Klonopin worked its way through my system. And I thought about the lesson I'd learned then, which was the same lesson I'd learned on the floor, listening to Gaga with Erin: a drug can loosen your brain up so that you can more readily come to revelations, or it can soothe your anxious nervous system so that it can accept the comfort of others, but substances are only part of the equation; nothing works, nothing really matters, without other people.

CHEMICAL VERSUS EXPERIENTIAL EFFECTIVENESS

Though it's undoubtedly a good thing that many drugs are becoming decriminalized and destigmatized, and that money is being poured into researching them, I worry that in doing so, we will forget that the context in which we take drugs matters. For me, ketamine would not have been healing if I hadn't done it with a friend. Its effectiveness was not only from the chemical changes it produced in my brain, but in the experience it opened up for me—of feeling closer to people I loved, of letting the healing power of music seep into my psyche.

Shame, then, that capitalism seems intent on cleaving these things—drugs and community, healing, and love—from each other. Ketamine clinics, in which patients are infused with the drug for several sessions over several months, are now a $3.4 billion industry. The industry is expected to double in size by 2030.[29] And in the mid-2010s, the giant pharmaceutical company Johnson & Johnson heavily lobbied the US government to approve Spravato, an isolated isomer of ketamine mixed into a nasal spray that, unlike normal ketamine, was patentable, even though it has shown no efficacy beyond nonpatentable ketamine. The government quickly approved Spravato, and Johnson & Johnson began charging thousands of dollars per month for the drug[30] (nonpatented ketamine is extremely cheap to produce, costing about $50 to $100 a month).[31]

What's happening to ketamine is happening to virtually all hallucinogens and dissociatives—they're getting absorbed into the mainstream medical-industrial complex. And though there's some benefits to this—increased access, increased research—it also, in a way, neuters these drugs' potential.

If drugs are not just about neurons, but about enabling us to reexperience our lives, then it seems logical that the more—more chaos, more joy, more perspective—one can experience on these drugs, the more helpful they can be.

And that jibes with my experience, and the experience of many others I know who love drugs like ketamine. Few want to sit in a white-walled room alone and get high. The chemicals are not the point—they're experience-modulators. They can open us up to something new, but only if we do the searching for the new thing ourselves.

One frequent ketamine user once told me that the reason ketamine works is because it breaks down rules, both internal and external. We live in an increasingly rule-bound world, forced to act and think in certain ways by our jobs, our schooling, and our social norms. And, especially these days, forced into algorithmic ways of thinking by our technology-saturated existences: our next favorite song, our next thought, our next piece of entertainment decided not by friends or communities or ourselves but by a few large corporations whose main focus is not our mental betterment, but the betterment of their own bottom lines. Ketamine, he said, randomizes all this, makes you feel less computer-generated. It de-algorithmizes you.

As the journalist Kyle Chayka argued in his 2024 book *Filterworld: How Algorithms Flattened Culture*, this constant deluge of algorithmically targeted content is a kind of drug in itself. And, like any drug-use cycle, it can cause both excitement and numbness and anxiety.

"The dopamine rushes become inadequate, and the noise and speed of the feeds overwhelming," Chayka wrote. "Our natural reaction is to seek out culture that embraces nothingness, that blankets and soothes rather than challenges or surprises, as powerful artwork is meant to do. Our capacity to be moved, or even to be interested and curious, is depleted."

Ketamine may be the drug of our moment because of its ability to temporarily scramble people's psyches. In a culture so controlled by machines and rules, it's nice to have a reprieve—a chance to dissociate from the algorithmic order.[32]

Ketamine, or any other drug, might not cure anything in a chemical sense, but for the twenty or thirty minutes you feel high, floating above the world and yourself, alienated from that which creates those deep and deeply unsettling feelings of loneliness, of disconnection, of anger and anger-turned-inward (and thus anxiety and depression), you might be able to look down, down at your brain, and down at the world, and understand, even if just for a second, exactly what you see, and then begin to rearrange it.

Which is why the medicalization of these drugs is such a double-edged sword. Drugs once considered by Timothy Leary and other trailblazers as tools to oppose unjust and oppressive systems are now becoming absorbed by the systems they once stood in opposition to.

As philosophy professor Olúfẹ́mi O. Táíwò writes in his book *Elite Capture*,[33] the history of capitalism and colonialism is largely a history of this kind of successful absorption. Building on the work of Frantz Fanon, Táíwò points to the liberation struggles of African countries living under European rule. When the colonists realized they could no longer use only violence to keep peoples under their control, they allowed for a form of controlled liberation in which the more direct and obvious violence of European imperialism was supplanted by the softer, bureaucratic violence of a multiracial managerial class that, while on paper more diverse, still kept populations in poverty and still dependent on the elite.

This same process can be seen the world over—in how the most radical demands of antiwar and civil rights protesters from the 1960s and '70s morphed into an ever-growing nonprofit-industrial complex; in how the often anticapitalist LGBTQ liberation struggles of the 1980s morphed into a narrowly focused fight for gay marriage and rainbow-branded consumerism. Fifty years ago, both of these movements were linked to anticapitalist struggles; they weren't just about acceptance or normalization, but about changing the oppressive systems under which we live.

Similarly, hallucinogens and other drugs were theorized to be part of a larger movement against oppression. Timothy Leary and Terence McKenna saw LSD and DMT (dimethyltryptamine) and psilocybin as a way to separate ourselves from the banal brutality of everyday life, to imagine a life beyond this. And antipsychiatry thinkers and organizers argued that the very way we see our own brains was constructed to support our own oppression, and fought to get people to rethink the way they viewed their minds, their "disorders," their very states of being.

This way of viewing the brain, and of viewing substances that can alter it, provided hope to countless people. As the poet Tao Lin wrote, "After McKenna, my alienation regained the earlier meaning, became shared and justified. Instead of a glum, demoralizing, indirectly satisfying sensation, alienation now seemed once again action-oriented and hope-filled and analysis-demanding. It indicated something about my relationship with society."

But now, what always happens, that process of absorption, is happening: Drugs, particularly hallucinogens and dissociatives, are becoming tools of adjustment rather than tools of liberatory alienation. As the scientific and medical establishments pushes for ketamine, mushrooms, and other drugs to be used as medicines, avenues of capitalization are opened—corporations step in. Drugs have become just another way to allow us to keep going.

| | | | |
| | | | |

I wanted to see this process of absorption into capitalism up close. I wanted to know what a future in which psychedelics and dissociatives were completely managed and dispensed by corporations was like. So I went to Miami.

On a humid night on a small and expensive island between the city proper and Miami Beach, about a hundred people—guys in overly tight colored khakis and denim and polo shirts and button-downs, girls in sparkly and bright party dresses—clamored to get inside a large, white house; security was slow. Inside the minimansion and around its pool, which overlooked Biscayne Bay, another hundred or so people milled about. The space was cavernous and dark. No one seemed to live there—only a few pieces of furniture were strewn about. I picked at a plate of sad-looking carrots and watery hummus (there was also guacamole and fettuccini Alfredo on offer) as the people around me talked about the big day, tomorrow, the first day of Wonderland, the "premier global event for psychedelics, mental health and longevity." Anything that said "Wonderland" on it also said "PRESENTED BY ALGERNON PHARMACEUTICALS."

The next day, the same sweaty people, plus a couple hundred more, rolled up to a conference center—a big box in a humungous parking lot in one of the city's "hip" neighborhoods. Algernon branding was everywhere. I'd later learn they are a "clinical-stage, Canadian drug development and repurposing company investigating drugs and naturally occurring compounds for unmet global medical needs."

Booths for dozens of psychedelic-inspired drug and supplement companies—Cubed Biotech ("crafting psychedelic betterment"), KGK Science, MycoLife ("where the world connects with a universe of adaptogens"), Woke Pharmaceuticals (yes, really)—lined the floors of the conference hall.

On two stages, panel after panel of researchers and execs from small pharmaceutical companies presented their findings, or pitched their products, or both. The first panel, on microdosing, began with an acknowledgment that the conference was being held on land stolen from Indigenous people, and that they were the true pioneers of the field of psychedelics. Then, three CEOs and a "transformational coach" spoke for an hour on how taking small doses of drugs could treat a host of mental health problems. Another panel, another land acknowledgment. Another panel.

It was fascinating to be in this space that, to the people around me, represented the future, when it so much felt like the mind-numbing present. Despite the words "revolutionary" and "breakthrough" being used over and over again, I felt as if this represented the worst possible outcome of the mainstreaming of drugs.

It, frankly, made me feel depressed—to see these things that had given me so much hope in the world, that changed my perspective so much, absorbed into this blandness. If this was the future, I wanted no part of it.

I'd planned to stay for two days, but by the time the "MDMA-Assisted Therapy for PTSD: Blazing the Path Toward Patient Access, Insurance Coverage, and Mass Mental Health" panel came up, I couldn't take it anymore. I left. I ate a burrito down the road and felt angry.

I spent the next day wandering around Miami, searching for something redeeming in this voyage. The more I walked, the more despondent I got. Yes, the conference was strange and in many ways bleak. But I couldn't stop thinking that maybe these people were right—not that drugs should be manufactured and distributed by strange corporations who convene in Miami, but that drugs were just medications like any other.

I'd spent the past year or so searching for a new experience, one that would give me the same kind of revelations I'd had on acid and ketamine during the depths of my hell years. Yes, those years were horrible, but that horribleness was the grounds for constant transformation. And now I wanted more. I wanted to feel like there wasn't an endpoint, that the revelations would keep coming, that the future wouldn't be so similar to the rest of life. I wanted to believe that my experimentation with drugs would lead me somewhere new. Not only healed, but reborn.

But as I walked across the city, down this bridge linking two islands, I took stock of my life and realized that I really was just back at normalcy. My years of hell did not change the world. I did not envision a new existence. I got better. I healed, largely back into the same shape I'd begun in. Healthier, for sure—fewer boxes in my brain, fewer monsters and fires in the corners. And definitely different, a little more confident in who I am, more willing to stake my claim to an identity regardless of whether people understand. And there is, for sure, a miracle in that. But I wanted all I'd been through, all the holes I'd fallen down, to lead me somewhere with a beauty I could only through struggle have come to understand. I wanted my pain to have meaning.

But as the sidewalkless streets of Miami; and the SUVs; and the ugly glass buildings filled with rich people, buildings that were sure to collapse into the ocean in the next few decades thanks to global warming; and the invasive lizards everywhere (cute but not great for the environment, and a sign of government neglect); and the old guys with potbellies and ugly, white hats, and ugly, white soul patches and impossibly hot wives on their arms, kept reminding me: The world, the world, it was still the world. And all the drugs I'd taken, my entire journey, had done nothing to change that.

8

SEARCHING FOR COLLECTIVE BREAKTHROUGH

TRYING TO FIND COMMUNAL FREEDOM;
THE RAVE AS COLLECTIVE EXPERIMENTATION;
THE LIMITS OF DRUGS IN OUR LIBERATION

To break open, to spill all that's boxed up out onto the floor and sort through it with every tool you have at your disposal—drugs, therapists, bodywork—over six excruciating years was hard enough. It was made harder by what I'd discovered afterward: that no matter how much you awaken to yourself and the world, no matter how much you change your brain, the rest of the world still, in many ways, sucks.

After Miami, this feeling weighed on me. That this couldn't be it. It terrified me to think that my reward for the hardest years of my life was to be back where I was before Charlottesville—stable, fine, the end. I wanted more.

Which is how I ended up high out of my mind on ketamine and mephedrone in a dark room in Brooklyn, shoved up against hundreds of other sweaty people, my ears so close to a gargantuan set of speakers that were so loud, so so loud; loud enough and the music fast enough to cause intense and uncomfortable vibrations through my whole body, which in turn made me feel like my brain would, just maybe, at any moment, explode.

To rave, I'd been told, was to give in to something larger than yourself; to give in to an experience of communality and blissful oneness; to let go of your individual brain and become a small part of a much larger one, one heaving back and forth and to and fro at 120 or 128 or 140 or however many beats per minute.

To accomplish this mind melding you do not have to be on drugs, but it sure helps. The ketamine detaching you from yourself, the GHB or molly or mephedrone attracting you to other bodies like proton to electron until you are each integral parts of one atom. The speed or coke keeping you there and buzzing through the night so that the neon or whatever element you have collectively formed does not go dark too soon. If one of you leaves, the whole thing changes, but it is still a whole, just a different whole, plutonium to neptunium.

There are many places where we get high together—people using heroin on the streets of Vancouver, tech execs in the forests of Peru attempting to right their minds with ancient-culture-inspired ayahuasca ceremonies, a college classroom where everyone is on Adderall or SSRIs or both; bars and alcohol, of course.

But the rave is where that collective usage inspires long essays and books about the politics of partying, about what it means to leave normative society in search of a larger and more radical *something*.

It turned out that I did not have to go very far to find that something, because that something had already found me. It was closing in on me from all sides—a new techno warehouse to the north of my New York City apartment; a friend and then another one and then another one who'd meet me for dinner with bloodshot and deep-purple-bagged eyes and a white tank top and some sunglasses on, apologizing because they hadn't been to bed yet. The rave was taking over New York's queer scene. Absorbing us all not by force but with a promise of meaning and community and that ever-elusive *something more*—perhaps an escape from the sky of New York one summer when it was tinged with a deep orange from massive wildfires hundreds of miles away; perhaps an answer to the ennui so many of my friends felt from working forty or fifty or sixty hours a week only to expend half or more of what they earned on rent; perhaps a solution to loneliness and sexlessness faced by so many young people today. All you had to do was put on a stupid little outfit, and pay a few dozen dollars, and all of that could be yours.

The psychologist Erich Fromm wrote eloquently of becoming "nothing but the drop of water on the crest of a wave" of humanity. He argued that in order to do that, you needed to both become yourself fully, and open yourself up to the experience of others:

"To be open is the condition to enable me to become filled with him, to become soaked with him, as it were; but I need to be I, otherwise how could I be open," he wrote.[1]

Beyond seeming incredibly horny, this also seemed undoubtedly true: that in order for me to understand my fellow man, I needed to also understand myself as much as possible. And I'd felt that I'd accomplished the latter—self-actualization and all that. I'd been in therapy for six years; I'd done enough mind-altering substances to kill a horse, or at least make him really high. But I still felt confused about my fellow man—about how we all collectively go through this ever-oppressive life, and how we can make that ever-oppressive life easier, if we do it together.

The rave, to me, was the clearest representation of Fromm's cresting wave.

"By entering into this space, you are agreeing to enter into struggle against this system," the writer Hannah Baer said of raves. "Even as you give us money, even as you strive for power and acceptance under these structures, you agree to nurture the seed of liberated reality that exists in your imagination and has a germ of possibility in every moment, you agree to cleave to this specter even as you grapple with the reality of contamination, harm, limitation, fracture. You want to get free and you want everyone else to get free, and for better or for worse, that is why you came here tonight."[2]

There are plenty of forms of community in this life. Church. Sports. Reading groups. Activist meetings. I'd tried a few of those. And they'd helped. But, with the exception of the more fundamentalist elements of church, which I did not have much interest in joining, none promised the ecstasy, the release, the transformation into a living collective that the rave did. I'd gotten really into tennis a few years prior, and while it really did make me feel better about myself and my life, no one claimed it was the vanguard, the way to envision a different world.

But then again, most people playing tennis or joining knitting circles or talking politics aren't on multiple hard drugs at a time and sleepless for thirty-six or forty-eight or seventy-two hours straight, so perhaps they've just seen things more clearly.

From everyone who is anyone in the scene, I am told there is one person I should meet if I want to be a drop on the crest of a wave, because she embodies that duality—individual and community, a central, integral part of a larger whole.

I meet Alaska at a house in Bushwick, which has become the kind of center of the New York rave universe, on a Friday night. An actual house, not an apartment. Two floors, an L-shaped couch and glass coffee table and huge speakers below a huge television. Alaska's friend lives here alone. He's gay. A production designer or something that makes him a lot of money. He gives the trans girls, the dolls as they're called, lots of free drugs (though that's not why Alaska is friends with him).

Alaska is running late. It's eleven p.m. Which is early.

She shows up in a car, three other gorgeous trans women behind her. Grand entrance. I sit on a couch. Someone puts rap on. Nicki Minaj, Cardi B—"MotorSport." I drink an espresso martini, which is delicious (thank you to our gracious host, the gay guy). There's Halloween candy on the table. It's spring now. We talk about how much we all love Reese's Pieces. No one eats the candy, except for me. Our host complains that no one here eats, which is ruining his plan for a birthday dinner. People laugh.

Then he whips out a gold, sandwich-bag-size bag filled with a white powder. Ketamine. He buys an ounce at a time. Which is a lot.

The bag goes around the group and each of the dolls takes a small, metal spoon, takes a little scoop, and delicately insufflates it up their nose. Alaska does a little dance as she snorts, her curly, long black hair bouncing along; her body in her skintight gray dress and chunky, heeled boots which go up to her knees, vibing to the beat.

More people arrive, including a DJ who's playing later tonight.

People talk about an upcoming party for a big fashion label. Alaska does some modeling. A lot of her friends work in fashion too.

"I need to shake down some twink for some Adderall," someone says.

More laughter.

A few people take a bit of coke.

I take a bit of coke and ketamine too. Just a small amount. The combo, in these circles, is called Calvin Klein. Ketamine alone is called "kundle," and coke alone is called "bundle."

Alaska is looking at her phone. So is everyone else. She's taking a video selfie and singing along to the music. The ketamine goes around again. Alaska does a few bumps in a row and winces at the burn. She has a bit of the powder between her nostrils now. Actually, basically everyone does. I realize I do too.

A few minutes pass, and people are really bouncing around now. Alaska sits down next to me and starts talking about her journey with ketamine. She's glad I'm here because, while she talks a lot about this stuff with other people in the scene, she doesn't get the opportunity to talk to someone a bit outside of it, like me. Plus, she says, she likes the sound of her own voice.

"I have a different reaction to ketamine than most people," Alaska tells me. "It's not a stimulant, but it stimulates me. I don't know if it's just because it's fun. But it puts me in my zone. With coke, I'm just anticipating the comedown. With ketamine, I can go as long and as hard as I want."

It surprises me to learn Alaska is twenty-three years old, and moved here only a few years ago, because she exudes a confident balance of personality I usually only see in people who've been here for much longer—knowing when to be loud, when to be soft, when to be sexy, when to back off.

To her, the rave, the drugs, they're all part of that—learning to be a full person. Learning to grow up, move on from a past she's often been reluctant to talk about.

"Ketamine's been really healing and I don't feel shame in saying that," she says over the loud music. "Does this mean it's an addiction? Is addiction immoral? I'm still working though all that. But my general answer is no. . . . If I'm maintaining agency over my life, if I'm staying grounded spiritually and materially, then I don't have to punish myself for liking it. It's shamanic down."

"Down" as in . . . it just kind of means you're emphasizing something, but more than that. Like, you're wearing a hot outfit, so that outfit is cunt down. "Cunt" as in hot. "Down" as in very. "Kundle" as in K. "Doll" as in a hot trans woman. Trans girl slang, which is also raver slang, which is also Black slang. They all swirl together here into something confusing to outsiders, which, I think, is part of the point—not everyone is meant to be here, not everyone is invited to the party.

More bumps, and then it's time to go—the DJ sets are about to start. The venue, not one of the girls' favorites but the one where their friends are getting paid to play tonight, is down the block. Next to a bunch of other ones. An infamous corner of chaos, where thousands of people just like us, coming from hundreds of apartments and houses in the surrounding neighborhoods, the pregame spots, meet up each weekend.

We file out the door around midnight. Someone's phone blares a CNN news alert about a mass shooting in some faraway state. Someone else says to not talk about it. It's a buzzkill. I think everyone hears anyway.

The club is two floors and, by New York standards, cavernous and immediately extremely loud as soon as you walk in. Colorful lights shoot down from the ceiling and smoke up from the floor and music from all sides. A bar greets you when you walk in, but few people ever walk up to it—most people are on enough drugs already. Security circulates to make sure no one is doing drugs, or, really, that no one is doing drugs extremely obviously, so that if the cops come they have plausible deniability.

This eve, the top floor is very straight. Lots of guys in button-downs awkwardly sipping beers and the kind of canned techno you'd hear in a movie scene in a techno club. Downstairs is where Alaska goes, where the dolls go. Where the kids who know go. The ceilings are low here and it's smoky and darker—to the point you can barely see in front of you. Within a few minutes, Alaska and her friends are already surrounding the DJ booth, shaking their asses against it, like they've practiced this before. They pull out their phones and record and tag the DJ on Instagram. It's a show of support for a friend.

We're here early, but soon twenty people becomes forty, and then forty becomes a hundred, and then the small basement space is packed with maybe three hundred people.

I do a little more K discreetly.

The DJ, Alaska's friend, is good. One of the best I've heard.

He's mixing so many different things at once—bounce music from New Orleans slowed way the fuck down, trap from Atlanta sped way the fuck up, pop from wherever, some kind of prayer music or something. It builds and builds and builds, like a sandcastle in fast-forward; then a wave of sound comes crashing down over it until all is flat again. Sparse.

A few more minutes pass and something else is being built now. An industrial beat so heavy it makes your stomach rumble. More drums. Then a sample: "If it wasn't for you, I'd be alone." Over and over again. "If it wasn't for you, I'd be alone. If it wasn't for you, I'd be alone."

Sped up and up, higher- and higher-pitched. The combination of the deep bass in my stomach and the overspeed lyrics bashing my brain makes me feel like I am a potato being mashed. I am quickly losing form. It's a bit scary. Destabilizing. Where did my shape go?

And then The Thing happens. I've experienced it many times before. But it feels equally novel each time: a combination of drugs and sounds and bodies against me until I no longer feel myself in the best way possible. I feel part of something larger. The wave. Maybe the best thing to call it would be transcendence. I feel empty. My brain has become a balloon, and thus there is no space for thoughts. There is no space for anything except me and us in that moment. My movements become looser, they feel automatic. I feel automatic.

And every time this happens, I start to get it. The pull to all this. Because this feels fucking great. To be with all these people, who are no longer really people in the sense of people with jobs and names, but just like, friendly bodies, drops coalescing, becoming something together, mushing together, fusing into an unthinking body of vibes. A shortcut to zen.

And then, whoa, I realize. This is where I was nearly six years ago. Six nights before my mental breakdown. Doing those pea-size bumps of cocaine and dancing with a friend. In this exact same space, which back then had a different name. Ah! Weird thought. I try to reconcentrate, or, rather, re-un-concentrate—to become part of the larger thing again. But the thoughts keep coming back. Maybe I feel as happy now as I did then, all those years ago, I realize. Which scares me, takes me out of it. I start, I guess, going on a minispiral, wondering why it took me six years to get back here, to the starting point. Six years of work to return to baseline. I want to get back to zen. But it's fading.

Alaska and her friends are really into the music now, thrashing around, jumping. They're experts at maintaining the chaotic zen; I still need to build my skills up. And that lack of practice eventually gets to me—I can't keep up. I keep snapping back. To my head. To my thoughts. I do more ketamine. It doesn't work. The wave has crashed. It's over. Maybe it's not; maybe I can will myself to get to where Alaska is. But I feel defeated. I want to be back there, in that state, with all of them, but I can't figure out the path back. So I want to leave.

But Alaska, she's not done. She's not ready to leave at all.

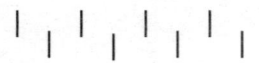

| ' | ' | ' | ' |

Alaska was adopted when she was three. She lived in a group home, the parents Southern Baptists, very religious. The home in Bonifay, Florida, which is not the Florida you're thinking of, with, like, beaches—it's one of the panhandle towns, of tiny and isolated and economically depressed communities; of deeply conservative Christians and the trans girls trying to run away from them. The mom homeschooled all the kids. There were always new kids too—kids coming in and out. Alaska was both completely surrounded by people and completely isolated. She hated it.

And then, at age twelve, Alaska was put into a privately run housing program with very little oversight, a home similar to a "troubled teen" home. In Palatka. Another small town, but thankfully not quite as small. The program was even more Christian, even more conservative. She hated it even more.

As soon as she was eighteen, she broke free.

"At eighteen I had the legal standing to reclaim my agency over the way I live and the way I identify and what I believe about the world and myself," Alaska told me. "So I took that opportunity as soon as it presented itself. I didn't really have it in me to not take that chance for myself."

She bounced around. To a secret boyfriend's house. To the house of the parents of a friend she'd only known online, in Stillwater, Oklahoma. To Saint Augustine, about forty-five minutes away from where she grew up, with some friends.

She began drinking and doing drugs—mostly MDMA and coke. Sometimes too much of it, her serotonin "shooting up and down constantly." And she began transitioning, becoming the woman she always wanted to be.

"Being on my own allowed me to realize who I was and actualize the version of myself that I am now," she said. "But socially and materially, it was just a very, very stale part of my life."

In 2020, when Covid hit, Alaska felt her life was in chaos. The world was locked down. But people were rebelling against state violence. Protests growing and growing. And Alaska joined them. At a protest in Jacksonville, a bigger city about an hour away, the cops cracked down. Alaska was arrested with twenty other people. And during her arrest, after she mentioned she was trans and didn't want to be jailed with men, she was sexually assaulted by a cop.

A few days later, when she was released, she found out she'd lost her job. She broadcast her story on Twitter. It went viral. A lawyer reached out and wanted to represent her, pro bono. Alaska wanted to sue, wanted justice for what was done to her.

But as that was all happening, a representative from IMG, one of the largest modeling agencies in the world, reached out to her via TikTok. She'd been scouted. It was her only chance. She sold her car, found an Airbnb in New York and, with $500 to her name, left Florida for good.

"It was just about getting here," she said. "I had been telling my parents since I was eight that I wanted to live here. I didn't know why. But I was willing to do pretty much whatever it took. Because I knew once I was here it would be clear why I was here. I knew things would fall into place, and they have so far."

When Alaska arrived in the city she didn't know where to begin. But just a few days after moving, someone DM'd her on Instagram and told her to come to a party with her. It was the Covid era—the clubs weren't open, so people partied illegally in lofts, on rooftops, under bridges, in parking lots.

"It was really invigorating at first," she said. "I didn't have anything else to do but party. No one did. And you could feel this energy in the air. People wanted to carry [a word that means, basically, party hard], and take it as far as they could. The feeling that we weren't supposed to be doing it. It was so exciting for a twenty-year-old little me who had never done that before. . . . I never really knew nightlife was a pillar of this culture. I didn't know it was its own living and breathing thing. It felt really rebellious."

I remember those Covid raves. I'd just moved back to New York and, at the time, felt relatively cautious about Covid—I was scared of being sick, and thus scared of other humans. But slowly, New York whittled me down. Most people here did not seem to care—they partied through the early days of the pandemic as TV stations and politicians told everyone to stay indoors. And people called it reckless, because, in many ways, it was. But what I kept hearing was that it also kept people alive. Queer people, often isolated from family and ostracized by the rest of society, needed those connections. They needed a respite from low-wage work and tiny apartments shared with however many roommates. For so many queers, me included, going out in whatever form was integral to our development. It's where I could be seen, where I could prove myself and my identity and have it validated back at me and find friends and release stress and just take a fucking break from the ever-present stressfulness of being queer and trans. So, reckless or not, I understood why people went. There was indeed something invigorating about being under a bridge in industrial Brooklyn while everyone else was home. It did feel rebellious. I do not know if it was necessary, for me personally, in an I-will-die-if-I-don't-do-this sense. But I do know that once I broke the seal, it was hard to go back.

But, I think, for many people, it really is that necessary. That's what they mean by community and transcendence—they are transcending an extremely isolating and hard life. Over the past ten years, the average American has become more and more lonely—the hours we spend alone rising by nearly ten per week.[3] Covid exacerbated this trend, but it did not start it. So while I acknowledge that raving and clubbing and any form of social interaction carries risk, I think so too does isolation—the risk of depression, drug addiction, a death of despair. And doubly so if you're trans or queer.

But that radical-feeling closeness born out of the pandemic has receded now. Raves still exist within capitalism, with all its inequalities and clout-chasing incentives and all the rest. The scene is different now. People have dispersed back into their corners, back into their cliques, to a certain degree. The clubs and their owners have taken back over and remonetized everything. But the scene in New York is also bigger than ever—more clubs, more parties, more people—and Alaska still stands at the center of it.

At first, it was mostly a weekend thing, like one night a week, pure escapism—a respite from the stress of a new city, a new identity, a new life. But within a year or two, it had become much more. Raves filled with queer and trans people in Brooklyn and Queens (and occasionally Manhattan) were where Alaska found community and support, where she made friends, where she learned to express herself. It became a form of therapy too. And drugs, especially ketamine, became integral to all of it.

"The community I've found in the scene is what keeps me in it," Alaska said. "I could exist in that community without drugs. But I don't think there's a reason for the scene to exist without drugs. I don't know if it could."

Alaska does ketamine several times a week. And she goes out several times a week, often staying out for twenty-four or forty-eight hours straight. She used to feel like her life was chaotic because of this, but she's grown into it, and grown to not care about the judgment others might have over the kind of life she leads.

"Most, or almost all of my social life, exists at night," she said. "Outside of social media and my few really close friendships with my roommates, or a few other close friends who I see throughout the day, ninety percent of my social life exists at night. And I think that that sort of is, like, one of the biggest points of difference: there can be twenty or thirty of us at the club, people I would call my friends, at the same event. It's community for us. Not just entertainment. I spend so much time with them. At the party, at the afters [which is what people call the after-parties that go long into the day, after the clubs have closed, usually at people's apartments]. There's such a stark difference between the way we interact with each other and ingest the experience, versus the energy you can feel from people who only go out on a Friday."

And that's the key difference between this and a knitting circle or bowling league or a church—for a certain group of people, this *is* church. Because there is no other space where people like Alaska feel equally at home; the only place they can feel within their own bodies and not pressured to conform to the straight world, and simultaneously the only place where they do not have to think of their bodies and minds at all. I get this, even if I'm less involved in the scene. I get needing a space where you can feel yourself and feel surrounded by people who are more like you than not. And I get how rare that is, especially for queer people, for trans people, for so many other marginalized groups.

The drugs aren't a requirement for that, but they certainly help. In the same way a club provides external space in which you get to finally let go, drugs can provide an internal one—enough breathing room in your brain to leave all the other shit behind, at least for a moment.

The drugs help Alaska open up, process, be present on the dance floor and at the after-parties. Pretty much everyone she knows feels the same. Drugs are different here than they were back home in Florida. They're just a fact of life. They're always there, or a phone call and thirty minutes away.

This—the clubs, the drugs, the community—is her life.

Which doesn't mean Alaska doesn't care about the world outside the rave. She talks to her friends about injustice, about cops, about gentrification and worrying whether she's part of it—wanting to make sure she's giving the city as much as she gains from it. But she has a different perception of what's important now, what community even means.

"After my arrest, the people who surrounded me, it just felt more political than personal," she said. "So I feel like since then, seeing how Black people and women and trans people, seeing how, post what liberals called a revolutionary moment, how much harm has still been caused since then, how much Western liberalism or even leftism or whatever you want to call it only served as talking points as opposed to material change. My experience is that me and my friends take care of each other. Dolls looking out for dolls. Gays looking out for gays. It's mutual aid because we are friends, not because we're motivated by guilt. It's material experiences I can see happening and am invested in in my world, that I can see and touch, that's not just online. It's reworked my understanding of what it means to fight for people."

Alaska used to feel guilty if she wasn't posting infographics and going to protests and making it known that she cared with a capital *C*. She's working to not feel that guilt anymore, because she says she's found a more meaningful politics, a more meaningful life, in what she does now.

"I don't like being too connected to something that I can't actually feel," she told me. "It's hard to have that conversation because there's so much guilt-tripping if you're not participating in the machine. But that just doesn't make sense to me anymore."

Alaska, and many others in this scene, are not radicals, but in a world of isolation and desperation, it's an important question they must ask themselves: What helps the world more—signaling your support for a cause, or being a part of something, anything, larger?

As Huw Lemmey, who specializes in queer history, argues, there has never been a clear line between activism and joy in queer spaces. Pride parades have been protests. Bars have been sites of organizing and activism.[4] And in a world that actively discourages community, that incentivizes connection only in the form of cisgender, heterosexual nuclear family units, the very act of coming together across genders and sexualities might be a necessary corrective.

After the first club, Alaska takes a car to another, kind of the main club that everyone likes. The one that's considered cool. The spot to be. It's usually pure chaos, which is what people like about it. Tonight, a friend has hidden Easter eggs filled with ketamine around the space, which Alaska thinks is cute.

She stays there until sunrise on Saturday, and then goes to an afters at someone's apartment in Williamsburg. She stays there until the evening, then goes and sees a play her friend is starring in. Then back to the same afters until six the next morning. Alaska goes home, goes to bed for a few hours, and wakes up to friends texting her telling her to come to a different afters, one for a party that started on Saturday night. She takes a cab to Greenpoint. All her main friends are there. In the evening, they go see a friend of a friend play a concert at a venue in Manhattan. Then from there go back to Brooklyn, back to that chaos intersection in Bushwick, just down the street from where the night (or really, two nights prior) had begun. A friend is playing a set there. And then, finally, at around four in the morning on Monday, Alaska and her friends end up at their friend Z's house. He's a fashion stylist and a DJ and well known in the scene.

"I wasn't super high," Alaska says. "But I'd been doing drugs for an extended period of time."

She is on GHB, mephedrone, and a little bit of ketamine. "A nice little cocktail."

She's in a back room with her friends, and they get to talking, and somehow Alaska's childhood comes up. And it turns into something she hasn't experienced before—a depth of feeling and sharing about what she went through she never reached.

"It was such a shift in the way I was able to humanize my experience," she tells me. "Before then, I had always had parts that I had held on to for myself. To be able to be in a space where I felt safe, where everyone was listening intently—not listening because they had to but because they wanted to—and to have that extra little push from the drugs to loosen up and feel things as intensely as I wanted to or needed to."

That was healing, she said.

"And to just have all those environmental factors create a material space that I've wanted for so long—for so long I've wanted to put this out into the world and for the first time I'm able to do that and be so intimate, and for it to be so well received."

In some ways, I envied Alaska and people like her. She has been able to throw herself into something so completely that she becomes part of it, and it part of her. I'd never been able to do that before. I'd processed my traumas in therapy (somatic and psychoanalytic), I'd done yoga and acupuncture and all the rest to reset my nervous system. And I'd done plenty of drugs—Klonopin and ketamine and LSD and cocaine and 2C-B. But it rarely felt collective or communal—which it seemed to me is what Alaska found so beautiful about rave culture. You weren't healing alone.

Yet after my nights out with Alaska, I kept wondering what I was missing—was it my fault that I couldn't fully integrate into this culture? I wondered if I was too tightly wound to fully give in, to become one drop on the crest of the wave over and over again.

So I kept going out. I kept finding myself at clubs at four or five or six or seven a.m., trying to find some religious ecstasy. And I'd sometimes feel bits of it. Straggling home on shrooms one night, right before the sun came up, the sky a dark, dark blue, my neighborhood looking like some kind of mythical forest, feeling the beauty of the whole world, even the beauty of Bushwick.

But then I'd wake up, and life would be back to what life always was. I still did the same things each day when I wasn't raving—I wrote and I watched movies and I saw friends. Going out, doing drugs, searching for revelation. At a certain point, I began to wonder if that was a kind of addiction. Not the drugs, but the need for something more—a greater meaning or purpose—as if that would somehow change the circumstances of my life.

The rave, according to some, began as a method of resistance. Specifically Black resistance. A form of, as the Black culture theorist DeForrest Brown Jr. writes, "sonic world-building and coded information exchange born out of a centuries-long lineage of African American struggle and insurrection."[5] In Detroit and Chicago and other predominantly Black cities, people developed sounds and spaces that allowed for exploration beyond the life prescribed by white mainstream culture.

Rave spaces made for and by Black people are about "forcefully taking up physical and sonic space with our imaginations," the artist Kumi James, aka BAE BAE, writes. "It is an act of collectively refusing the world and making new realities. Our space argues that we can constitute new material and imaginative realities, even if it's for six hours in the middle of the night."[6]

Of course, since then, as Brown Jr. writes, it's become something much different from that: commodified, made safer for white audiences, profited off of by people in Berlin and New York and elsewhere, while the Black originators of techno and house get left with little credit.

"Today's raves are hardly a situation that prefigures utopia," the theorist McKenzie Wark writes. "They cannot prefigure futures when there may not be any."

Yet, for some, despite its gentrification, despite its bastardization, the rave represents all hope, all community, all that's good with the world. For Wark, who is trans, it's one of the only places she can feel free of the burdens of the world that surrounds it.

"A good rave, on a good night—that is where I can feel like my body is not an anomaly, or rather: not the *only* anomaly," she writes. "It's a distribution of anomalies without a norm, anomalous only to each other."[7]

Few claim the rave, at least as it's configured today, is inherently revolutionary. But, to many, it's a space where we can at least imagine a world different from our own, even if we have to work to pay rent and feed ourselves once we leave the club. And the club still requires labor, often underpaid labor—of bartenders and cleaners and security guards and DJs. But often there isn't a hard line between these groups. The DJs are also partiers; and it's a trope that every raver eventually becomes a DJ. But it's a good reminder, when you see a bored security guard wandering around, or a bartender sweating and wearing a mask to protect themselves from Covid, that sometimes, participating in the fantasy of creating a new and better world is only available to those who have the time and space and energy to do so.

Yet I cannot cynically dismiss what happens in these spaces. They do, often, feel like the start of *something*. Not revolution, but a sliver of an opening toward a less sexually and mentally and socially repressed world.

In Freud's view, each and every society required a form of repression—of our sexual drives, of our violent fantasies—if it was to function. To Freud, this meant humans had to sublimate, or redirect, those drives, into forms of release—art, writing, dance, whatever. And for some of us, that need of sublimation is greater. For those who carry the burden of oppression—whether because of race or gender or sexuality—the need for a space to transform not only one's own desires, but the demands of others placed on our psyches every day, having spaces in which we can get the lead out is a matter of life and death. The psychic weight of normal life is too great to bear without these outlets.

And, if we can create space within these outlets, space to imagine and feel free and feel unburdened, it feels possible we can take that and run with it.

That, I think, feels like the radical potential of the club, and of drugs writ large—once you know that normal life is not all there is, once you know that there is something better, you start to become enamored with that feeling. You push for more of it, because the rest of life feels dreadful in comparison.

"Whoever publicly insists on her or his own fantasy opens this path for the world entire," the theorist Todd McGowan writes. "It is through fantasy that one sees the possibility of the impossible."[8]

It echoes what Gilles Deleuze and Félix Guattari said about fantasy—that in a world of repression, every desire, no matter how small, is "capable of calling into question the established order of a society."[9]

To give in to our desires. To allow our imaginations to flourish. That is the point; that is the promise. It's very easy to feel one has no space for desire of their own these days. Our lives filled with carrying out the desire of others—to be productive, to remain isolated and autonomous from one another, to remain grounded in a boring and staid reality. The rave is not a protest or a riot. But like a protest or riot it creates a space where desires usually shunned by polite society can flourish. And, perhaps, that can be built on.

"In a little microcosmic way it feels transcendent," one raver friend named Vince told me. "When you're in the back rooms at a club and fully closed off from the outside world, where time is completely fungible, where you can pack a bunch of people in and do a bunch of drugs, and completely forget what life is for forty minutes, and then have this insane, fun conversation that has nothing to do with work or jobs or capital. It feels very free."

I've been there too. In those spaces that feel like, Wow, what if the world could always be like this? What if life was always about feeling good, or at least relaxed—surrounded by friends and community, not tied to a desk or a register? And that's a feeling that being administered ketamine or MDMA or shrooms in a doctor's office cannot replicate—because the point is not only the drugs, but the fantasy they help enable.

But so often after that, after that feeling, there is a crash. Because the feeling is so temporary, the spaces so temporary. We push, we desire more, we fight for more space and more time in which we can desire more. We use drugs to access those spaces. But then, the sun comes up.

In that way, going to raves reminded me of Charlottesville, or any other protest—of course very different in their stated, material purposes, but perhaps similar in their interior, emotional ones. What attracted me to activism before Charlottesville wasn't just the idea that I could help change the world, but the idea that there were other people like me, people who felt the world was bad enough to warrant action. It felt freeing and healing to be surrounded by others like me. Marching down the streets, running from the cops—it was, in a way, a high. It felt, much as doing ketamine at three a.m. does, like a peek, a small opening into something greater—a future world.

But then there is, as with any high, the comedown—not only after Charlottesville, but nearly every protest. So often pushing for a better world is met with violence. The obvious sort like police brutality and pushback from the Far Right; but also the less obvious emotional kind—the exhaustion that comes from doing the work, the alienation one feels from living in a society in which most people have blinders on.

At protests, I've caught a glimpse into another world. And then it's over. And I feel worse than I did before. Cynicism develops. We become stuck. We start fighting for smaller and smaller things—not a better world, but better words to use, or a more correct identity to inhabit. In place of collective change, we accept personal change. What we fought for becomes a slogan on skincare products.

That, I think, is where we are now. Stuck, realizing there is something much deeper and greater and more fulfilling, but only able to make that fantasy a reality for brief periods, whether through collective action, or collective partying.

"Maybe the focus is smaller now," Vince said. "We don't really have a belief that we can change the world like the hippies did. So maybe the best thing we can do is change the outcome of our lives and our little communities."

As he waits for a world filled with less nihilism, the rave acts as a kind of stand-in. Giving Vince and others the sense that the world is bigger than what we've been conditioned to believe it to be.

That's what we go back for. That's why we do the drugs. That's a large part of the appeal—to feel temporarily more alive.

I ask Vince if afterward, after the party ends, or the drugs wear off, it feels disappointing—the crash of having transcended, and then reentering the world we consider real, the one with sunlight and jobs and such.

"It's hard," he says. "I used to feel horrible and guilty when the sun came up. Back when I was doing lots of coke and drinking . . . But if you go back, and do more of whatever the fuck you're doing, and you're high as shit, then you're out worshipping the sun coming up. So it's all a matter of perspective. And of having the right drugs."

| | | | |

The emotional whiplash of seeing the possibility of a better world and then realizing, over and over again, that that world is nowhere close to fruition, is enough to turn even true believers into cynics.

When I first meet Z, he is always around. I see him at a bar my friends frequent in Brooklyn, surrounded by little tweaker boys on mephedrone and speed who've been up for three days; the boys asking for a glass of water from the bartender to mix their GHB in, making sure to clarify a glass glass, because GHB melts plastic. Z is there when our mutual friend takes too much GHB and nearly faints. I console the friend in an alleyway and make sure he drinks water. Z is there at the afters with Alaska. He's there at the club the next weekend.

He's a fixture, but he's not like many other people here. He exudes calm and stability. He holds down several jobs. He DJs. He travels a lot. He's the eye in the center of the storm of wasted twinks and dolls whirring around the dance floor.

It took him a while to get to this place, to a place where the rave provides purpose, but where the real world still feels real and workable. For many others, that balance is ever elusive. They become addicted, if not to the drugs, then to the feeling of escape from mundanity. I see two friends in quick succession succumb to this: they start at the same place Z did, using the rave as a reprieve until it becomes the entire focus of their lives, their jobs and schooling and passions and many of their friendships falling to the wayside.

"People have told me that they're worried about me, or concerned for me," one person I know, a smart one who dropped out of a good school to move to New York and party, tells me one day. "I think I need to be more careful and remember who I am and take my time with things."

The next time I see them, their eyes are glazed over. They've been up for a few days. And they no longer want to talk to me about their experience. A few months after that, they post a handwritten poem on Instagram: "When you left home on that warm Tuesday night in July and knew you would never return did you know that you would never feel the feeling of home again, except in the place you choose to rest your head on any given night?"

This full absorption into the scene, this giving of one's life to it, never happened for Z.

He moved to New York from the South—Virginia, south side of Richmond. The most rural place possible, as he calls it. He needed to get away from the simple country life; he "always knew there was more."

Twelve years ago, when Z first moved here, there wasn't much of a rave scene to speak of. People would go to Berlin if they wanted to club. New York was still a cocaine and champagne city. No one had heard of GHB. But slowly, the culture started pouring over, taken in one drop at a time, and one bottle of GHB at a time, from the club heads returning from Europe. Z didn't know he wanted that scene. When he first got to New York, he went to drag events and a few sporadic parties.

But then things started building up.

A party called GHE20G0TH1K. A party called Fruits and

Vegetables. He remembers, around 2017, being in an industrial loft in Sunset Park, Brooklyn, on the waterfront, with a view of the Statue of Liberty out the window and feeling like this was the place for him. He began dancing more, DJing more, going out more. And doing ketamine more—he found it helped foster a feeling of togetherness.

"The drug supports something bigger," he says. "It helps this actual community; it's not just doing drugs for the sake of doing drugs, most of the time."

The drugs, the music, the dancing, all felt like therapy for Z. He'd dance into a trance, a meditative state. When he'd enter these spaces, things would bubble up from his subconscious—minor annoyances, childhood traumas, stress at the world.

"Afterward, I sometimes don't know what was solved, but I know the experience was real, that something was processed in that moment," he says. "Even if I'm not so conscious of it now."

That's why he calls the music he plays "temple techno." To him, the club, at its best, is really a church. A place of collective processing and healing and transcendence.

"That is to me why, whether they're saying it or not, why people come back," he said. "Why else would you put your body and your mind through that? Staying up so late; the drugs. It's because we want to leave with something, it's because we are filled with something, or have let something go. I'm not going week after week because I want to find a dick or a person or whatever; it's because I want a word, in the same way somebody goes to their place of worship every week. I want to receive something. Some nourishment."

In 2017, when Z was in his early thirties, GHB started getting really popular. People like it because it loosens you up, makes you sexual, but without making you feel really high, unless you take too much. It's a controversial drug. Ravers often go too far with it. People "G out"—collapse on the dance floor and need to be taken to the hospital. One of my friends called it a "hungry drug"—it creates a need for itself; people end up going out just to do it, people end up surrounding themselves with people who do it and cutting out people who don't. Some DJs hate it. One DJ told me he feels like he now plays to crowds full of zombies. Z started seeing all of this happen.

"I've seen too much," he said. "People's lives turn. People convulsing and losing color in their face and thinking they're dying. Seeing death flash in their eyes. So I was like, maybe this isn't my thing, maybe the risks outweigh the benefits for me."

And then, a few years ago, someone did die. A friend of Z's. From an overdose of GHB.

"Out of respect for him, I don't do it," Z said. "A lot of people around me still do, and I see what it can open up for them, but I'm honoring him, so I choose not to. I'm learning from his life."

I never do G either for this reason. Because I've seen how far people take it. I see their lives change, bending to the will of the drug. And I see that this is hard for people within the scene to really acknowledge. Some clubs put up signs discouraging its use. But mostly people mourn the deaths and move on. I try not to be judgmental with drugs. But I'd be lying if I said G didn't worry me. It's understandable, relatable, to use drugs as an escape from the world, but a drug that creates a need for itself can end up becoming the point, rather than the tool. The line is always there, really with any drug, but especially with G, what you want from it is not an enabling of something larger that you can carry back into your non-high life—community, reprieve, understanding, solace—but simply the drug itself.

Deaths from GHB are relatively rare—there were seventy-four deaths from GHB between 2000 and 2019.[10] Most people who take too much simply get revived with a little speed, or some lemon water; or, if they're in a really bad state, one friend told me, an ice cube up the ass works. But it's changed the scene. It's changed my friends. It's changed Z's life too many times now.

To the point of the community he'd been in for over a decade cracking, fracturing, until, basically, he had to flee it.

| | | | | | | | |

At some point, rumors began spreading about Z. He'd had sex with a straight guy in Europe over the summer. To Z, the sex was consensual. But GHB was involved. The guy might have been too high. The guy, months later, decided he hadn't been into it.

A few months after the incident, a few other DJs began approaching clubs and telling them about the incident, and asking them to cancel Z's gigs. The clubs obliged. Z lost thousands of dollars in income. And he began to lose his community.

Z maintains he did nothing wrong, as do several other people I've spoken to with knowledge of the situation. But that's the thing with GHB in particular. I know of at least five people who've been accused of sexual impropriety when the drug was involved. What may have seemed chill in the moment, in the light of sobriety now feels different.

Z has attempted to repair his standing. Reaching out to clubs.

Reaching out to his accuser. Z is Black, his accuser is white and straight. He can't help but feel like that's part of what led to his shunning. He started feeling like people weren't listening to him. That they were too quick to believe anything and everything about him.

But it was more than that.

It was the scene writ large. It had changed. Z started seeing more friends G out, be crazier, stay up too long, lose the point of the experience—it was no longer temple for many, but just an excuse to get high.

I saw this too. At a certain point, friends started looking worse: pale, tired, joyless in the sunlight. They stopped doing other things—music, poetry, whatever; they were too busy raving or recovering.

"I feel like people don't realize how much they matter," Z told me. "If you knew the nobility inside of you . . . I don't know, maybe it would be different. There's this duality. Of this place where people feel like they've found themselves, they feel like they've found a safe haven. And then that develops into something unsafe. They've drifted past this place of intention."

Z started going out less. And he started having anxiety, sometimes panic attacks, when he did. Then, another friend died. Likely from GHB too.

So Z left.

He still technically lives in New York, but he's been spending most of his time in Berlin. Where the scene feels a little more open to him. And a little less dark—there's something that still feels more exciting there, less on death's edge.

Every time he's there, Z goes to a museum that houses the bust of Nefertiti, the ancient Egyptian queen. Z has worn a pendant of Nefertiti on his neck forever. In some way, the bust makes him feel like he's supposed to be there in Berlin. Kismet.

"It's in this kind of tall, round room," Z tells me. "She's the only thing in it. And she stands eyeball to eyeball with you."

Nefertiti, to Z, is what people are missing in their life—what makes them take it too far, what makes the scene get dark. The self-respect. The knowledge that you are, in your own way, a queen.

The last time he visited Nefertiti, a couple of friends in tow, he felt the statue opened something spiritual in him. The same kind of thing he can get from the rave, when the rave is at its best.

"It's opening that divine intimacy again," he said. "I was in the room for thirty minutes, just looking at her."

When he came to, he realized his friends had long ago left.

| | | | |

There are specks of time where, as Mark Fisher writes, you can see the current world is just as much of a fantasy as any fantasy of a better one we can conjure. That it is a "dreamwork that has forgotten it is a dream, and which seeks to make us forget too, by sweeping us up in its urgencies, by perplexing us with its lugubrious dementia, or by terrifying us with its sudden, unpredictable and insatiable violence."

Once you see this, once you see that reality is not stagnant; once you become conscious of the fact that for your entire life you have over and over again been unconsciously surrendering to the world as it has been envisioned for us, living life as you once did becomes much harder. Once the space has been opened, by ketamine, or acid, or the club, or whatever, so that you can see that there is another world, it's impossible to forget. Even if that other world feels so temporary, or far away, down a black hole that you've only reached the other side of once, with the tip of one finger, you want to keep trying. You want to keep going. The world as it stands today loses its point when you realize a better one is right down the street, or one snort or pill or dropper away.

So I keep going. I keep trying. I keep doing drugs. I keep going to raves.

On a sunny spring Sunday not too long ago, I prepare to head to a day rave. I take a microdose of acid in the morning to get me going. And then meet four of my friends for breakfast at a fancy pastry shop, which for them is a pit stop between the previous rave that ended a few hours ago and the one we're headed to now. Vince is there in a black tank top and leather pants and gas station sunglasses. After $15 egg sandwiches, we pile into Vince's old SUV and one of our friends blasts a technofied version of the Italian protest song "Bella Ciao," written in the late 1800s as an antiwork anthem and later remembered as an antifascist one. (I ask the friend who puts it on if he's aware of its history; no, he says, it's just a fun song that lots of people play these days.) My friends take out drinking glasses to dose GHB; I decline. Then they take out thick, black plastic cards made specifically to crush and snort mephedrone and speed and ketamine. I partake. We all get high, and then drive a few blocks, and then we arrive at about noon.

The industrial-but-gentrifying neighborhood is mostly empty—it's Sunday so the warehouse workers and mechanics and such aren't there, but it's too early for the newer residents to have gotten their days started.

But in the middle of one block, there's twenty people standing in the bright and hot sun, smoking cigarettes and doing bumps of K or coke or other substances I can't identify. One buff man is shaking . . . vibrating, his hands unable to keep still, presumably from a combination of drugs and a lack of sleep. My friends say their hellos to the outside group and then we walk inside the warehouse.

It's dark. Very dark. And the air is damp and filled with fog and vape smoke and the body odor of a few dozen dancers. The music is loud and pulsating. I spot a group of G'd-out twinks lying on a ratty couch at the back of the room. I see Alaska and her friends. I see former roommates, a girl from my high school. And, to my surprise, I see Lucas. The last time I saw him he was at death's door, nodding off from fentanyl. He comes up and hugs me. He's no longer on fentanyl, he tells me. He just completed a stay at rehab. He's totally sober. The only thing he's drinking at the rave is yerba maté, the caffeinated tea popular in South America and certain areas of Brooklyn.

Lucas tells me he got his life together after ODing and almost dying once more, saved again by Narcan. He got kicked out of his apartment. Then kicked out of a hotel. After that, he called up his parents and they brought him back home to Virginia. He got back on Suboxone. And then weaned off that. And then went to a rehab center in New Jersey. He and his boyfriend broke up. He, thankfully, kept his job. His life is surprisingly together, he says. And I'm very happy he's here. I'm very happy he's not dead. He seems happy too. Taking selfies with his rave friends. Cracking jokes. Dancing. Later he tells me he's in a really good place. And I believe him. And he tells me he's worried about some people in the scene. They're doing too many drugs; it's dark, he says. I tell him I agree.

I don't know exactly where the line is between drug use that feels fun, or even healing, and drug use that feels bleak. Maybe it's when drugs stop functioning as modulators of *other* things—party enhancers or perspective shifters—and become the thing in and of themselves. Getting high not to accentuate or shift, but to feel high. That line is different for everyone, and constantly shifting for me. In my darkest days, drugs felt like tools of survival. And then they became something else—a way to rewire my brain and rewrite my life. But now, at this rave, I'm not sure what function they serve anymore. In the moment they feel mostly like a way to keep me there—in that dim and dingy and sweaty space. I'm not sure I'd be there without them.

I hug Lucas again and then go find my friends to ask for another line of ketamine.

A friend of a friend cuts some lines on top of her phone. I do a tiny bump. Another friend offers me speed. I do another tiny bump. And then I go to the dance floor with two friends. It's not packed, which is nice. Everyone is in their own little world, rocking their hips and flailing their arms about in their small, personal bubbles. Someone I don't like is there, and I try to use them as a test, to see if I can stop caring what they, and thus what everyone else, thinks about me or how I'm dancing. To just live in the moment. I want to recapture that experience that faded so quickly the last time I went out. And it works. I lose inhibition.

I'm getting into the music. I feel loose. At this point, I feel a bit practiced. I can get into that state. The lobotomy. The zen. And I can stay there for a bit longer. Not as long as many people I know. But longer than I could a few months ago.

Alaska comes up to me. "It's the Lord's day!" she yells. She has a bit of a glassy-eyed stare. She's been up for a while. Then she adds that she's so fucking high. And then she disappears into the crowd.

I keep dancing. It's so hot. My makeup has melted off my face. It looks like I'm crying a purple tear, a friend tells me.

We dance more. *This state is nice*, I think. I push the questions I have about what the point of this all is—whether I'd be there without the drugs, whether this serves me in any way—to the back of my mind. We dance more. I grind and sweat on Vince, and he grinds and sweats on me.

After twenty or so minutes, I take a break from the dance floor to cool down and do another few bumps of K and speed in the back. And then back to the dance floor. Back and forth and back and forth until a few hours pass and I begin to feel tired.

I do a little bit of a mephedrone to get me back into it. The hand of the guy who gives it to me is shaking.

I vacillate between thinking that everyone here has figured out the solution to life, and feeling like I want to put every single one of them into rehab. *Shhh*, I tell myself, *just keep dancing. Keep getting into that state.*

Another hour passes.

I go outside to get some air.

Now about fifty ravers are out there, more people outside than in, smoking, vaping, wearing tiny black outfits that barely cover anything. The bouncer tells us to move down the block. The neighbors are complaining.

I go back in. I dance a bit more.

But that thing is starting to happen—the bubble bursting. I try to keep dancing, but my body is pushing back. My arms stop swaying; my legs perform a monotonous tap. I tell myself to get back into it. It's not working. I push my way through the dance floor and go to the back of the warehouse and ask a friend for more ketamine. I wait for my will to come back. But my head floating above me doesn't do much for me this time around. Yes, it's shifted my perspective, but I've seen this perspective before too. Many times. In New Orleans. In Philadelphia.

I go back to the dance floor and give it one more try. But the people around me are beginning to feel less like people, are more like a blob of energy—and not in the drop-on-the-crest-of-the-wave sense... but in a kind of... who-are-you-all sense.

A small jolt of panic hits me in my stomach and I leave.

The sun immediately quells the agitation. I put my head down so I don't have to say bye to anyone smoking and talking outside. And I begin my walk toward home. Past a bunch of trash. Past a family getting into a minivan. Past some young girls laughing at something. Past a group of cops doing nothing, looking at their phones. I stop at the deli a block away from my apartment and order a turkey sandwich with American cheese and lettuce and tomato and mayo and, while I wait, stare at the meats and cheeses and lettuce and tomato made cartoonishly colorful either by the bright blue illuminative power of the glass case's fluorescent lights, or by whatever amount of LSD is still in my system from that morning, or both. The store is crowded. Everyone there looks tired. I wonder what each has done with their Sunday and what each will do with the rest of it. I make my way to the back and grab a Diet Coke.

I thank the deli man and I slowly walk the remaining block to my building. The trees are swaying and vibrant and green.

I get home.

I put on a Mets game.

I eat the turkey sandwich. It's dry. But good.

The baseball game progresses. The LSD slowly wears off, though I don't know when. I don't really notice; I just see the colors on my TV gradually become slightly less vibrant.

The bubbly scratchiness of the soda feels good going down my throat.

The Mets win.

It's 7:23 p.m.

Through my window, the sun is setting. It's hazy and gray outside, though, so you can't really see it.

AFTERWORD

TOWARD A NEW, COLLECTIVE NARRATIVE

The world, I don't need to tell you, is bad. I write this on one of many 90-plus-degree days in New York City this summer, in what will likely be one of the hottest years ever recorded on earth, a record which will likely be broken again and again in the years that follow. I write this as the US helps wage violence against countless populations abroad, using our tax dollars for bombs while many of us struggle without health care. I write this as it seems much of the country has given up on the idea that capitalism works, that democracy works, that anything works. I write this as several of my friends recover in isolation from a virus politicians claimed to have gotten rid of years ago, as other friends struggle to leave the house because they're depressed, as others visit medical professional after medical professional attempting to get their mental health in order (and as others bide their time until they have enough money or sufficient insurance to start that process).

I go online to distract myself from these things and instead encounter thing after thing that reinforces them—articles blaming trans people for humanity's predicaments, pundits blaming the oppressed for their oppression, and, perhaps most depressingly of all, videos by normal people, teens in their bedrooms, millennials on their couch next to their cats, therapists in front of bookshelves, telling the camera, you, the viewer, all of us, that it's all in our heads—that the reasons we feel the way we do have nothing to do with the world and everything to do with our brains; that we are too ADHD or BPD or MDD to function in this world; that the solution to our woes is often chemical and always individual. That it is not the polluted water in which we swim making us ill; we just don't have the right wetsuit. Or gills.

It's like we're all looking for scapegoats because the real causes of our distress are too large, too complex, too scary to confront. It's easier to find the locus of control within ourselves than it is to imagine that we could ever find, much less disentangle, the roots of our distress. And the worse things get, it seems, the more we're willing to individualize our problems, to find the fault of capitalism in people rather than systems, to, essentially, go backward.

A year after I traveled to Vancouver to meet with harm reduction activists, police raided the offices of the Drug User Liberation Front. It had been just over twelve months since DULF had begun their experiment of handing out tested, pure, and affordable drugs on the Downtown Eastside. And things were going well. Vince Tao told me that the two founders of DULF, Eris Nyx and Jeremy Kalicum, had recently presented preliminary findings on their "compassion club": zero deaths, overdoses halved, better health outcomes.[1] And then, a few days later, police kicked down the doors of Eris's and Jeremy's apartments, confiscated their computers (along with, for some reason, Jeremy's grandmother's ashes), and charged them with drug trafficking. They were out of jail within a few days, but the duo still face a slew of charges.[2] They've also been banned from setting foot in the Downtown Eastside, despite the fact that Eris lives there.

The arrests, Tao said, while unexpected in their timing, were not exactly surprising, given how quicky the tides had turned against decriminalization across Canada and the United States. It only took a few months after DULF had opened its doors for politicians and the media to realize that railing against homeless people and drug users was an effective strategy to win the hearts and minds of Vancouver's public.

"Vancouver is a confluence of every single capitalist engine of misery, and that's leading people to die on the streets. And that makes people uncomfortable. Which they should be," Vince Tao told me. "So decriminalization became this floating signifier—it began to mean nothing and everything. Every single social ill could be blamed on it."

That strategy—blaming the increasingly obvious social misery of society and the drug use that misery causes on those most harmed by capitalism—has become de rigueur across much of North America, even in the most "progressive" of cities. In Philadelphia, a new wave of politicians brought with them an actively hostile approach to organizations like Prevention Point, where I'd watched volunteers and staff hand out syringes and medical supplies and Narcan and undoubtedly help save many lives in the process. In 2023, the city council passed a ban on any safe consumption sites, places where drug users can inject drugs under the supervision of medical professionals.[3] And then in 2024, Democrat Cherelle Parker became mayor of the city and promptly began a campaign to cut funding for syringe exchange programs.[4]

Across the country in Oregon, Democratic and Republican lawmakers declared decriminalization a failure and rolled back many of their lenient policies.[5] And in New York, Mayor Eric Adams took a tough-on-crime approach, attempting to arrest his way out of a homelessness crisis.

Part of the problem is that this has all been set up to fail: politicians took half measures (or, really, less-than-half measures), did not adequately fund rehabilitation or health programs, did not educate the public on harm reduction, and then declared harm reduction useless or dangerous after a few months or years.

But Vince Tao told me that the main issue is larger than local policy failures. It's that we're entering a new era, one in which capitalism's fatal flaws are becoming too obvious to ignore, even for the most privileged among us. So people are left with two options: either work to dismantle capitalism and build a brighter future—more housing, more health care, more compassion—or put the blinders up even higher and go further into denial, creating a false barrier between the people who are most visibly affected by increasing inequality and poverty, and those who can, at least for now, claim to be beneficiaries of the system.

Every mainstream narrative we have about drugs, Tao told me, ignores that *why*. That people are in pain, that capitalism has pushed physical and mental anguish into some bodies and minds more than others, but really and increasingly into everyone's body and mind, and that people are simply looking for relief.

"The entire system is falling apart," Tao said. "As that continues to happen, it's not gonna just be the homeless guy. It's gonna be everyone who slips through the ever-widening, disintegrating social net. It's gonna be all of us."

As I have reported in this book, that connecting thread became clearer to me. Whether a drug user on the street of Philadelphia or Vancouver, or someone in their own house like Lucas, or someone with relative privilege like Melissa or her brother or me, whether the drug of choice was fentanyl or SSRIs or Adderall, everyone seemed to be attempting to hold the increasingly frayed fabric of society together within their own psyches; as if we could patch up an external, systemic problem internally and individually.

Two years after meeting Melissa in Chicago, I called her again, and things were similar but different. She'd halved her Prozac dose and was feeling stable. Her baby and husband were doing well. But she'd moved back home, to the same town she grew up in in Wisconsin, right down the street from her parents.

"I have to grapple a lot with whether I'm giving in," she told me. "Shouldn't I be stronger? Am I smaller now because I moved back?"

But she believed she needed to—she needed to be somewhere she felt safe. Back in Chicago one day, she'd taken her son to a street fair and a vivid scene played out in her mind of him being shot in the head. She could see it as if it were real. It shook her.

In Wisconsin, on an acre of land on a dead-end street, she said she feels much more comfort, protected from the increasing chaos of the country.

"When we talk about the state of the world, we talk about how we're safe up here," she said. "In our house on the hill."

Yet there's still a lot to worry about. A few days before we last talked, a middle schooler brought a pellet rifle to school just twenty minutes from Melissa's house. Police shot and killed him when he refused to drop the gun.[6] Melissa told me she worries about what it'll be like to send her kid to school in America. She worries what will happen if he becomes an angsty teen like she was—will she be able to help him out more than her parents could help her? Will she even know why he's struggling? Her parents certainly didn't know why she and her brother did.

She tries to keep this all in check, if not for her sake then for the sake of her son. It's less that Melissa has cured her anxieties, and more that she's accepted them—accepted that in this world, anxiety is a given; that yes, sometimes it feels unbearable, but that it's just what one must deal with: take the Prozac, take the lorazepam to get to sleep when needed, go for a run, text your husband that you're having an urge to self-harm again, squeeze two ice cubes in your fists to feel a bit of pain. You can't get rid of the demons, but you can get them down to a manageable level. An ice cube level, instead of a razor blade level. And, Melissa said, she's begun to realize that maybe everyone is the same way.

"I'll never forget the first time I told my therapist that walking past knives freaks me out, because I'm worried I'm going to pick one up and hurt myself or stab someone," she said. "And my therapist said, 'Everyone thinks that; your brain isn't that special.'"

That—knowing it wasn't just her—somehow helped.

"I don't think I ever thought about knives like that again," she said.

That, in the end, is how I felt too—not healed, but comforted by the fact that no one is, that no one can be.

After years of using drugs in an attempt to heal from my traumas—to find stability, and then to find a new life—I sensed that, by and large, the tools had served their purpose. For years, I had wanted so badly to move beyond just healing—to not only be stable or capable of making it through the day without meltdowns; I wanted something more. I wanted my past pain to serve a future purpose and imbue my life with new meaning. It seemed unfair to go through so much only to end up back in the same place—a different person in some ways, but in the same world.

The drugs had helped me survive the darkest time in my life; they'd helped me envision a new life beyond trauma, they'd helped me reach deep into my brain and figure out whom I wanted to be—that I was trans, that I needed more community, that I needed to work through a lifetime of traumas large and small, that I needed to allow myself to care less about what other people thought of me. But they didn't fix much else—they didn't stop the world from being the world. I'd gone down the rabbit hole, and it turned out the other side looked a lot like the one I'd left behind.

Everywhere I looked, it appeared many others were looking for drugs to do something similar. Constant ads on social media promised healing through ketamine clinics. Article after article published about the promising new field of psilocybin- or MDMA-assisted therapy for veterans or cancer patients. Part of me felt glad that society was acknowledging that drugs, even until recently illegal ones, could help people heal. But I began to wonder if the same thing that happened with SSRIs, or benzos before them, or whatever the mental health wonder-drug-du-jour was in a given decade, was happening with these less traditional drugs: that we were asking too much from them; that we were putting false hope into the idea that this new crop of substances would finally be the one to do the trick, would finally be the thing that made us less depressed or anxious or traumatized. Red herrings, giving us a few more years or decades of being able to ignore that *why*—that the drugs are often useful tools to quell or understand or move past our pain, but that they are needed because there is an immense amount of pain in this world to begin with, and that they cannot help with that.

I was, for a time, unsatisfied with this. I pushed to find more. I went to raves and parties and found communities that used drugs collectively—as tools to become closer to one another, and perhaps closer to a vision of a kinder, freer, less isolated future. But even there, the liberation was temporary. Drugs may help people envision a better reality, but when the drugs wore off, so too did the vision.

So, increasingly, I found myself giving up the search. Not giving up on the possibility of a better future, but giving up on the idea that a new world could be found within myself, within my own mind.

Yet I realize that on most days, these days, I feel more hopeful than I ever did before my long journey of recovery, before my life's narrative was scrambled.

It's been nearly seven years since that day in Oakland, the day I thought my life ended. And, it turns out, it didn't. Perhaps that's the simplest explanation for my increased faith in humanity—if I could survive what I survived, if I could rebuild my life with the help of drugs and therapy and all the rest, if my psyche was capable of transforming so radically, then what isn't possible?

That's what I saw in my reporting too—people who refused to accept the narrative imposed on them by society and who pushed beyond it. Jeremy and Eris and Vince in Vancouver, LaDonna Smith in Philadelphia, even the ravers in New York. All led very different lives, yet all were united in an attempt to build a future beyond the isolating and depressing one we've been handed, and often using drugs to do those things.

Whether those efforts to rewrite our collective narrative will succeed is unclear. Anyone who attempts to challenge our social or political mores will be met with repression, whether that repression is direct and violent in the form of police and punitive politicians, or more subtle and psychic—the ostracization one can face from normative society when they attempt to create an alternative. Like the ostracization people like Lucas faced from the time he was a teen until today.

But that, in the end, despite the inevitable repression, is where my hope really comes from—from the people who fight on to build something new and kinder.

And the fact that those people exist and keep fighting gives me a new perspective when I begin to dwell on how bad life can feel right now. When I see those articles on how trans people are to blame for everything, when I see politicians attempt to criminalize drug users and homeless people, when I see people cling for dear life to pseudoscientific and individualistic views of mental health, I see a society that is, yes, bad, but bad for a specific reason. It's becoming ever clearer that a new path is being forged, that young people want to live in new ways, in new configurations and communities, as new genders, with different goals than the generations before them.

As those desires are realized—as they are externalized from individual fantasy to collective reality, nascent and fragile but no less real, on dance floors and on the streets—it makes sense that the people and institutions invested in the old order need to push back harder and harder and attempt to keep those desires within people's minds and bodies and out of the material world. In other words, the world feels so bad right now partly, or maybe even entirely, because it's changing for the better. The only way out is through.

Desire, as Deleuze and Guattari wrote, is explosive. Desire can change the world.

Right now, though, we are still relatively atomized—pushing for a new world but mostly siloed into communities unaware that we are fighting for the same things. The people fighting for drug users in Philadelphia and Vancouver, and the people attempting to embody a collective consciousness in the raves, and the people isolated in their rooms using drugs to quell the pain of being forced to live in a society that's not built for them, and the people who take SSRIs or Adderall to get through the day without imploding are, on paper, very different. Yet all are united by a recognition that the current narrative doesn't work for them, that they need something more.

Rewriting a life, as I'd discovered, is a powerful thing.

Imagine how powerful it'd be to do it together.

ACKNOWLEDGMENTS

Thank you first to my editor, Stephanie Hitchcock, who, from the first time we discussed this book, immediately understood why I wanted to write it and what it could be, despite its unconventional tone, style, and content. Without her shepherding this manuscript from start to finish, without her brilliant edits and questions and feedback, this book could not exist.

Thank you also to my agent, Melissa Flashman, who has advocated for me at every step, answered all my annoying questions, and kept me calm and focused as I undertook the biggest project of my life.

I am blessed to have perhaps the most supportive family on earth, people who've never questioned what I wanted to do with my life, even though at certain points I'm sure "freelance writer" sounded like the worst possible idea in the world. To my mom, Sally; my dad, Michael; my brother, John; my sister-in-law, Christina; my nephew, Julian—thank you for not only believing in me, but pushing me to be the best version of myself, and giving me the support needed to do the things I've always wanted to do. And thank you to everyone else in my extended family

ACKNOWLEDGMENTS

too, people too numerous to name, who've always been there for me, and who've been an integral part of my life every day, week, month, and year of my existence.

Thank you to my therapist, Dennis, who helped me reconfigure my entire mind and entire life. And thank you to my professional mentors over the years, especially Fred Bever.

Okay, and now for the friends, many of whom I am going to forget to mention because there are too many of you. Please know that if we've ever gotten a drink at Singers, you likely mean the world to me, and I likely would not be alive without you. But here we go: First, Erin "Storm Chaser" Corbett, my trauma-bonded bestie, my forever partner in crime, I love you so much and look forward to annoying you incessantly until we die in a nursing home or in a fiery car crash running from the law together. And also to: Vince, Jack, Gavin, Kacper, Justin, Molly, Erik, Mike, Will, Ary, Michelle, Michael, Hesse, Amber, Tal, Reid, Drew, Caleb, Kelly, April, Camille, Grace, Charlotte, Rex, Chris, Dick, Anand, Jake, Kaye, Harron, Emily, Nick, Henry, and Zarina. I never really understood what community meant until I found all of you. I couldn't imagine living any other way.

And, finally, I'd like to thank everyone who participated in the reporting of this book. To me, journalism is a collaborative process. So, in a way, you've all written this book with me. Thank you for your time and for your brilliant insights that have allowed me to understand the world more fully, and enabled me, and hopefully others, to feel less alone. Thank you, thank you, thank you.

NOTES

INTRODUCTION

1. Qingqing Liu, Hairong He, Jin Yang, Xiaojie Feng, Fanfan Zhao, and Jun Lyu, "Changes in the Global Burden of Depression from 1990 to 2017: Findings from the Global Burden of Disease Study," *Journal of Psychiatric Research* 126 (July 2020): 134–40, https://doi.org/10.1016/j.jpsychires.2019.08.002.
2. Dan Witters, "U.S. Depression Rates Reach New Highs," Gallup, May 17, 2023, https://news.gallup.com/poll/505745/depression-rates-reach-new-highs.aspx.
3. Avgi Saketopoulou, *Sexuality Beyond Consent: Risk, Race, Traumatophilia* (New York: New York University Press, 2023), 22.
4. Marianne Williamson, *A Return to Love: Reflections on the Principles of A Course in Miracles* (New York: HarperOne, 1996), chap. 1, Apple Books.
5. Parul Sehgal, "The Case Against the Trauma Plot," *The New Yorker*, December 27, 2021, https://www.newyorker.com/magazine/2022/01/03/the-case-against-the-trauma-plot.

NOTES

6. Parul Seghal, "The Tyranny of the Tale," *The New Yorker*, July 3, 2023, https://www.newyorker.com/magazine/2023/07/10/seduced-by-story-peter-brooks-bewitching-the-modern-mind-christian-salmon-the-story-paradox-jonathan-gottschall-book-review.

CHAPTER ONE: MY BREAKDOWN

1. Lee T. Wyatt, *The Industrial Revolution* (Westport, Conn: Greenwood Press, 2009), 62.
2. Will Self, "A Posthumous Shock," *Harper's*, December 2021, https://harpers.org/archive/2021/12/a-posthumous-shock-trauma-studies-modernity-how-everything-became-trauma/.
3. "Meprobamate," PubChem database, National Center for Biotechnology Information, National Library of Medicine, n.d., https://pubchem.ncbi.nlm.nih.gov/compound/Meprobamate.
4. Anne Harrington, *Mind Fixers: Psychiatry's Troubled Search for the Biology of Mental Illness* (New York: W.W. Norton & Company, 2020), chap. 3, Apple Books.
5. Harrington, *Mind Fixers*, chap. 3, Apple Books.
6. Jeannette Y. Wick, "The History of Benzodiazepines," *The Consultant Pharmacist* 28 (September 2013): 538–48, https://doi.org/10.4140/tcp.n.2013.538.
7. Sujata Gupta, "Mother's Little Helper: A Brief History of Benzodiazepines," *Mosaic*, Wellcome Trust, March 17, 2015, archived at https://web.archive.org/web/20230223032855/https://mosaicscience.com/story/mothers-little-helper-brief-history-benzodiazepines/.
8. W. W. Rosser, "Benzodiazepines: Part of Lifestyle in the 1980s," *Canadian Family Physician* 30 (January 1984), 193–98, https://pmc.ncbi.nlm.nih.gov/articles/PMC2154007/pdf/canfamphys00215-0195.pdf.

9. Heather Zeiger, "Our Uneasy Tranquility," *The New Atlantis*, Spring 2019, https://www.thenewatlantis.com/publications/our-uneasy-tranquility.
10. C. L. DeVane, M. R. Ware, and R. B. Lydiard, "Pharmacokinetics, Pharmacodynamics, and Treatment Issues of Benzodiazepines: Alprazolam, Adinazolam, and Clonazepam," *Psychopharmacology Bulletin* 27, no. 4 (1991): 463–73.
11. "We Are All Very Anxious," Plan C, April 4, 2014, https //www.weareplanc.org/2014/04/we-are-all-very-anxious/.

CHAPTER TWO: A PERSONAL BREAKDOWN

1. "Suicide," National Institute of Mental Health, n.d., https //www.nimh.nih.gov/health/statistics/suicide.
2. Erica Pandey, "Gun Deaths Among Children Are Soaring," *Axios*, April 10, 2023, https://www.axios.com/2023/04/10/gun-deaths-among-children-are-soaring.
3. Jillian McKoy, "Depression Rates in US Tripled When the Pandemic First Hit—Now, They're Even Worse," Boston University, October 7, 2021, https://www.bu.edu/articles/2021/depression-rates-tripled-when-pandemic-first-hit/.
4. "Mental Health Care," Household Pulse Survey, 2020–2022, National Center for Health Statistics and US Census Bureau, Centers for Disease Control and Prevention, February 22, 2023, https://www.cdc.gov/nchs/covid19/pulse/mental-health-care.htm.
5. "Mental Health Facts and Statistics," Mind, June 2020, https://www.mind.org.uk/information-support/types-of-mental-health-problems/mental-health-facts-and-statistics/.
6. John J. McGrath, Ali Al-Hamzawi, Jordi Alonso, Yasmin Al-waijri, Laura H. Andrade, Evelyn J. Bromet et al., "Age of Onset and Cumulative Risk of Mental Disorders: A Cross-National Analysis of Population Surveys

from 29 Countries," *The Lancet Psychiatry* 10 (September 2023): 668–81, https://doi.org/10.1016/s2215-0366(23)00193-1.

7. "Fentanyl DrugFacts," National Institute on Drug Abuse, National Institutes of Health, June 2021, https://nida.nih.gov/publications/drugfacts/fentanyl.

8. "Drug Overdose Deaths: Facts and Figures," National Institute on Drug Abuse, National Institutes of Health, August 2024, https://nida.nih.gov/research-topics/trends-statistics/overdose-death-rates.

9. "Commonly Used Terms," Centers for Disease Control and Prevention, April 19, 2024, https://www.cdc.gov/overdose-prevention/glossary/.

10. Emmanuel Darcq and Brigitte Lina Kieffer, "Opioid Receptors: Drivers to Addiction?" *Nature Reviews Neuroscience* 19 (August 2018): 499–514, https://doi.org/10.1038/s41583-018-0028-x.

11. Andrew Rosenblum, Lisa A. Marsch, Herman Joseph, and Russell K. Portenoy, "Opioids and the Treatment of Chronic Pain: Controversies, Current Status, and Future Directions," *Experimental and Clinical Psychopharmacology* 16 (October 2008): 405–16, https://doi.org/10.1037/a0013628.

12. Aurélie Salavert, Antoine Zazzo, Lucie Martin, Ferran Antolín, Caroline Gauthier, François Thil et al., "Direct Dating Reveals the Early History of Opium Poppy in Western Europe," *Scientific Reports* 10 (November 20, 2020), https://doi.org/10.1038/s41598-020-76924-3.

13. Svend Norn, Poul R. Kruse, and Edith Kruse, "Opiumsvalmuen og morfin gennem tiderne [History of Opium Poppy and Morphine]," *Dan Medicin Historisk Årbog* 33 (2005): 171–84, https://pubmed.ncbi.nlm.nih.gov/17152761/.

14. "Lotus-Eater," *Encyclopaedia Britannica*, n.d., https://www.britannica.com/topic/Lotus-Eater.

15. Aristotle, "On Sleep and Sleeplessness," trans. J. I. Beare, Philosophy, Religion, and Humanities Department, Austin Community College, n.d.,

https://liberalarts.austincc.edu/philosophy-religion-humanities/on-sleep-and-sleeplessness/.

16. Dan Chiasson, "The Man Who Invented the Drug Memoir," *The New Yorker*, October 10, 2016, https://www.newyorker.com/magazine/2016/10/17/the-man-who-invented-the-drug-memoir.

17. Thomas De Quincey, *Confessions of an English Opium-Eater and Other Writings*, ed. Robert Morrison (Oxford: Oxford University Press, 2013), Apple Books.

18. De Quincey is quoting the *Odyssey*.

19. De Quincey, *Confessions*, Apple Books.

20. Thomas De Quincey, *Confessions of an English Opium-Eater*, ed. Joel Faflak (Peterborough, Ontario: Broadview Press, 2009), Apple Books.

21. Daisy Hay, "Guilty Thing: A Life of Thomas De Quincey by Frances Wilson—Review," *The Observer*, April 3, 2016, https://www.theguardian.com/books/2016/apr/03/guilty-thing-a-life-of-thomas-de-quincey-by-frances-wilson-review.

22. "Prescription Opioid Epidemic: Know the Facts," American Medical Association Alliance, July 2019, https://amaalliance.org/wp-content/uploads/2019/07/Opioid-White-Paper_Final_Template.pdf.

23. "Drug Overdose Deaths: Facts and Figures," National Institute on Drug Abuse.

24. Jessica Dickler, "Home Prices Are Now Rising Much Faster than Incomes, Studies Show," CNBC, November 10, 2021, https://www.cnbc.com/2021/11/10/home-prices-are-now-rising-much-faster-than-incomes-studies-show.html.

25. "One in Four People Could Be Forced to Turn Off Their Heating and Hot Water When Energy Bill Increases Come in This Autumn," Citizens Advice, August 21, 2024, https://www.citizensadvice.org.uk/about-us/media-centre/press-releases/one-in-four-people-could-be-forced-to-turn-off-their-heating-and-hot-water/.

26. Sigmund Freud, *Beyond the Pleasure Principle and Other Writings*, trans. John Reddick (London: Penguin, 2003), Apple Books.

27. Naomi I. Eisenberger, Matthew D. Lieberman, and Kipling D. Williams, "Does Rejection Hurt? An fMRI Study of Social Exclusion," *Science* 302 (October 10, 2003): 290–92, https://doi.org/10.1126/science.1089134.

28. Paolo Riva, James H. Wirth, and Kipling D. Williams, "The Consequences of Pain: The Social and Physical Pain Overlap on Psychological Responses," *European Journal of Social Psychology* 41 (October 2011): 681–87, https://doi.org/10.1002/ejsp.837.

29. Maria Gudmundsdottir, "Embodied Grief: Bereaved Parents' Narratives of Their Suffering Body," *Omega: Journal of Death and Dying*, 59 (November 2009), 25–69, https://doi.org/10.2190/OM.59.3.e.

30. Charles Veltri and Oliver Grundmann, "Current Perspectives on the Impact of Kratom Use," *Substance Abuse and Rehabilitation* 10 (July 2019): 23–31, https://doi.org/10.2147/SAR.S164261.

31. Anne Case and Angus Deaton, "Mortality and Morbidity in the 21st Century," Brookings Institution, March 23, 2017, https://www.brookings.edu/bpea-articles/mortality-and-morbidity-in-the-21st-century/.

32. Maureen R. Benjamins, Abigail Silva, Nazia S. Saiyed, and Fernando G. De Maio, "Comparison of All-Cause Mortality Rates and Inequities Between Black and White Populations Across the 30 Most Populous U.S. Cities," *JAMA Network Open* 4 (January 20, 2021), https://doi.org/10.1001/jamanetworkopen.2020.32086.

33. Carol Graham, "Why Are Black Poor Americans More Optimistic than White Ones?" Brookings Institution, January 30, 2018, https://www.brookings.edu/articles/why-are-black-poor-americans-more-optimistic-than-white-ones/.

NOTES

34. Carol Graham, "Racial Gaps in Hope, Ill-Being, and Deaths of Despair," Brookings Institution, February 27, 2020, https://www.brookings.edu/articles/racial-gaps-in-hope-ill-being-and-deaths-of-despair/.
35. "Suicide Statistics," American Foundation for Suicide Prevention, n.d., https://afsp.org/suicide-statistics/.
36. "Prescription Opioid Trends in the United States," IQVIA, December 16, 2020, https://www.iqvia.com/insights/the-iqvia-institute/reports-and-publications/reports/prescription-opioid-trends-in-the-united-states.
37. "Prescription Opioid Trends in the United States," IQVIA.

CHAPTER THREE: THE UNEQUAL DISTRIBUTION OF BREAKDOWN

1. "Mental Health Treatment Among Adults: United States, 2020," Centers for Disease Control and Prevention, October 2021, https://www.cdc.gov/nchs/products/databriefs/db419.htm.
2. *Key Substance Use and Mental Health Indicators in the United States: Results from the 2021 National Survey on Drug Use and Health*, § (2023), Center for Behavioral Health Statistics and Quality, Substance Abuse and Mental Health Services Administration, December 2022, 16, https://www.samhsa.gov/data/sites/default/files/reports/rpt39443/2021NSDUHFFRRev010323.pdf.
3. Lauren Mayk and Brian X. McCrone, "Mehmet Oz Picks Up Used Needle in Kensington on Campaign Stop in Philly," WCAU/NBC10 Philadelphia, September 19, 2022, https://www.nbcphiladelphia.com/decision-2022/mehmet-oz-picks-up-used-needle-in-kensington-on-campaign-stop-in-philly/3366873/.
4. "Opioid Epidemic Updates: 'Frankenstein Opioids' and Xylazine-Induced Skin Ulcers," *American Family Physician Community Blog*, February 13, 2023, https://www.aafp.org/pubs/afp/afp-community-blog/ent

ry/opioid-epidemic-updates-frankenstein-opioids-and-xylazine-induced-skin-ulcers.html.

5. Brooke A. Lewis, "The History of the Disease Concept of Substance Dependency" (master's thesis, Northern Michigan University, 2016), 2, https://commons.nmu.edu/cgi/viewcontent.cgi?article=1109&context=theses.

6. Joanna S. Fowler, Nora D. Volkow, Cheryl A. Kassed, and Linda Chang, "Imaging the Addicted Human Brain," *Science and Practice Perspectives* 3 (April 2007): 4–16, https://pmc.ncbi.nlm.nih.gov/articles/PMC2851068/.

7. "Drug Misuse and Addiction," National Institute on Drug Abuse, National Institutes of Health, July 2020, https://nida.nih.gov/publications/drugs-brains-behavior-science-addiction/drug-misuse-addiction.

8. Jenny Valentish, "Why Addiction Isn't a Disease but Instead the Result of 'Deep Learning,'" *The Age*, August 21, 2015, https://www.theage.com.au/national/why-addiction-isnt-a-disease-marc-lewis-seo-here-20150810-givho9.html.

9. "Stigma and Discrimination," National Institutes of Health, February 28, 2024, https://nida.nih.gov/research-topics/stigma-discrimination.

10. Annette Mary Mendola, "A Critique of the Disease Model of Addiction" (PhD diss., University of Tennessee, 2003), https://trace.tennessee.edu/utk_graddiss/5156.

11. Carl Erik Fisher, *The Urge: Our History of Addiction* (New York: Penguin Press, 2022), chap. 2, Apple Books.

12. David L. Herzberg, *White Market Drugs: Big Pharma and the Hidden History of Addiction in America* (Chicago: University of Chicago Press, 2020), chap. 1, Apple Books.

13. Herzberg, *White Market Drugs*, chap. 3, Apple Books.

14. Herzberg, *White Market Drugs*, chap. 3, Apple Books.

15. Edward R. Bloomquist, "The Addiction Potential of Oxycodone (Percodan)," *California Medicine* 99 (1963): 127–30, https://pmc.ncbi.nlm.nih.gov/articles/PMC1515192/.
16. David T. Courtwright, *Dark Paradise: A History of Opiate Addiction in America* (Cambridge, Mass.: Harvard University Press, 2001), 2.
17. Herzberg, *White Market Drugs*, chap. 5, Apple Books. "Overdose deaths were similarly disproportionate."
18. Herzberg, *White Market Drugs*, chap. 1, Apple Books.
19. Wendy Sawyer and Peter Wagner, "Mass Incarceration: The Whole Pie 2022," Prison Policy Initiative, March 14, 2022, https://www.prisonpolicy.org/reports/pie2022.html.
20. Ashley Nellis, "The Color of Justice: Racial and Ethnic Disparity in State Prisons," The Sentencing Project, October 13, 2021, https://www.sentencingproject.org/reports/the-color-of-justice-racial-and-ethnic-disparity-in-state-prisons-the-sentencing-project/.
21. Ben Westhoff, *Fentanyl, Inc.: How Rogue Chemists Are Creating the Deadliest Wave of the Opioid Epidemic* (New York: Atlantic Monthly Press, 2019), chap. 2, Apple Books.
22. Harry G. Levine, "Review of *The Globalisation of Addiction: A Study in Poverty of the Spirit* by Bruce K. Alexander," *Harm Reduction Journal* 6 (June 23, 2009): 12, https://harmreductionjournal.biomedcentral.com/articles/10.1186/1477-7517-6-12.
23. Friedrich Engels, *The Condition of the Working Class in England* (originally published in 1847; Panther edition, 1969, Institute of Marxism-Leninism, Moscow), https://www.marxists.org/archive/marx/works/1845/condition-working-class/.
24. Jeremy Scahill and Ruth Wilson Gilmore, "Ruth Wilson Gilmore Makes the Case for Abolition," *Intercepted* (podcast), June 10, 2020, https://

theintercept.com/2020/06/10/ruth-wilson-gilmore-makes-the-case-for-abolition/.

25. "Illicit Drug Toxicity," Coroners Service, Ministry of Public Safety and Solicitor General, British Columbia, Canada, January 31, 2023, https://www2.gov.bc.ca/assets/gov/birth-adoption-death-marriage-and-divorce/deaths/coroners-service/statistical/illicit-drug-type.pdf.

26. Rhianna Schmunk, "B.C. Marks 3rd Straight Month with More Than 170 Overdose Deaths," CBC News, August 25, 2020, https://www.cbc.ca/news/canada/british-columbia/bc-overdose-numbers-july-2020-1.5698795.

27. "Letters of Support," Drug Users Liberation Front, n.d., https://dulf.ca/wp-content/uploads/2025/02/dulf-sec-56-los-complete.pdf.

28. "Average Rent in Vancouver, BC," Zumper, October 30, 2023, https://www.zumper.com/rent-research/vancouver-bc.

INTERLUDE TWO: HOW TO EXTERNALIZE THE BREAKDOWN

1. Dino Franco Felluga, "Cathexis," Introductory Guide to Critical Theory, 2011, https://cla.purdue.edu/academic/english/theory/psychoanalysis/definitions/cathexis.html.

2. Carlos Nordt, Ingeborg Warnke, Erich Seifritz, and Wolfram Kawohl, "Modelling Suicide and Unemployment: A Longitudinal Analysis Covering 63 Countries, 2000–11," *The Lancet Psychiatry* 2 (March 2015): 239–45, https://doi.org/10.1016/s2215-0366(14)00118-7.

3. Jeffrey Pfeffer, *Dying for a Paycheck: How Modern Management Harms Employee Health and Company Performance—And What We Can Do About It* (New York: HarperBusiness, 2018), chap. 5, Apple Books.

4. Sigmund Freud, *Beyond the Pleasure Principle: And Other Writings*, trans. John Reddick (New York: Penguin Books, 2003), Apple Books.

5. Kelly Oliver, *The Colonization of Psychic Space: A Psychoanalytic*

NOTES

Social Theory of Oppression (Minneapolis: University of Minnesota Press, 2004), 43.

6. Bessel van der Kolk, *The Body Keeps the Score: Brain, Mind, and Body in the Healing of Trauma* (New York: Penguin Books, 2015), chap. 8, Apple Books.

7. Thomas Helbling, "Externalities: Prices Do Not Capture All Costs," *Finance & Development*, International Monetary Fund, n.d., https://www.imf.org/external/pubs/ft/fandd/basics/38-externalities.htm.

8. Judith Butler, "Melancholy Gender—Refused Identification," *Psychoanalytic Dialogues* 5 (January 1995): 165–80, https://doi.org/10.1080/10481889509539059.

9. Karl Marx, "A Contribution to the Critique of Hegel's Philosophy of Right" (originally published in 1844; ed. Andy Blunden, 2005, and Matthew Carmody, 2009), Marxist Internet Archive, https://www.marxists.org/archive/marx/works/1843/critique-hpr/intro.htm.

10. For more on this, see Sarah Schulman, *The Gentrification of the Mind: Witness to a Lost Imagination* (Berkeley: California University Press, 2013).

11. Gilles Deleuze and Félix Guattari, *Anti-Oedipus: Capitalism and Schizophrenia*, trans. Robert Hurley (Minneapolis: University of Minnesota Press, 2008), xxiii.

12. See Tobi Haslett on the George Floyd protests: Tobi Haslett, "Magic Actions," *N+1*, Summer 2021, https://www.nplusonemag.com/issue-40/politics/magic-actions-2/.

CHAPTER FOUR: PUTTING MYSELF BACK TOGETHER

1. Cynthia Allen, "The Potential Health Benefits of Meditation," *ACSM's Health & Fitness Journal*, November/December 2020: 28–32, https://www.researchgate.net/publication/361335763_The_Potential_Health_Benefits_of_Meditation.

NOTES

2. Van der Kolk, *The Body Keeps the Score*, chap. 4, Apple Books.
3. Wei He, Xiaoyu Wang, Hong Shi, Hongyan Shang, Liang Li, Xianghong Jing et al., "Auricular Acupuncture and Vagal Regulation," *Evidence-Based Complementary and Alternative Medicine* 2012: 786839, https://doi.org/10.1155/2012/786839.
4. "America's State of Mind Report," Express Scripts, April 16, 2020, https://www.express-scripts.com/corporate/americas-state-of-mind-report.
5. Alan Mozes, "In Long Run, Antidepressants Don't Improve Quality of Life: Study," *U.S. News & World Report*, April 20, 2022, https://www.usnews.com/news/health-news/articles/2022-04-20/in-long-run-antidepressants-dont-improve-quality-of-life-study.
6. "Antidepressant Use Among Adults: United States, 2015–2018," NCHS Data Brief No. 377, Centers for Disease Control and Prevention, September 2020, https://www.cdc.gov/nchs/products/databriefs/db377.htm.
7. Nirmita Panchal and Justin Cho, "Exploring the Rise in Mental Health Care Use by Demographics and Insurance Status," KFF, August 1, 2024, https://www.kff.org/mental-health/issue-brief/exploring-the-rise-in-mental-health-care-use-by-demographics-and-insurance-status.
8. "Pain in the Nation 2022," Trust for America's Health, May 24, 2022, https://www.tfah.org/report-details/pain-in-the-nation-2022/.
9. "Country Health Profiles 2023," European Commission, December 15, 2023, https://health.ec.europa.eu/state-health-eu/country-health-profiles/country-health-profiles-2023_en.
10. "Chapter 2: Mental Health in Cumberland," Cumberland Public Health Annual Report, 2023/4, Cumberland Council, United Kingdom, May 7, 2024, https://www.cumberland.gov.uk/cumberland-public-health-annual-report-20234/chapter-2-mental-health-cumberland.
11. "Overview—Selective Serotonin Reuptake Inhibitors (SSRIs)," National

NOTES

Health Service, United Kingdom, n.d., https://www.nhs.uk/mental-health/talking-therapies-medicine-treatments/medicines-and-psychiatry/ssri-antidepressants/overview/.

12. P.E. Moskowitz, "Breaking Off My Chemical Romance," *The Nation*, March 23, 2022, https://www.thenation.com/article/society/ssri-antidepressant-side-effects/.

13. A. L. Montejo, G. Llorca, A. Izquierdo, and F. Rico-Villademoros, "Incidence of Sexual Dysfunction Associated with Antidepressant Agents: A Prospective Multicenter Study of 1022 Outpatients. Spanish Working Group for the Study of Psychotropic-Related Sexual Dysfunction," *The Journal of Clinical Psychiatry* 62, Suppl. 3 (2001): 10–21.

14. Rif S. El-Mallakh, Yonglin Gao, and R. Jeannie Roberts, "Tardive Dysphoria: The Role of Long-Term Antidepressant Use in Inducing Chronic Depression," *Medical Hypotheses* 76 (2011): 769–73, https://doi.org/10.1016/j.mehy.2011.01.020.

15. Moskowitz, "Breaking Off My Chemical Romance."

16. Mark Abie Horowitz and David Taylor, "Tapering of SSRI Treatment to Mitigate Withdrawal Symptoms," *The Lancet Psychiatry* 6 (June 2019): 538–46, https://doi.org/10.1016/s2215-0366(19)30032-x.

17. Alfredo C. Altamura, Anna R. Moro, and Mauro Percudani. "Clinical Pharmacokinetics of Fluoxetine," *Clinical Pharmacokinetics* 26 (1994): 201–14, https://doi.org/10.2165/00003088-199426030-00004.

18. "Prolonged Grief Disorder," American Psychiatric Association, May 2022, https://www.psychiatry.org/patients-families/prolonged-grief-disorder.

19. Alice Walker, *Living by the Word: Selected Writings, 1973–1987* (New York: Amistad, 1989), Apple Books.

20. Carina del Valle Schorske, "Melancholy," *The Point*, June 16, 2015, https://thepointmag.com/examined-life/melancholy/.

NOTES

CHAPTER FIVE: A TENUOUS STABILITY

1. Benedict Carey, "Panel to Debate Antidepressant Warnings," *The New York Times*, December 13, 2006, https://www.nytimes.com/2006/12/13/us/13suicide.html.

2. Benedict Carey, "Antidepressant Paxil Is Unsafe for Teenagers, New Analysis Says," *The New York Times*, September 16, 2015, https://www.nytimes.com/2015/09/17/health/antidepressant-paxil-is-unsafe-for-teenagers-new-analysis-says.html.

3. Joanna Le Noury, John M. Nardo, David Healy, Jon Jureidini, Melissa Raven, Catalin Tufanaru et al., "Restoring Study 329: Efficacy and Harms of Paroxetine and Imipramine in Treatment of Major Depression in Adolescence," *British Medical Journal* 351 (September 19, 2015), https://www.bmj.com/content/351/bmj.h4320.

4. T. M. Hillhouse and J. H. Porter, "A Brief History of the Development of Antidepressant Drugs: From Monoamines to Glutamate," *Experimental and Clinical Psychopharmacology* 23 (February 2015), 1–21, https://doi.org/10.1037/a0038550.

5. "Mental Health Treatment Among Adults: United States, 2020," Centers for Disease Control and Prevention, October 2021, https://www.cdc.gov/nchs/products/databriefs/db419.htm.

6. Benedict Carey and Robert Gebeloff, "Many People Taking Antidepressants Discover They Cannot Quit," *The New York Times*, April 7, 2018, https://www.nytimes.com/2018/04/07/health/antidepressants-withdrawal-prozac-cymbalta.html.

7. "Pharmaceutical Market," OECD Data Explorer, Organisation for Economic Co-Operation and Development, https://stats.oecd.org/Index.aspx?DataSetCode=HEALTH_PHMC.

8. "The Top 300 of 2020," ClinCalc, https://clincalc.com/DrugStats/Top300Drugs.aspx.

NOTES

9. "Industries: 2024," OpenSecrets, https://www.opensecrets.org/federal-lobbying/industries.

10. Julia Faria, "Pharma DTC Ad Spend in the U.S. 2021," Statista, January 6, 2023, https://www.statista.com/statistics/686906/pharma-ad-spend-usa/.

11. Hal Arkowitz and Scott O. Lilienfeld, "Is Depression Just Bad Chemistry?" *Scientific American*, March 1, 2014, https://www.scientificamerican.com/article/is-depression-just-bad-chemistry/.

12. C. M. France, P. H. Lysaker, and R. P. Robinson, "The 'Chemical Imbalance' Explanation for Depression: Origins, Lay Endorsement, and Clinical Implications," *Professional Psychology: Research and Practice* 38 (2007): 411–20, https://doi.org/10.1037/0735-7028.38.4.411.

13. Moskowitz, "Breaking Off My Chemical Romance."

14. Benedict Carey, "How to Quit Antidepressants: Very Slowly, Doctors Say," *The New York Times*, March 5, 2019, https://www.nytimes.com/2019/03/05/health/depression-withdrawal-drugs.html.

15. "Butisol Advertisement, 1969, *JAMA: The Journal of the American Medical Association*, Vol. 207, No. 6, p. 1206," Bonkers Institute for Nearly Genuine Research, http://www.bonkersinstitute.org/medshow/cope.html.

16. "Miltown Advertisement, 1967, *JAMA: The Journal of the American Medical Association*, Vol. 202, No. 1, pp. 54–56," Bonkers Institute for Nearly Genuine Research, http://www.bonkersinstitute.org/medshow/fembps1.html.

17. Charles Fain Lehman, "The Downer About Uppers," *New Atlantis*, November 28, 2023, https://www.thenewatlantis.com/publications/the-downer-about-uppers.

18. Sarah Lohmann, "No Comment, Vintage Edition: You Can't Set Her Free," *Ms.*, September 7, 2010, https://msmagazine.com/2010/09/07/no-commentvintage-editionyou-cant-set-her-free/.

19. Jeffrey Geller, "The Rise and Demise of America's Psychiatric Hospitals: A

Tale of Dollars Trumping Sense," *Psychiatric News*, March 14, 2019, https://psychnews.psychiatryonline.org/doi/10.1176/appi.pn.2019.3b29.

20. Jonathan Metzl, *The Protest Psychosis: How Schizophrenia Became a Black Disease* (Boston: Beacon, 2011), chap. 16, Apple Books.
21. David Lowell Herzberg, *Happy Pills in America: From Miltown to Prozac* (Baltimore: Johns Hopkins University Press, 2010), 4.
22. Herzberg, *Happy Pills*, 23.
23. Herzberg, *Happy Pills*, 33.
24. "What Is Psychiatry?" American Psychiatric Association, January 2023, https://www.psychiatry.org/patients-families/what-is-psychiatry.
25. "Miltown: A Game-Changing Drug You've Probably Never Heard Of," CBC News, August 7, 2017, https://www.cbc.ca/radio/ondrugs/miltown-a-game-changing-drug-you-ve-probably-never-heard-of-1.4237946.
26. Leon W. Powell, Geoffrey T. Mann, and Sidney Kaye, "Acute Meprobamate Poisoning," *New England Journal of Medicine* 259 (October 9, 1958): 716–18, https://doi.org/10.1056/nejm195810092591504.
27. Herzberg, *Happy Pills*, 38–39; Victor G. Laties and Bernard Weiss, "A Critical Review of the Efficacy of Meprobamate (Miltown, Equanil) in the Treatment of Anxiety," *Journal of Chronic Diseases* 7 (June 1958): 500–519, https://doi.org/10.1016/0021-9681(58)90168-1.
28. Wick, "History of Benzodiazepines."
29. Advertisement in the *American Journal of Psychiatry* in 1965, The Open University, https://www.open.edu/openlearn/mod/oucontent/view.php?id=3718&extra=thumbnailfigure_idm576.
30. "Benzodiazepines (Benzos)," Cleveland Clinic, January 3, 2023, https://my.clevelandclinic.org/health/treatments/24570-benzodiazepines-benzos.

NOTES

31. Jonathan Leo and Jeffrey R. Lacasse, "The Media and the Chemical Imbalance Theory of Depression," *Society* 45 (February 2008): 35–45, https://link.springer.com/article/10.1007/s12115-007-9047-3.

32. Linda M. McMullen and Kristjan J. Sigurdson, "Depression Is to Diabetes as Antidepressants Are to Insulin: The Unraveling of an Analogy?" *Health Communication* 29 (2014), 309–17, https://doi.org/10.1080/10410236.2012.753660.

33. Victor Cohn, "Charting 'the Soul's Frail Dwelling-House,'" *The Washington Post*, September 5, 1982, https://www.washingtonpost.com/archive/politics/1982/09/05/charting-the-souls-frail-dwelling-house/061ae189-ddb4-4061-b73a-71751a149d68/.

34. Harrington, *Mind Fixers*, chap. 4, Apple Books.

35. "Bayh-Dole Act," Office of Research & Innovation, Drexel University, n.d., https://drexel.edu/research/innovation/technology-commercialization/bayh-dole-act.

36. Harrington, *Mind Fixers*, chap. 5, Apple Books.

37. Chris Koyanagi, "Learning from History: Deinstitutionalization of People with Mental Illness as Precursor to Long-Term Care Reform," Kaiser Commission on Medicaid and the Uninsured, August 2007, https://www.kff.org/wp-content/uploads/2013/01/7684.pdf.

38. "NHS Hospital Bed Numbers: Past, Present, Future," The King's Fund, November 5, 2021, https://www.kingsfund.org.uk/insight-and-analysis/long-reads/nhs-hospital-bed-numbers.

39. Milt Freudenheim, "The Drug Makers Are Listening to Prozac," *The New York Times*, January 9, 1994, https://www.nytimes.com/1994/01/09/business/the-drug-makers-are-listening-to-prozac.html.

40. Drug Usage Statistics, United States, 2013–2022: Fluoxetine Summary for 2022," ClinCalc, https://clincalc.com/DrugStats/Drugs/Fluoxetine.

41. "Drug Usage Statistics, United States, 2013–2022: Sertraline Summary for 2022," ClinCalc, https://clincalc.com/DrugStats/Drugs/Sertraline.

42. "Drug Usage Statistics, United States, 2013–2022: Escitalopram Summary for 2022," ClinCalc, https://clincalc.com/DrugStats/Drugs/Escitalopram.

43. A. John Rush, Maurizio Fava, Stephen R. Wisniewski, Philip W. Lavori, Madhukar H. Trivedi, Harold A. Sackeim et al., "Sequenced Treatment Alternatives to Relieve Depression (STAR*D): Rationale and Design," *Controlled Clinical Trials* 25 (February 2004): 119–42, https://doi.org/10.1016/S0197-2456(03)00112-0.

44. Becky Mars, Jon Heron, David Kessler, Neil M. Davies, Richard M. Martin, Kyla H. Thomas, and David Gunnell, "Influences on Antidepressant Prescribing Trends in the UK: 1995–2011," *Social Psychiatry and Psychiatric Epidemiology* 52 (November 2016): 193–200, https://doi.org/10.1007/s00127-016-1306-4.

45. Radu C. Racovita and Maria D. Ciuca, "Wastewater Treatment Approaches for the Removal of Antidepressant Residues," in *Wastewater Treatment and Sludge Management Systems*, ed. Başak Kılıç Taşeli, Eduardo Jacob-Lopes, Mariany Costa Deprá, and Leila Queiroz Zepka (IntechOpen, 2024), https://www.intechopen.com/online-first/1181144.

46. Steven E. Hyman, "Psychiatric Drug Development: Diagnosing a Crisis," *Cerebrum* (April 2, 2013): 5.

47. Irving Kirsch, "Antidepressants and the Placebo Effect," *Zeitschrift für Psychologie* 222 (January 2014): 128–34, https://doi.org/10.1027/2151-2604/a000176.

48. Kirsch, "Antidepressants and the Placebo Effect."

49. Moskowitz, "Breaking Off My Chemical Romance."

50. Omar A. Almohammed, Abdulaziz A. Alsalem, Abdullah A. Almangour, Lama H. Alotaibi, Majed S. Al Yami, and Leanne Lai, "Antidepressants and

NOTES

Health-Related Quality of Life (HRQoL) for Patients with Depression: Analysis of the Medical Expenditure Panel Survey from the United States," *PLoS One* 17 (2022): e0265928, https://journals.plos.org/plosone/article?id=10.1371/journal.pone.0265928.

51. Joanna Moncrieff, Ruth E. Cooper, Tom Stockmann, Simone Amendola, Michael P. Hengartner, and Mark A. Horowitz, "The Serotonin Theory of Depression: A Systematic Umbrella Review of the Evidence," *Molecular Psychiatry* 28 (2022), https://doi.org/10.1038/s41380-022-01661-0.

52. Montejo et al., "Incidence of Sexual Dysfunction Associated with Antidepressant Agents."

53. Carey and Gebeloff, "Many People Taking Antidepressants."

54. D. T. Wong and F. P. Bymaster, "Subsensitivity of Serotonin Receptors After Long-Term Treatment of Rats with Fluoxetine," *Research Communications in Chemical Pathology and Pharmacology* 32 (1981): 41–51, https://pubmed.ncbi.nlm.nih.gov/6974884/.

55. Yan Luo, Yuki Kataoka, Edoardo G. Ostinelli, Andrea Cipriani, and Toshi A. Furukawa, "National Prescription Patterns of Antidepressants in the Treatment of Adults with Major Depression in the US Between 1996 and 2015: A Population Representative Survey Based Analysis," *Frontiers in Psychiatry* 11 (2020): 35, https://doi.org/10.3389/fpsyt.2020.00035.

56. "Suicide Mortality in the United States, 2000–2020," National Center for Health Statistics, Centers for Disease Control and Prevention, March 2022, https://www.cdc.gov/nchs/products/databriefs/db433.htm.

CHAPTER SIX: THE STABILITY TRAP

1. Avgi Saketopoulou, *Sexuality Beyond Consent: Risk, Race, Traumatophilia* (New York: New York University Press, 2023), 100.

NOTES

2. "New APA Poll: One in Three Americans Feels Lonely Every Week," American Psychiatric Association, January 30, 2024, https://www.psychiatry.org/news-room/news-releases/new-apa-poll-one-in-three-americans-feels-lonely-e.

3. Lyman Stone, "Sexless America: Young Adults Are Having Less Sex," Institute for Family Studies, January 21, 2025, https://ifstudies.org/blog/sexless-america-young-adults-are-having-less-sex.

4. Associated Press, "Insanity Ascribed to Some Authors," *The New York Times*, May 15, 1935, https://timesmachine.nytimes.com/timesmachine/1935/05/15/94608186.pdf.

5. Metzl, *Protest Psychosis*, 32.

6. Harry Olsen, "Check on Society's Defectives Seen as Urgent Need of Nation," *The New York Times*, September 2, 1923, https://www.nytimes.com/1923/09/02/archives/check-on-societys-defectives-seen-as-urgent-need-of-nation.html.

7. Metzl, *Protest Psychosis*, 33–34; E. Fuller Torrey and Robert H. Yolken, "Psychiatric Genocide: Nazi Attempts to Eradicate Schizophrenia," *Schizophrenia Bulletin* 36 (2010): 26–32, https://doi.org/10.1093/schbul/sbp097.

8. Walter Bromberg and Franck Simon, "The 'Protest' Psychosis: A Special Type of Reactive Psychosis," *Archives of General Psychiatry* 19 (August 1968): 155–60, https://doi.org/10.1001/archpsyc.1968.01740080027005.

9. David Pilgrim, "Drapetomania." Jim Crow Museum, November 2005, https://jimcrowmuseum.ferris.edu/question/2005/november.htm.

10. Jonathan M. Metzl and Dorothy E. Roberts, "Structural Competency Meets Structural Racism: Race, Politics, and the Structure of Medical Knowledge," *The Virtual Mentor* 16 (September 2014): 674–90.

11. Jordan A. Conrad, "A Black and White History of Psychiatry in the United States," *Journal of Medical Humanities* 43 (2022): 247–66, https://doi.org/10.1007/s10912-020-09650-6.

12. Charles M. Olbert, Arudanti Nagendra, and Benjamin Buck, "Meta-Analysis of Black vs. White Racial Disparity in Schizophrenia Diagnosis in the United States: Do Structured Assessments Attenuate Racial Disparities?" *Journal of Abnormal Psychology* 127 (2018): 104–15, https://pubmed.ncbi.nlm.nih.gov/29094963/.
13. Sebastian M. Barr, Dominic Roberts, and Katharine N. Thakkar, "Psychosis in Transgender and Gender Non-Conforming Individuals: A Review of the Literature and a Call for More Research," *Psychiatry Research* 306 (2021): 114272, https://doi.org/10.1016/j.psychres.2021.114272.
14. Andrew E. Skodol and Donna S. Bender, "Why Are Women Diagnosed Borderline More Than Men?" *Psychiatric Quarterly* 74 (2003): 349–60, https://link.springer.com/article/10.1023/A:1026087410516.
15. Frantz Fanon, *Toward the African Revolution* (New York: Grove Press, 1964), chap. 1, part 1.
16. Mark L. Ruffalo, "The Fall of Psychoanalysis in American Psychiatry," *Psychology Today*, December 30, 2019, https://www.psychologytoday.com/us/blog/freud-fluoxetine/201912/the-fall-psychoanalysis-in-american-psychiatry.
17. Jerome Agel, *The Radical Therapist: The Radical Therapist Collective* (New York: Ballantine, 1971), https://dokumen.pub/the-radical-therapist-the-radical-therapist-collective-1974-printingnbsped-345223837125.html.
18. Insane Liberation Front, "Insane Liberation Manifesto," in *The Radical Therapist*.
19. Insane Liberation Front, "Insane Liberation Manifesto."
20. Christina Caron, "Teens Turn to TikTok in Search of a Mental Health Diagnosis," *The New York Times*, October 29, 2022, https://www.nytimes.com/2022/10/29/well/mind/tiktok-mental-illness-diagnosis.html.

21. Christopher Marc Bettis Moreland, "The Unbreakable Circle: An Intellectual History of Michel Foucault" (master's thesis, California State University, San Bernardino, 2014), https://scholarworks.lib.csusb.edu/cgi/viewcontent.cgi?article=1009&context=etd.
22. Michel Foucault, *Mental Illness and Psychology* (Berkeley: University of California Press, 1987), xxvi.
23. Alina Surís, Ryan Holliday, and Carol S. North, "The Evolution of the Classification of Psychiatric Disorders," *Behavioral Sciences* (Basel, Switzerland) 6 (2016): 5, https://doi.org/10.3390/bs6010005.

INTERLUDE THREE: FEAR OF FREEDOM / FREEDOM FROM FEAR

1. Donna Bach, Gary Groesbeck, Peta Stapleton, Rebecca Sims, Katharina Blickheuser, and Dawson Church, "Clinical EFT (Emotional Freedom Techniques) Improves Multiple Physiological Markers of Health," *Journal of Evidence-Based Integrative Medicine* 24 (January 2019), https://doi.org/10.1177/2515690x18823691; Nicola König, Sarah Steber, Josef Seebacher, Quinten von Prittwitz, Harald R. Bliem, and Sonja Rossi, "How Therapeutic Tapping Can Alter Neural Correlates of Emotional Prosody Processing in Anxiety," *Brain Sciences* 9 (2019): 206, https://doi.org/10.3390/brainsci9080206.
2. D. W. Winnicott, "Fear of Breakdown," *International Review of Psychoanalysis* 1 (1974): 103–7, https://winnicottisrael.com/wp-content/uploads/2020/10/ogden-fear-of-breakdown-1.pdf.
3. "Stress in America 2024," American Psychological Association, October 22, 2024, https://www.apa.org/pubs/reports/stress-in-america/2024.
4. Thomas H. Ogden, "Fear of Breakdown and the Unlived Life," *The International Journal of Psychoanalysis* 95 (April 2014): 205–23, https://doi.org/10.1111/1745-8315.12148.

NOTES

CHAPTER SEVEN: BECOMING ALIVE

1. Juan José Fuentes, Francina Fonseca, Matilde Elices, Magí Farré, and Marta Torrens, "Therapeutic Use of LSD in Psychiatry: A Systematic Review of Randomized-Controlled Clinical Trials," *Frontiers in Psychiatry* 10 (2020): 943, https://doi.org/10.3389/fpsyt.2019.00943.

2. Charles L. Raison, Gerard Sanacora, Joshua Woolley, Keith Heinzerling, Boadie W. Dunlop, Randall T. Brown et al., "Single-Dose Psilocybin Treatment for Major Depressive Disorder: A Randomized Clinical Trial," *JAMA: The Journal of the American Medical Association* 330 (2023): 843–53, https://jamanetwork.com/journals/jama/fullarticle/2808950.

3. Jennifer M. Mitchell, Michael Bogenschutz, Alia Lilienstein, Charlotte Harrison, Sarah Kleiman, Kelly Parker-Guilbert et al., "MDMA-Assisted Therapy for Severe PTSD: A Randomized, Double-Blind, Placebo-Controlled Phase 3 Study," *Nature Medicine* 27 (2021): 1025–33, https://doi.org/10.1038/s41591-021-01336-3.

4. Rachel Nuwer, "A Balm for Psyches Scarred by War," *The New York Times*, May 29, 2022, https://www.nytimes.com/2022/05/29/health/mdma-therapy-ptsd.html.

5. Nicola König, Sarah Steber, Josef Seebacher, Quinten von Prittwitz, Harald Bliem, and Sonja Rossi, "How Therapeutic Tapping Can Alter Neural Correlates of Emotional Prosody Processing in Anxiety," *Brain Sciences* 9 (August 19, 2019): 206, https://doi.org/10.3390/brainsci9030206.

6. Greg Miller, "Open Your Mind to the New Psychedelic Science," *Wired*, April 26, 2013, https://www.wired.com/2013/04/psychedlic/.

7. F. J. Carod-Artal, "Hallucinogenic Drugs in Pre-Columbian Mesoamerican Cultures," *Neurologia* 30 (2015): 42–49, https://doi.org/10.1016/j.nrl.2011.07.003.

8. Carod-Artal, "Hallucinogenic Drugs."

NOTES

9. "ELSI Research Report: State Regulation of Psilocybin: Recommendations for the Oregon Health Authority," Project on Psychedelics Law and Regulation, Petrie-Flom Center for Health Law Policy, Biotechnology, and Bioethics, Harvard Law School, December 12, 2021, https://www.oregon.gov/oha/PH/PREVENTIONWELLNESS/Documents/ELSI%20Report%20Draft-%20Historical%20and%20Indigenous%20Use.pdf.
10. "ELSI Research Report."
11. Gordon R. Wasson, "Magic Mushrooms," *Life*, May 13, 1957, https://www.cuttersguide.com/pdf/Periodical-Publications/life-by-time-inc-published-may-13-1957.pdf.
12. Ahmed Kabil, "This Mexican Medicine Woman Hipped America to Magic Mushrooms, with the Help of a Bank Executive," *Medium*, January 5, 2017, https://medium.com/timeline/with-the-help-of-a-bank-executive-this-mexican-medicine-woman-hipped-america-to-magic-mushrooms-c41f866bbf37.
13. Kabil, "Mexican Medicine Woman."
14. Scotty Hendricks, "How the CIA Used LSD to Fight Communism," Big Think, August 5, 2021, https://bigthink.com/the-past/mkultra-cia-lsd/.
15. Greg Miller, "Timothy Leary's Transformation from Scientist to Psychedelic Celebrity," *Wired*, October 1, 2013, https://www.wired.com/2013/10/timothy-leary-archives/.
16. "Timothy Leary," Harvard University Department of Psychology, n.d., https://psychology.fas.harvard.edu/people/timothy-leary.
17. Timothy Leary, "Turn On, Tune In, Drop Out," The Library of Consciousness, 1966, https://www.organism.earth/library/document/turn-on-tune-in-drop-out.
18. "COINTELPRO," FBI Records: The Vault, May 5, 2011, https://vault.fbi.gov/cointel-pro.

NOTES

19. Branko Marcetic, "The FBI's Secret War," Jacobin, August 31, 2016, https://jacobin.com/2016/08/fbi-cointelpro-new-left-panthers-muslim-surveillance.
20. Marcetic, "FBI's Secret War."
21. "COINTELPRO: New Left," Federal Bureau of Investigation, 1970, Internet Archive, https://archive.org/details/COINTELPRONewLeft/100-HQ-449698-01/mode/2up.
22. Joan Didion, "Slouching Towards Bethlehem," *The Saturday Evening Post*, September 23, 1967, https://www.saturdayeveningpost.com/2017/06/didion/.
23. "Prison Population over Time," The Sentencing Project, n.d., https://www.sentencingproject.org/research/.
24. Malcolm Harris, *Palo Alto: A History of California, Capitalism, and the World* (New York: Little, Brown and Company, 2023), chap. 3, Apple Books.
25. "McNature," *Psychedelic Salon* podcast, no. 197, September 16, 2009, https://psychedelicsalon.com/podcast-197-mcnature/.
26. Lin Tao, *Trip: Psychedelics, Alienation, and Change* (New York: Vintage Books, 2018), Apple Books.
27. Mark Fisher, "Acid Communism (Unfinished Introduction)," Blackout (blog, Peter Bouscheljong), https://my-blackout.com/2019/04/25/mark-fisher-acid-communism-unfinished-introduction/.
28. Mark Fisher, *Capitalist Realism: Is There No Alternative?* (Winchester, UK: Zero Books, 2009), Apple Books.
29. "U.S. Ketamine Clinics Market Size, Share, & Trends Analysis Report by Treatment (Depression, Anxiety, PTSD, Others), by Therapy (On-site Therapy, Online Therapy), and Segment Forecasts, 2024–2030," Grand View Research, n.d., https://www.grandviewresearch.com/industry-analysis/us-ketamine-clinics-market-report.
30. Eric Sagonowsky, "Cost Watchdogs Scold J&J for 'Overpricing' Its New Ketamine-like Antidepressant," Fierce Pharma, May 10, 2019, https://

www.fiercepharma.com/pharma/icer-takes-issue-johnson-johnson-s-spravato-price-questions-breadth-data.

31. Chris Hamby, "A Fraught New Frontier in Telehealth: Ketamine," *The New York Times*, February 20, 2023, https://www.nytimes.com/2023/02/20/us/ketamine-telemedicine.html.

32. Kyle Chayka, *Filterworld: How Algorithms Flattened Culture* (New York: Doubleday, 2024), Apple Books.

33. Olúfẹ́mi O. Táíwò, *Elite Capture: How the Powerful Took over Identity Politics (and Everything Else)* (Chicago: Haymarket Books, 2022), Apple Books.

CHAPTER EIGHT: SEARCHING FOR COLLECTIVE BREAKTHROUGH

1. Erich Fromm, *Beyond the Chains of Illusion: My Encounter with Marx and Freud* (London: Bloomsbury, 2017), chap. 11, Apple Books.

2. Hannah Baer, "Dance Until the World Ends," Artforum, December 2021, https://www.artforum.com/features/hannah-baer-on-rave-and-revolution-251091/.

3. Bryce Ward, "Americans Are Choosing to Be Alone. Here's Why We Should Reverse That," *The Washington Post*, November 23, 2022, https://www.washingtonpost.com/opinions/2022/11/23/americans-alone-thanksgiving-friends/.

4. Huw Lemmey, "Party and Protest: The Radical History of Gay Liberation, Stonewall and Pride," *The Guardian*, June 25, 2020, https://www.theguardian.com/world/2020/jun/25/party-and-protest-lgbtq-radical-history-gay-liberation-stonewall-pride.

5. DeForrest Brown, *Assembling a Black Counter Culture* (Brooklyn: Primary Information, 2022), as cited in McKenzie Wark, *Raving* (Durham, NC: Duke University Press, 2023), 6.

NOTES

6. Kumi James, "Hood Rave LA: Framing the Black Femme Underground," *e-flux Journal*, December 2022, https://www.e-flux.com/journal/132/508444/hood-rave-la-framing-the-black-femme-underground/.
7. McKenzie, *Raving*, 14.
8. Todd McGowan, *Enjoying What We Don't Have: The Political Project of Psychoanalysis* (Lincoln: University of Nebraska Press, 2013), 211.
9. Gilles Deleuze and Félix Guattari, *Anti-Oedipus: Capitalism and Schizophrenia* (New York: Penguin Books, 2009), xxiii.
10. Shane Darke, Amy Peacock, Johan Duflou, Michael Farrell, and Julia Lappin, "Characteristics and Circumstances of Death Related to Gamma Hydroxybutyrate (GHB)," *Clinical Toxicology* 58 (November 2020): 11, 1028–33, https://doi.org/10.1080/15563650.2020.1726378.

AFTERWORD

1. Jeremy Kalicum, Eris Nyx, Mary Clare Kennedy, and Thomas Kerr, "The Impact of an Unsanctioned Compassion Club on Non-Fatal Overdose," *International Journal of Drug Policy* 131 (September 2024), https://doi.org/10.1016/j.drugpo.2024.104330.
2. "Vancouver Drug Policy Advocates Face Trafficking Related Charges," CBC News, June 7, 2024, https://www.cbc.ca/news/canada/british-columbia/dulf-advocates-charged-1.7229040.
3. Nicole Leonard, "Philadelphia City Council Passes Near-Total Ban on Future Supervised Injection in Most Parts of the City," WHYY, September 15, 2023, https://whyy.org/articles/philadelphia-city-council-passes-near-total-ban-on-future-safe-consumption-overdose-prevention-sites/.
4. Anna Orso and Aubrey Wheelan, "Mayor Parker Proposes Cutting Nearly $1 Million in Syringe Exchange Funding for Prevention Point," *Philadelphia Inquirer*, April 15, 2024, https://www.inquirer.com/politics/philadel

NOTES

phia/mayor-cherelle-parker-prevention-point-syringes-funding-20240415.html.

5. Zach Fannin, Joe LoCascio, Mack Muldofsky, Aria Young, and Ivan Pereira, "Oregon's Drug Decriminalization Law Rolled Back as Homelessness, Overdoses on the Rise," ABC News, March 12, 2024, https://abcnews.go.com/US/oregons-drug-decriminalization-law-rolled-back-homeless-overdoses/story?id=107841625.

6. "Investigators Say Student Killed by Police Outside Mount Horeb School Pointed Pellet Rifle," Associated Press, May 9, 2024, https://www.wpr.org/justice/investigators-say-student-killed-by-police-outside-mount-horeb-school-pointed-pellet-rifle.

INDEX

A

Abilify (aripiprazole), 190, 204, 213
acetaminophen, 47, 68
acid. *See* LSD (lysergic acid diethylamide)
activism, 1–4, 206, 246–48, 280, 281, 287–88. *See also* harm reduction
acupuncture, 70, 77, 127–28, 129, 149
Adderall, 27, 65, 75, 78, 92, 95, 173, 198, 204, 213, 266, 307, 312
addiction
    of benzos, 177
    blaming poor people and immigrants for, 89–90
    as a disease, 87–89
    dislocation theory of, 93–94
    morphine, 93
    needing higher doses with, 62–63
    opioids, 54, 55–59
    pain medication, 66–67
    to tranquilizers, 177
ADHD diagnosis/meds, 6, 46, 173, 197–201, 209, 213, 215, 218. *See also* Adderall

advertisements, pharmaceutical, 137, 164, 171–73, 208
Africa, European colonization of, 259–60
Alaska (trans woman), 269–71, 272–83, 298
alcohol use/alcoholism, 38, 101, 135, 183, 187, 242
Alexander, Bruce, 93–94
Algernon Pharmaceuticals, 262
alienation, 222–24, 249, 250–61
amitriptyline, 166
amphetamines, 91, 92, 173, 197–201, 247. *See also* Adderall
antidepressants, 6, 133–46
    author's side effects from, 137–41
    author's use of, 27, 33, 132–33, 135–46
    Effexor, 133–34, 135, 136, 142, 144, 145–46
    expectations of, 142–43
    getting off of, 134–35, 143–47, 168–69
    prevalence of using, 134, 135, 163, 180, 182

INDEX

antidepressants (*cont.*)
    questioning efficacy of, 180–82
    taking since childhood, 157–62, 166–70
    theory of, 136–37
    withdrawal from, 144, 145–46
anxiety, 38, 42, 43, 46, 135, 146, 172, 173, 220–21, 242, 308
Aristotle, 54
Aronowitz, Shoshana, 79, 80, 82
Ativan (lorazepam), 168, 308
Australia, 135, 163

B

Baer, Hannah, 268
Bayh-Dole Act (1980), 179
benzodiazepines, 40–41, 173, 177, 215.
    See also Klonopin; Xanax
Berle, Milton, 176–77
Berlin, Germany, 75, 290, 294–95
Bever, Fred, 202
Black Americans
    dementia praecox/schizophrenia diagnosis and, 206–7, 208–9
    drug use by white Americans versus, 91
    incarceration rate, 93
    mortality rate, 70–71
    "protest psychosis" and, 208
    raves and, 284
Black Panthers, 246
Bobbi, 44, 256
The Body Keeps the Score (van der Kolk), 229
borderline personality disorder (BPD), 209, 215, 304

brain
    addiction and, 87
    antidepressants and, 136
    benzos and, 40, 177
    chemical model of the. *See* chemical model of the brain
    depression and chemical imbalance in, 164–65
    opioid receptors, 49, 52, 69, 74
    rethinking the way we view the, 260
    trauma and, 127
breakdown, personal
    of author, 5–6, 13–14, 21–26
    author's life after, 5–6, 26–37, 43–44, 117–31
    author's recovery, 117–23, 125–34, 135–52
    costs related to, 77–78
    diagnosis of depression after, 132–34
    drug use and, 57
    fear of, 230–33
    feeling alone after, 45, 46
    refusal to go backward from, 204–5
breakdown, societal. *See* societal breakdown and decay
breathing exercises, 70, 106, 121
Britt, 219–22
Brown, DeForrest Jr., 284
buprenorphine, 49
bupropion (Wellbutrin), 163, 166, 215
Butisol, 171–72
Butler, Judith, 110

C

capitalism/capitalist society, 211–12
    attendant affect of, 41–42

blaming social ills on those most
    harmed by, 305–6
the church and, 111
counterculture of the 1960s and, 249–50
drugs becoming absorbed into,
    257–58, 259, 261–63
internalization of brutality from,
    224–25
ketamine clinics and, 257
meaning making and, 224
pain caused by, 103, 306–7
trauma in, 38, 223
"capitalist realism," 249–50
Carmichael, Stokely, 212
Case, Anne, 70
cathexis, 107, 111, 113
Charlottesville, Virginia, rally (2017),
    1–4, 31–32, 122–23, 126, 151, 287
Chayka, Kyle, 258–59
chemical imbalances, 164–65, 219, 220,
    221
chemical model of the brain, 178–79
    Britt's story on, 221–22
    dismissing the *why* of mental distress,
        175
    efficacy of SSRIs and, 180–81
    prescription drugs and, 164–65,
        174–75
    radical movement opposing, 210–12
    SSRI popularity and, 183
Chinese immigration/immigrants, 89
Chromatica (Lady Gaga), 253–54
civil rights movement, 208, 260
class
    disease model of drug use and, 92–94
    influencing false divide between drugs
        and medications, 89–92

influencing resources and support
    related to drug use, 77–78, 85–86
opium addiction and, 89
clonazepam. *See* Klonopin
clubs/clubbing, 272–74, 278–79,
    281–82, 286–87
cocaine, 86
    author's use of, 22, 27, 95, 141, 238, 252
    DULF and, 96, 98, 99
    taken with ketamine, 270
    used in the 1980s, 248
collective grieving, 110–11
colonization, 224, 259–60
The Colonization of Psychic Space
    (Oliver), 224
community/communality, 266–69,
    277–83
compassion club (DULF), 98–100, 304
Confessions of an English Opium-Eater
    (De Quincey), 55–59
Courtwright, David T., 91
Covid-19 pandemic, 64, 78, 97, 203,
    276–77, 278
CPTSD, 11
crystal meth, 92
cutting, 160–61, 162
Cymbalta (duloxetine), 162, 168–69,
    171

D

Daffy Duck, 18
"deaths from despair," 8, 71, 182
Deaton, Angus, 70, 71
decriminalization, 101, 257, 305, 306
Deleuze, Gilles, 112, 286, 311
dementia praecox, 206–7
Demerol, 90

INDEX

Dennis (therapist), 23–24, 30–31, 34, 77, 118–19, 122, 127, 130, 148, 150, 241
depression. *See also* antidepressants
   author's diagnosis of, 132–34
   chemical imbalance and, 164–65
   efficacy of antidepressants for, 180–82
   increase in rates of, 135
   James's story on, 187–88, 189
   LSD and, 242
   Percocet use and, 49
   physical pain with, 68–69
   prevalence of, 8, 45
   psychedelics helping people with, 241–42
   purpose of, 147–50
   questioning cause of, 183–84
De Quincey, Thomas, 55–59
Dexedrine, 173, 198, 200
dextromethorphan, 189
diagnosis(es), 9, 129–30
   of ADHD, for author, 198–99
   author no longer wanting a, 204–5
   escaping, 213–22
   finding an identity outside of, 170–71
   finding space outside of, 222–25
   history of, 206–13
   racism and, 206–9
diazepam. *See* Valium
Didion, Joan, 247–48
Dilaudid, 90, 101
Disch, Hilary, 81
dissociation, 5, 17, 26, 105, 205
dissociatives, 232, 257–58, 261. *See also* ketamine
DMT (dimethyltryptamine), 260
doctors, pharmaceutical companies and, 163–64

dopamine, 87, 88, 174, 259
drapetomania, 208
Dreyfus, Hubert, 222
Dr. Jim (psychiatrist), 203–4
drug dealing, DULF (Drug User Liberation Front) and, 95–103
Drug Enforcement Administration, 177–78
drug industry. *See* pharmaceutical industry
drugs, 10, 12–14. *See also* medication(s); prescription drugs; psychedelics; specific names of drugs
   becoming absorbed into mainstream medical industrial complex, 257–58, 259, 261–63
   chemical versus experiential effectiveness of, 257–61
   creating a space for desires and fantasy, 285–87
   experiential versus chemical effectiveness of, 257–59
   false divide between medicine and, 89–91
   prescription drugs compared with illicit, 43
   providing an internal space, 280
   raves and, 266, 273, 286–89
   rewriting collective narrative with, 310–12
   rewriting your life with, 298, 309
drug use. *See also* addiction; safety of drug use
   addiction memoir (1821) on, 55–57
   by author, 10, 12–13, 252–56, 266, 296, 298, 299, 307–9
   author's LSD experience, 238–41

INDEX

cuts on harm reduction programs, 304–6
disease model of, 87–89, 92–95
to ease pain, 6, 37–38, 70, 113, 309–10
economic inequities and, 77–78, 85–86
envisioning a better world with, 285–87, 295–96, 310
feeling bleak versus feeling fun, 297–98
guardrails for those without privileges for, 95–103
"harm reduction" approach to, 80–82
imagining a different world with, 250–51, 287–89
by James, 187–90
maintenance program for, 50, 75
with others, 256–57, 266–67
prevalence of, 78, 163
race and class influencing view of, 89–90
raves and, 289–90, 296–97, 298–300
societal factors and, 78, 93–94, 306–7
in trans community, 269–73, 278–79, 280, 282
while listening to music, 253–57
without oversight or support by others, 66
Z's story on, 291, 292
DULF (Drug User Liberation Front), 95–103, 304
duloxetine (Cymbalta), 162, 168–69, 171
dysphoria, 197

E

eating disorders, 217
economic disparities. *See* class
Effexor, 133–34, 135, 136–39, 142, 144, 145–46
Eli Lilly, 180

Elite Capture (Táíwò), 259
emotional pain, 68–69, 72
Engels, Friedrich, 94
England, 89, 135, 163. *See also* United Kingdom (UK)
Erin, 1–2, 3, 141, 251, 252–54, 256
escitalopram. *See* Lexapro

F

Facebook, 214–15
Fanon, Frantz, 108, 209, 224, 259
fantasy, 286, 287, 295
FBI (Federal Bureau of Investigation), 208, 246–47
fear of breakdown, 230–33
fentanyl, 52, 70, 307
  deaths related to, 47
  DULF and, 97–98, 99, 100, 101
  heroin and, 81, 101
  Kensington, Philadelphia, and, 79
  Narcan/overdoses and, 74
  OxyContin and, 52
  in Percocets, 47–48, 73
  pharmaceutical industry and, 93
  Serenity House and, 83, 85
  tranq and, 81
F. Hoffman–La Roche, 39, 40
Fields, James Alex Jr., 3, 42
Filterworld: How Algorithms Flattened Culture (Chayka), 258
Fisher, Mark, 249–50, 295
fluoxetine. *See* Prozac
Foucault, Michel, 212, 222, 223
Freedom of Information Act, 181
Freud, Sigmund, 30, 68, 107, 108, 175, 176, 285
Fromm, Erich, 109, 267–68

INDEX

G

GABA (gamma-aminobutyric acid), 40, 177
gabapentin, 166
gender
    pharmaceutical ads and, 172–73
    suicide rates and, 72
gender identity, 17, 34–35, 152, 196. *See also* trans community
Germany, 211–12
GHB, 86, 266, 282, 289, 290, 292–93, 296
GlaxoSmithKline, 161
grief, 8, 110–11, 147–48, 151, 152–53
Guattari, Félix, 112, 286, 311

H

Haldol, 208
hallucinogens, 6. *See also* psychedelics
    becoming absorbed into mainstream medical industrial complex, 257–58
    history of, 243
    medicalization of, 250, 257–58, 261
    as a movement against oppression, 260
    as tools to change the world, 248–49
    Wasson's photo-essay on, 243–44
harm reduction, 80–85, 95–103, 304–5, 306
Harrington, Anne, 39, 174
Harvard University, 245–46
healing. *See also* therapy
    by author after mental breakdown, 117–29
    fear of breakdown and, 229–33
    releasing energy and, 108–9
    through acupuncture, 127–28
    through yoga, 127

    trauma-to-healing narrative, 9–10, 11–12
    using drugs to, 308–10
heroin, 70, 102. *See also* fentanyl
    DULF (Drug User Liberation Front) and, 96, 97, 98, 99–100, 101
    fentanyl and, 48, 81, 85
    James's story on, 167, 188, 189
    maintenance program for, 50
    overdoses, 167, 189
    OxyContin and, 52
    pharmaceutical industry and, 93
    prescription drugs and, 90, 91
    supplanting LSD, 247, 248
Herzberg, David, 89–91, 175
Heyer, Heather, 4
Hillman, D. C. A., 53, 54
Hofmann, Albert, 245
Holocaust-surviving families, 30, 32, 151, 230–31
Huber, Wolfgang, 212
hydrocodone, 61
Hyman, Steven, 180–81

I

Iceland, 163
immigrants, 55, 89, 206–7
individualism, 216, 222, 223
Industrial Revolution, 38, 41
Insane Liberation Front (ILF), 211
Instagram, 217, 218–19, 276, 290
institutionalization/deinstitutionalization, 174, 179
Internet, 69, 139, 145, 214–20

J

James, 167, 184–193, 195, 214
James, Kumi, 284

INDEX

Janssen Pharmaceuticals, 93
Johnson & Johnson, 93, 257

K

Kalicum, Jeremy, 98, 99, 100, 304–5, 310
Kensington neighborhood, Philadelphia, 79–87, 109
Kesey, Ken, 248
ketamine, 6, 86, 291
    Alaska's use of, 270–71, 278–79, 281, 282
    author's use of, 253–56, 270, 283, 299
    de-algorithmizing user, 258, 259
    healing power of, 241–42
    medicalization of, 257–58, 259
    raving with, 266, 296–97
    taken with cocaine, 270
    in trans community, 269–70
ketamine clinics, 257, 309
King, Martin Luther Jr., 247
Kirsch, Irving, 181
Klonopin, 66, 78, 171, 177
    author's use of, 24–25, 29, 34, 37, 46, 66, 106, 110, 118, 145, 149, 241, 252, 283
    history of, 39–40
    life of, 40–41
    Melissa's use of, 169
kratom, 69–70, 78, 110, 149

L

Lady Gaga, 253–255
Leary, Timothy, 243, 245–46, 249, 259, 260
Lemmey, Huw, 281

Levine, Peter, 108
Lewis, Marc, 88
Lexapro, 33, 34, 136, 145, 163, 166, 168, 180, 191, 220–21
LGBTQ liberation struggles, 260
Librium, 40
life narrative, 6–13
lorazepam (Ativan), 168, 308
LSD (lysergic acid diethylamide), 6, 185, 238–39, 241–42, 245, 248, 260, 296, 300–301
Lucas, 46–51, 59–67, 73–76, 214, 297, 311

M

Maddie, 214–16
Malcolm X, 208
marijuana use, 84, 161–62, 169, 187, 188, 192
Marx, Karl, 111
Maude, 217–19
McGowan, Todd, 286
McKenna, Terence, 249, 260
MDMA, 241–42
medication(s). *See also* prescription drugs; specific names and types of medications
    alleviating social conditions, 210–11
    false divide between drugs and, 89–92
    fear of going off of, 162, 171
    idea of achieving happiness and stability through, 162–63
    James's story on, 187–88, 190–92
meditation, 149, 153, 238
Melissa, 156–62, 165–71, 192, 195, 214, 307–8

INDEX

mental health/mental health issues
  biological view of the brain and, 179
  influence of prescription drugs on, 165
  oppressed populations and, 209–10
  prevalence of, 45–46
  shift from external to internal causes of, 171–74, 175–76, 183, 210–11
  societal oppression and, 209–10
  as a symptom of environmental issues, 213–14
Mental Patients Liberation Front, 211
mephedrone, 266, 282, 296, 299
meprobamate (Miltown). *See* Miltown (meprobamate)
meth, 92, 96, 98, 99
methadone, 82
Metzl, Jonathan, 206–7
Mexico, 243–44, 245
Miami, Florida, 261–64
Miltown (meprobamate), 38–39, 172, 174–75, 176–77, 183
Mind Fixers (Harrington), 39, 174
morphine, 47, 52, 89, 90, 93
Morrison, Robert, 55
mortality rate, 70–71
mushrooms. *See* psilocybin

N
Narcan (naloxone), 49, 64, 73–74, 81, 82, 84, 85
narratives
  on chemical model of the brain. *See* chemical model of the brain
  collective, 310–12
  diagnostic. *See* diagnosis(es)
  life, 6–13
  rewriting, 8, 10–12, 14, 310–12

National Alliance on Mental Illness, 179
National Institute of Mental Health, 178–79, 180
National Institutes of Health, 87–88, 89
needles/needle exchange, 79, 80, 81
Nefertiti, 294–95
neurotransmitters, 87, 134, 137, 146, 165, 174, 177. *See also* serotonin
New Orleans, Louisiana, 140–41, 144, 203, 251, 253
norepinephrine, 136–37
"North African syndrome," 209–10
Nyx, Eris, 97, 98, 99, 101–2, 304–5, 310

O
Odyssey (Homer), 53
Ogden, Thomas, 232
Oliver, Kelly, 108, 224
"On Sleep" (Aristotle), 54
opiates, 52, 92. *See also* opioids/opioid use
opioid receptors, 49, 52, 69, 74
opioids/opioid use
  addiction memoir on, 55–59
  deaths related to, 47, 72–73
  disease model of drug use and, 92–93
  to ease pain, 66–67
  good versus bad user of, 55
  history of, 52–54
  Lucas's story about, 46–51, 59–66, 73–76
  overdoses, 47, 49, 66, 73
  OxyContin and, 72
  prescriptions, 72, 91
  used in ancient societies, 52–54
  white-market drugs, 90
opium/opium poppy, 53–54, 89

INDEX

overdoses, 67
   deaths in British Columbia, 97
   DULF and prevention of, 97–99
   GHB, 292, 293
   heroin, 167, 189
   Lucas's story on, 66, 75, 76
   Narcan reversal, 64, 74, 82
   opioids, 47, 49, 66, 73
oxycodone, 47, 61, 90
OxyContin, 52, 55, 72, 90, 92, 163

P

pain
   capitalism creating, 103, 306–7
   connection between physical and emotional, 68–69
   drug use to ameliorate the, 37–38, 43, 46, 65–66, 78, 111, 309–10
   feelings of aliveness and, 232
   opioid use and, 47, 51, 66–67
   societal conditions changing amount of, 67–68
panic attacks, 22–23, 107, 118, 131, 201
Parker, Cherelle, 305
Paxil, 160, 161, 166
Percocets, 47–49, 52, 73
Percodan, 90
pharmaceutical industry, 89–90
   advertising, 137, 164, 171–72
   Bayh-Dole Act and, 179
   chemical imbalance theory promoted by, 164–65
   influence campaigns of, 163–64
   profit margins of, 176
   unpublished studies of, 181
   Wonderland event and, 261–62

Philadelphia. *See* Kensington neighborhood, Philadelphia
Plan C, 41
poppy plants, 52–53
Portugal, 163, 180
prescription drugs, 9. *See also* medication(s); specific names and types of drugs
   during the 1950s, 38–40
   advertisements for, 137, 164, 171–73
   author's use of, 203–4, 213
   author's use of amphetamines, 197–200
   "bad" drugs versus, 89–90
   chemical model of the brain and, 164–65, 174–75
   compared with illicit drugs, 43
   influence of manufacturers on, 163–64
   Melissa's story on, 157–62, 168–70
   opioids, 91
   percentage of Americans on, 45–46
Prevention Point, Kensington, Philadelphia, 80–82, 85, 305
The Protest Psychosis (Metzl), 206
protests(ing), 208, 276, 287–88. *See also* Charlottesville, Virginia, rally (2017)
Prozac, 134, 136, 145–46, 163, 178, 180, 181, 182, 187–88
psilocybin, 6, 241–42, 243, 245–46, 260
P. somniferum (poppy plant), 53
psychedelics. *See also* hallucinogens
   drugs and supplements inspired by, 262
   history of LSD experimentation, 245–46

INDEX

psychedelics (*cont.*)
   LSD experience, 238–41
   mainstreaming, 241–51
   in the 1980s and 1990s, 248–49
   revolutionary movement of the 1960s/1970s and, 246–48, 249–50
   in spiritual and shamanistic rituals, 243
   therapeutic use and effects of, 241–43, 250
psychiatry/psychiatric care, 32–33, 174, 198, 203–4, 210
psychoanalysis, 30, 122, 152, 175–76, 221. *See also* therapy
psychosis, 107, 201, 208, 209
psychotherapy, 134, 165, 174. *See also* therapy
PTSD, 5, 11, 38, 108, 127, 242
Purdue Pharma, 52, 90

Q

Queer Nation, 110
queers/queerness. *See also* trans community
   of author, 95, 125–26, 197
   feeling outcast and isolated by, 59
   more often diagnosed with ADHD, 209
   overdoses among, 67
   raving/clubbing and, 267, 277–78, 281

R

race and racism. *See also* Black Americans
   coping strategies and, 71–72
   dementia praecox/schizophrenia diagnosis and, 206–9
   disease model of drug use and, 92–94
   influencing false divide between drugs and medications, 89–92
   influencing resources and support related to drug use, 78, 85–86
   life expectancy and, 70–71
   of North Africans in France, 209
   opium use/laws and, 55, 89
Radical Therapist Collective, 211
raves, 266–68, 271, 277–80, 283–87, 289–90, 292, 295–300
Rebecca (therapist), 228–29, 231, 241
Reeder, Earl, 39–40
repression, 108, 112, 285, 286, 310–11
A Return to Love (Williamson), 10–11
Ritalin, 173, 198
RO-5-0690, 39–40
Robitussin, 189, 190

S

Sabina, Maria, 244
safety of drug use
   DULF (Drug User Liberation Front) and, 95–103, 305–6
   harm reduction program in Philadelphia, 80–82, 85, 305
   maintenance program and, 50, 75
   Miltown and, 177
   racial and class differences in, 65–66, 75, 91–92, 95
Saketopoulou, Avgi, 10, 205
Sandoz Laboratories, 245
schizophrenia, 190, 206–9
Schorske, Carina del Valle, 149
Seberg, Jean, 246–47
Sehgal, Parul, 11–12
Self, Will, 38

INDEX

September 11th terrorist attack, 31–32, 95, 123–25, 151, 196, 197, 199, 214
Serax (oxazepam), 173
Serenity House, Kensington, Philadelphia, 82–85, 86–87
serotonin, 88, 136–37, 163, 165, 174, 182
sertraline. *See* Zoloft (sertraline)
sexual dysfunction, antidepressants and, 139, 182
Shawn (heroin user), 100–101
Silicon Valley, California, 248
"Slouching Towards Bethlehem" (Didion), 248
Smith, LaDonna, 83–85, 86–87, 310
SNRI (serotonin and norepinephrine reuptake inhibitor), 136–37
social conditions and issues. *See also* capitalism/capitalist society; class; race and racism
  alienation/capitalism and, 222–25
  diagnostics of psychiatry versus mental issues in context of, 210–13
  medications used to alleviate, 210–11
  mental health and, 303
  rewriting collective narrative and, 310–12
  scapegoats for, 304
  social murder (Engels) and, 94
  those most harmed by capitalism blamed on, 305–6
  unfair diagnoses and, 209
  worrying about, 307–8
Socialist Patients' Collective (SPK), 211–12
social media, 217, 218, 309
social murder, 94

societal breakdown and decay. *See also* social conditions and issues
  addiction-as-disease framework and, 87–94
  addictions to cope with, 67–68
  drug use and, 43, 57, 93
  economic disparities and, 78
  externalizing, 105–13
  in Kensington, Philadelphia, 79–87
  pain from. *See* pain
  unequal distribution of, 77–78
SOL Collective, 79
somatic therapy, 77, 227–30, 241, 283
Spravato, 257
SSRIs (serotonin reuptake inhibitors), 166, 192, 307, 309. *See also* antidepressants; Prozac
  neoliberal economic revolution and, 183
  prescribed for mental breakdown, 33
  remaining the same, 242
  side effects, 139–40, 182
  in TV advertisement, 130
stability
  in author's life, 202–3, 227, 237–38
  feeling of tenuous, 167, 168
  idea of achieving through medication, 162–63
  selling the idea of, 171–76
Sternbach, Leo, 39
Suboxone, 49, 50, 61, 74–75, 297
suicide/suicidal behavior
  author entertaining idea of, 33–34
  gender differences in, 72
  increase in, 45, 71, 107, 135, 182–83
  James's story on, 187, 188, 193
  Jean Seberg and, 246–47
  Paxil and, 161

INDEX

Sutherland, Christy, 101
syringes, 81, 305
Szasz, Thomas, 212

T

Táíwò, Olúfẹ́mi, 259
Talia (therapist), 196–97, 201
Tao Lin, 260–61
Tao, Vince, 102–3, 109, 304, 305, 306
tapping, 228–29
Teotihuacán, mural in, 243
Thase, Michael, 165
therapy, 149
  for addiction, 88
  after author's mental breakdown, 34–35
  by author after mental breakdown, 23–24, 31
  author's use of, 117–19, 122, 126, 150, 196–97, 198, 201
  costs, 77
  James's story about, 190–91
  as a narrative process, 8–9
  releasing energy through, 108–9
  somatic, 227–30
  using psychotherapy in addition to, 241
Thorazine, 38
tranq, 81, 85
tranquilizers, 174–75, 176–77
trans community, 27, 209, 269–83, 304, 309, 311
trauma. *See also* PTSD
  in author's life/family, 30, 36, 95, 149, 203
  author's suppression of, 195–200
  author's therapy sessions and, 31–32, 34–35, 138, 231
  becoming a different person from, 205–6
  bonding with others over, 253
  the brain and, 127
  capacity to grow through, 8–11
  drug use and, 43, 95, 308–9
  efforts to "get better" from, 8–10
  in modern capitalistic society, 38
  somatic therapy and, 228, 229–30, 231
tricyclics, 166
Trump, Donald, 1
Turn Illness Into a Weapon (Socialist Patients' Collective), 211
2C-B, 6, 283
Tylenol, 47, 68, 188

U

United Kingdom (UK), 46, 67, 179, 180, 183
"Unite the Right" rally (2017), 1–4
US Office of National Drug Control Policy, 87

V

Valium, 40, 177–18
Vancouver, British Columbia, 95–103, 304–5
Van der Kolk, Bessel, 229
venlafaxine (Effexor). *See* Effexor
Vicodin, 60–61
Vince (raver friend), 286–87, 288, 296, 299

W

Walker, Alice, 149
Wark, McKenzie, 284–285
Wasson, R. Gordon, 243–45

INDEX

Wellbutrin (bupropion), 163, 166, 215
White Market Drugs (Herzberg), 89
white supremacists, Charlottesville "Unite the Right" rally and, 1, 2–3, 95
Williamson, Marianne, 10–11
Winnicott, Donald, 230
withdrawal
    after using Narcan, 74
    from amphetamines, 200–201
    from antidepressants, 144, 145–46
    from Effexor, 145
    from Klonopin, 41, 169
    from opioids, 49, 61, 65
    with Prozac, 146
    from Valium, 177
    from Zoloft, 169
Wonderland, Miami, Florida, 261–63

X

Xanax, 40, 61, 177, 215, 220
Xavi, 1–2, 3

Y

yoga, 69, 70, 77, 86, 127, 129, 149, 238

Z

Z (clubber/raver), 289–95
Zoloft (sertraline), 136, 145–146, 157–158, 164, 166, 168–169, 180

A NOTE ON THE AUTHOR

P.E. Moskowitz is a writer born and raised in New York City. Their writing has appeared in *New York* magazine, *GQ*, *The Nation*, and many other places. They run a popular Substack newsletter about psychology, psychiatry, and culture called *Mental Hellth*. When they're not writing, they're probably playing tennis, chilling with friends across the city, or watching the Mets lose again. For more information, visit their website at Moskowitz.xyz.